PARADIGMS OF MARGINALITY

PARADIGMS OF MARGINALITY:
A CRITICAL ASSESSMENT

Editors
Dr S. Chelliah
Dr Bijender Singh

KALPAZ

First Published, 2019

Published by

Kalpaz Publications
C-30, Satyawati Nagar,
Delhi – 110052
Ph.: 011-47034999, 9811692060
www.kalpazpublications.com
E-mail: kalpaz@hotmail.com

Printed at: G. Print Process, Delhi

Cataloging in Publication Data—DK
Courtesy: D.K. Agencies (P) Ltd. <docinfo@dkagencies.com>

Chelliah, S. *(Professor of English)*, **author.**
Paradigms of marginality : a critical assessment/
Dr S. Chelliah, Dr Bijender Singh.
pages cm
ISBN 9789353240868

1. Indic literature (English)—History and criticism. 2. Indic literature—History and criticism. 3. American literature—History and criticism. 4. Marginality, Social, in literature. 5. Women in literature. I. Singh, Bijender, author. II. Title.

LCC PR9484.6.C44 2019 | DDC 820.93552 23

Contents

Introduction

We define marginality as an involuntary position and condition of an individual or group at the margins of social, political, economic, ecological, and biophysical systems, that prevent them from access to resources, assets, services, restraining freedom of choice, preventing the development of capabilities, and eventually causing extreme poverty.

– (Gatzweiler et al. 3)

Marginalization is also termed as a social exclusion or simply embargo from social or religious activities. It is a position of disadvantage and relegation of an individual or a group of people to the margins or periphery of society. The term is widely used these days and it was first used in France. It is frequently used across various disciplines, like, literature, education, psychology, sociology, economics and politics. The process of Marginalization includes denial of complete access and claim to the available opportunities and resources, and rights, which are freely granted and are fundamental to other individuals or groups of individuals. These rights encompass the basic rights like employment, housing, health and nutrition, democratic involvement and other public engagements.

The shifting of a particular person or group of society to the periphery and resultant alienation from this process may be associated with a variety of factors, such as, their gender, class, race, culture, creed, colour, ethnic origin, age, education, family background, living standards, appearances, sexual orientations; or physical, mental, habitual, and/or psychological differences from others, especially those who constitute a dominant group in a specific place or time. Thus, in a broad sense, it may be stated that the practice of discrimination against people on the basis of any of the above listed factors prevalent in a human society anywhere in the world that pushes those, who are discriminated, to the fringes of the social set-up, leads to their Marginalization, and is called social exclusion. It implies that any person who seems to deviate or differ from expected norms or appropriate behaviour in a society or a population may be the victim of noticeable or subtle forms of Marginalization. The commonly marginalised groups or people include women, black, poor, illiterate, physically disabled, especially-abled, LGBTQ, drug addicted people, diasporic and minority population, old age people etc. The process of social exclusion prevents the affected population from participating freely and completely in the social, political, economic, and cultural life of the society in which they live. This may gradually lead to protests and demonstrations on the part of the marginalised population or individuals.

The emergence of Marginalization at an individual level or at group level is seen at four dimensional correlated stages, viz. inadequate access to social rights, deprivation of material possessions, restricted social involvement, and absence of normative assimilation in society. It is, thus considered as the mixed outcome of both – the individual risk and administrative, social and legal policies and practices.

To discuss a few forms of Marginalization and the individuals or groups of people as its victim, and the resultant protests on their behalf, women as the secondary gender and the feminist movement as an outcry of the process of Marginalization deserves the foremost right to be included in this book. Blacks and aboriginals have incessantly been struggling for their rights as equals to whites and mainstream community. Dalit demonstrations and Dalit literature as an expression to caste-based social exclusion, has gained momentum in a decade, especially in India. Similarly the LGBTQ community has been registering its demands of equal rights as those granted to heterosexuals in various parts of the world. The disabled population has also voiced its agony over the mistreatment and exploitation it receives from the abled individuals. The minority groups demonstrate their protests to claim their rightful equality and inclusion in society in which they live. Diaspora emerged as a literature of immigrants written by or/and about their lived and shared experiences.

Literature becomes an appropriate forum to offer a say to all those, whether individuals or groups of people, who have ever endured exclusion or Marginalization. Doubtlessly, it serves as a bridge between those at the periphery and those at the centre. It connects the two by lending a voice to the socially excluded, thereby relieving them off the burden of their suffering, dilemma and enigma; and creating a sense of awareness and empathy in the mainstream population through the narration of lived experiences and ordeal of the other group. Thus, we have a variety of literature that comprises of a different and separate category for each group, enriched with their stories, their version, their feelings and perceptions, their thought process and their point of view. All these forms and categories are incorporated under a single term, that is, Literature of Marginalization. A number of critics endeavour to further comprehend the marginalised literature of all kinds and study and bring it forth in a more lucid manner. Though, marginalised literature and its critical evaluation deals primarily with the phenomenon of social exclusion, yet it acts like an agent of social inclusion of all the marginalised groups and their population.

Dalits also come under the category of Marginalization. Zelliot writes in a letter to Gangadhar Pantawane about the definition of Dalits. This definition gives the clear pictures of Dalit people who face many challenges in their lives:

> To me, Dalit is not the caste. He is a man exploited by the social and economic traditions of this country. He does not believe in God, rebirth, soul, holy books teaching separatism, fate and heaven because they have made him a slave. He does believe in humanism. Dalit is a symbol of change and revolution. (Zelliot 3)

Apart from Dalits, women, LGBTQ, Kashmiri migrants, migrant people who fail to get equal status on a foreign land and many more socially or economically weak people come in this category but due to space constraint, we are unable to mention all the people who live under the dark and accursed shadow of marginality.

The anthology *Paradigms of Marginality: A Critical Assessment,* a collection of thirty papers, is an important addendum in the existing literature of marginality. Its subject matter and contents succinctly encapsulate and convey the message to all the people who are living their lives at the fringe or on the threshold of the mainstream and are striving hard to create their niche in the world which they think is not theirs.

This anthology attempts to address certain shades of marginality which are prevalent in the world. It further provides a fertile ground through the constructive insights and the meaningful explorations on the targeted topic. It is hoped that the book would bring positive changes in the human beings, create awareness and spread the message of humanity and will pave the way for the budding researchers to carry out further research on this topic.

The first paper of this anthology "Subalternity, Marginality and Untouchability as Projected in the Current Literary Scenario" is a joint effort by Dr S. Chelliah and Dr Bijender Singh. Their paper sheds light on the concept of subalternity, marginality and untouchability as projected in the realm of literature. It neatly derives these concepts and definitions and how these concepts are applied in the various stages of literary works. This paper further insists on the significance of these concepts in Western proletarian society, Afro-American society and Dalit society in India. These concepts gain more significance in the modern postcolonial literature depicting the realistic life of subalterns, untouchables and slaves all over the world.

The second paper of this anthology has been written by an eminent Gujarati Dalit writer Harsh Mangalam. In his paper titled "An Appraisal of Marginality in Select Dalit Short Stories", he has tried to give proper and broad definition of marginality by selecting a few very relevant and profound short stories "A Curse of Caste" by Baburao Bagul, "Chat of Chaturi Chamar" by B.L. Nayer, "The Trespasser" by Omprakash Valmiki and "The Flame" by Harish Mangalam etc. In the Hindu-India society, the scheduled castes people are more ostracised among all communities of marginals. The subjects of these short stories unfold our eyes and show the pictures visible of ground-naked reality removing all delusions of our ugly social system. Such obstacles are hurdles in the developing path of marginals. The writer of this article is desirous of a total revolution and to awaken consciousness of the downtrodden community.

Dr Ashok Verma's paper titled "Negotiating Marginality through Female Body: Revisiting Marginal Women Characters in Krishna Sobti's *Zindaginama*" is the third paper of this anthology. In his paper Dr Verma endeavours to critique the 'marginal' women characters of Krishna Sobti's *Zindaginama* (1979) who otherwise do not figure prominently in the main fabric and texture of the book; they however, successfully prevail upon their (fe)male counterparts by using their body as an agent of power rather than powerlessness, thus causing ripples in the 'seamless' harmony of life. These women are neither educated nor conscious of their rights as individuals. Like the modern-day feminists, they are able to negotiate marginality and assert themselves nonetheless. Thus, Dr Verma has tried to explore the subtle nuances of intra-family power play wherein 'marginal' women characters are seen negotiating their marginal status by using their bodies. He has also endeavoured to bring to the fore the inter/intra-gender ramifications of such moves.

Dr Shikha Saxena's paper titled "Displacement and Marginalization of Santhals in Hansda Sowvendra Shekhar's *The Adivasi Will Not Dance*" deals with a new type of discourse that presents the deprivation, displacement and exploitation of tribal people especially the Santhal community. In the current paper there is a threadbare analysis of the displacement of tribals particularly Santhal community in Hansda Sowvendra Shekhar's story collection *The Adivasi Will Not Dance*. Every story in the collection reveals the plights of Santhal tribals.

The fifth paper titled "Women's Search for Selfhood: Marginalised Women in Margaret Atwood's Select Novels" is an attempt to explore how the female characters of Anita Desai's novels feel dissatisfied and suffocated in the man-dominated society. These women take birth, breath, eat and die like other men, then why they are considered inferior to men, this point has been tried to explore by Dr Rumana Ashraf.

Dr C. Ramya's paper titled "Social Stratification, a Savage: A Comparative Analysis of Dr Ambedkar and Mulk Raj Anand" has been written with a view and vision to present a comparative analysis of formation of Indian society through the point of view of two legendary figures Dr B.R. Ambedkar and M.R. Anand respectively.

Dr Suruchi Sharma has penned the sixth paper of this anthology. In her paper she has tried to explore and analyse the candid and frank treatment of female subjugation in the poems of Kamala Das. Kamla Das was an iconoclast, a rebel who revolted against the hush prudery and conventionalism of Indian society in its attitude towards love and blunt treatment of sexual desires of women. Kamala Das remains a revolutionary figure who neither listened much to her family members nor to her husband and lived most of her life independently and with a carefree attitude.

K.M. Keerthika's paper "Shifting Attitude of Immigrant Women in Bharati Mukherjee's Select Fiction: An Analysis" focuses on immigrant women's shifting attitude in the cross cultural milieu and depicts the challenges faced by the immigrant in the alien land. All the novels of Mukherjee depict the life of an immigrant who longs for his mother land with pain and nostalgic feelings, and portrays their sufferings, pains, agony, and suppression suffered in the male-dominated society and shows how they manage to overcome difficult situations and sufferings. Tara, Dimple and Jasmine are the stereotyped protagonists who suffer, and whose attitudes are sandwiched between two identities. Tara is a split-up personality; Dimple is the wife as a psychic murderer and Jasmine is a pursuant of her American dream. As a major novelist, she has achieved an enviable position through her works.

Space and time have a fatal entanglement which holds the capacity to shape a society and author its history. The industrial revolution and economic restructuring began a saga of urbanization where space and time were redefined to fit in the historicity of a nation that was building. The urban space that defined itself according to the accepted patriarchal norms conveniently created a space that was meant to satiate desires and render pleasure, but only to the man. Prostitution bloomed with urbanization but the realities remained veiled as the prostituted women were never given a voice in the saga of development. Guni Vats' paper titled "Redefining Peripheries: Urbanization and Prostitution in Indian Literature" attempts to bring these to the light with a special emphasis to the short stories and begin an argument of the status of these women in the peripheries of urban spaces. The peripheries that are forgotten about are to be brought to the center so that the patriarchal structure deconstructs and a play of the urban space begins.

N. Kaushi Reddy's paper titled "Social Exclusion of Woman Characters in Select Novels of Bharati Mukherjee: A Brief Study" picturizes the highlights of social exclusion of women characters in Bharathi Mukherjee's novels, whose writings focused on the plights and subjugation of females under the dominance of male society. She projects the female marginalization at different causes like search for identity, alienation, sexual harassment, suppression of male chauvinistic behaviour, reinvention of 'self' and transformation. Through her writings, N. Kaushi Reddy envisages against the social exclusion of women and she protested to gain the prevailing rights to women to enjoy their freedom.

Dr Kusum Kanger has written the eleventh paper of this anthology. Her paper titled "Marginalised Status of Women in Anita Desai's Select Novels" is an effort to analyse that women are marginalised even in twenty-first century and sometimes they take such a bold step that may be fatal for the men as Maya kills her husband Gautama under depression in *Cry, the Peacock.* Through Anita Desai's other novels, it has been tried to show that the boys or men are given more importance than girls or women in their own home also.

Ramanuj Mahato's paper "(Re-)Defining the 'Marginal' Identity and 'Alternative Media' as a Voice of Democracy: Exemplifying Arundhati Roy's Fictional and Non-Fictional Works" seeks to explore the identity of marginal issues that need to be highlighted through the concept of 'alternative media' in respect of Arundhati Roy's vision about democratic rights, social and political awareness and national policies of Govt. Roy's emphasis lies on the role of 'alternative media' that opposes the 'mainstream media' and weighs the peripheral matters into focus through social media, web lectures, blogs and interviews etc. Roy has identified the broader goal of the nation and issues connecting the marginalised community and individual. She has brilliantly manifested her ideology as an activist more than a common writer.

Rekha Batta's paper "Rhetoric of Storytelling: Subverting the Colonial Ethos in *A Geronimo's Story*" examines the art of storytelling as a mean to subvert the master narratives. The performance of the native stories has allowed the presence of real tribal referent over its absence in the hegemonic discourse. The element of storytelling undermines the representation and subjugation of the tribes in the literature of dominance by creating a discourse that challenges the "final vocabularies" of terminal creeds. The search for Geronimo in the story exposes the colonial ethos of mainstream American society which has made every possible attempt to vanish the race of Native Americans. Nevertheless, Native Americans have contested treacherous ways of colonizers with equally contrived manners.

N. Padmapriyadharshini's paper titled "Evolution of subaltern consciousness of Women from 'Draupadi' of the *Mahabharata* to Mahasweta Devi's 'Draupadi': An Analysis" is a comparative study of the *Mahabharata* and Mahasweta Devi's Draupadi character focusing much on Mahasweta Devi's Draupadi. Padmapriyadharshini's paper claims that no matter a woman belongs to an aristocratic or a subaltern community, her strength and courage are unlimited and unstoppable. From ancient to the modern times, the sufferings and pains that women face in the society are uncountable. Every day they are subjected to some kind of physical as well as emotional assaults. Her paper presents all those treatments and tells how women get rid of subaltern consciousness using their strength and courage.

Anup Barman's and Sabuj Sarkar's joint paper titled 'The Policy of Exclusion': In Search of 'Marginal Voices' in Rushdie's *Midnight's Children*" makes an attempt to show how and why marginality is caused, and how some sections of the society are victim of it. In most cases, it is a process of social exclusion. Women are often marginalised in the society. The concerns of this paper are also to show different perceptions and perspectives of marginality.

In the research paper titled "The Journey of a Woman in Kavita Kané's *Lanka's Princess* and Manini J. Anandani's *Mandodari: Queen of Lanka*", Shikha Khandpur has taken up a feminist reading of the selected novels, which are a retelling of *Ramayana*, an epic tale from Hindu Mythology, from the perspective of the women of Lanka. Her paper traces the role of patriarchy in shaping a woman's character, and uses these characters and their tales in order to draw a parallel with the current place for women in a patriarchal society, and showcases the many ways in which women are silenced and marginalised in a misogynistic set up of society, and further discusses the need to address these concerns by questioning the prevalent notion of defined gender roles.

Dr Sumitra Singh has contributed seventeenth paper of this anthology. Her paper titled "Shades of Female Marginality in Toni Morrison's *Sula* and Alice Walker's *The Color Purple*" showcases the marginalised status of the Black women. Walker's novel *The Color Purple* describes the narrative of a black girl Celie who is molested by her own father. Alice Walker's novel *Sula* is a narrative of Nel and Sula and their self realisation, self-understanding and understanding of each other. The sufferings of Black women and their marginalised status is the core issue of Dr Sumitra's paper.

Dr Parveen Bala's and Dr Vijaylakshmi's joint paper titled "Humanism, Feminism and the Established Socio-Economic Order in Works of Shashi Deshpande" has been placed at serial number eighteenth. Their paper aims to explore humanism, feminism, and social vision of Shashi Deshpande in her works and to highlight the conflict of tradition and modernity in general and particularly in relation to the position of modern, educated, middle-class Indian women in a traditional society keeping in centre the protagonists of Deshpande's novels and how they strive to be independent in socio-economic matters.

Disha Sharma's paper titled "'Size-ism' in Literature: Marginalising Fat Women as Non-Brandish" exclusively details the hardships undergone by fat people, especially fat women in the society. These fat people are marginalised in the sense that they are made to be accepted only if they cut down their big bodies and fit into the mold of the society. Her paper evokes the struggle of women at two different stages of life; at childhood and adulthood. The fat female characters Linda and Carline are made to suffer and harassed at different times of the plots. Her paper thus, attempts to expose the psychological effects of these harassments engulfing the minds of fat women and their seeming urge to put an end to these events by culminating to diet culture.

S. Divya Bharathi's paper titled "The Mirror Images of Marginalization in M.R. Anand's *Untouchable* and Arundhati Roy's *The God of Small Things*: A Comparative Analysis" offers the comparative analysis of the two characters Bakha and Sohini from *Untouchable* and Velutha and Ammu's from *The God of Small Things*. These characters had to suffer due to the tyranny of caste, class and gender.

Dr Budhanath Pratihast has written the next paper of this book. In his paper he has analysed and explored that it is very difficult for a modern metropolitan girl to adjust in a conservative world. In the novel *Inside the Haveli*, the central female protagonist becomes a caged bird when she is asked to cover her face with *purdah* in front of men. Though, she faces a lot of problems in that tradition-ridden environment, yet she brings a lot of change also in the haveli through her innovative ideas and new approach towards life.

S. F. Filomine White Sheela's paper "Self Identity, Ambition and Womanhood in Mahesh Dattani's *Dance Like a Man*" is an attempt to show that it is very difficult for a man to enter the world of women. When Jairaj tries to learn Bharatanatyam against the wishes of his father, he is constantly threatened by his father. Jairaj is a victim of the tensed environment of his house where both his father and wife come on the way of his ambition to stand on his own legs as a dancer.

The next paper "Addressing the Euphemism of "Better Life" in Pratibha Ray's *The Primal Land*" of this anthology by Sumedha Bhandari's evaluates the notions of civilization; progress and development modeled on the dictums of western thought within the framework of tribal ecological consciousness. Believing in the role of literature in propagating action and activism for the betterment of the society, Pratibha Ray has extensively used the pen of her ink to evoke sensibilities towards the displacement of tribals on the pretext of gifting them "better life". The text questions the pace of development and re-defines the meaning of progress for the indigenous. It is a statement against the hazardous effects of western model of development on the indigenous ecology along with sending a lucid message that for the survival of tribal race the models of development and the euphemisms of "better life" need to be positively structured. The novel foregrounds the idea that by a mere addition of a "better life" tag to the lives of tribal people, a better life cannot be assured for them.

Anupama Rai's paper titled "Appropriation of Mythic Women through the Lens of Counter-Narration in Divakaruni's *The Palace of Illusions* and Parameswaran's *Sita's Promise: A Dance Drama*" endeavor to represent the mythic women characters who have carved their impressions on the psyche of Indian society from the time immemorial. It intends to analyse the mainstream Indian mythic tradition under the umbrella of contemporary counter-narrative. Consequently, its strong presence has created a bulk of writing which re-interprets the main text (the *Ramayana* and *Mahabharata*) from different perspective. Accordingly, there are few women litterateurs who have dismantled the very myth of myth creation and reception by constructing the sub-narrative or counter-narrative of the main texts. That leads finally to inauguration of a new epoch of re-construction and re-formation of myth and mythic characters which are push to the periphery of such narratives.

The research paper titled "Tracing the Distinctive Agendas of Dalits: The socio-Political Injustice with Reference to Vijay Tendulkar's *Kanyadaan*" by Abirami P. is about to express the social caste system and its impacts on individual's life. The play, *Kanyadaan* is more shows the problems of marriage and especially inter-caste marriage. In this article we discuss about the customs of marriage and the modernity in marriage which doubles the problems in marriage life and less about the common caste discrimination in the society. The issues here were discoursed through the three different lawyers of essential features accordingly first is the inter-caste marriage, second is the individual socio-cultural factors and the third is the caste as a custom identity. Finally, this article declares the dramatic changes from the seventies India and it's tradition of caste system in this twenty-first century.

Twenty-sixth paper of this anthology has been written by A.P. Pavithra Bhuvaneshwari. Her paper titled "Neoteric Dalit Ecoaesthetic Subaltern Rebellious Voice as Depicted in Bama's "Annachi": An Analysis" analyses the caste discrimination in the society. The protagonist of the story Ammasi's revolutionary steps and the caste has been depicted as a canker. The revolt, resistance and dalit consciousness are the key-focus of Pavithra Bhuvaneshwari's paper.

Dr S. Jayanthi's paper titled "African American Sojourn – An Attempt to Subvert the Literary and Power Traditions of the Dominant Culture" attempts to trace the development of African American literature. The paper explores the literature of the inspired black writers who made an effort to rise above the discrimination and racist attitudes of the dominant culture. Dr Jayanthi has given a picture of the women writers and dramatist who go back to the African culture to free themselves from the shackles that bind them.

Dr Arti Chandel's paper *"When I Hit You:* Marginalised Coming to the Fore" titled *'When I Hit You:* Marginalised Coming to the Fore' explores the process of liberation of a young Indian wife from an excruciatingly harrowing marriage, her journey and evolution from being forced to be silent, passive and marginalized woman to a strongly and powerfully voiced, active and established writer, speaking every bit of truth about her horrible experiences in marriage and of an extremely domineering pseudo-Marxist self-proposed loving husband, shaking the very foundation of the patriarchal society; thus coming to the fore, the centre and living her life the way she wants.

Dr P. Bala Shanmuga Devi has written the second last paper for this anthology. Her paper titled "When 'She' Smiles: Deontology in Indian

Puranas" aims at seeing how women are marginalised and treated as the other in the Indian *puranas* which supposedly is to be the highest form of guidance for the society for ages to come. A random study of marginalized female characters from the *Ramayana* and *Mahabharata* is taken up and empowered characterization of a smiling Sita in *Adbhut Ramayana* is also taken up in juxtaposition to the crying former.

Dr B. Manivannan has written the thirtieth and last paper of this anthology. His paper titled "Theorizing the Subaltern Representation as a Genre" is an attempt to explore more in to theoretical discussion across postcolonial concepts in general and between subaltern history and literature in particular. The first part of this paper aims not only at studying historical legitimacy involved in subaltern studies but also establishing of the view that subaltern theory is more Indian than any other western countries; it is neither Eurocentric, nor Anglo-American. The second part discusses how the motif and theme of the text are represented providing certain form for the product of subaltern discourse as a new genre.

This anthology would not have been be brought into this shape with the cooperation and dedication of many research scholars, researchers and faculty members who came forward to contemplate the concept of marginally from a literary angle. In this context, we are highly indebted to our esteemed contributing authors who took all the pains to explore multiple facets of marginality.

Apart from it, we place on record our indebtedness to our teachers, friends, critics, family members and all those unnamed names who inspired us or said something positive or negative that brought us onto this platform. We convey our countless thanks to the almightily God because without His blessings, we would never have completed this project.

Last but not the least, we are highly indebted to Mr Amit Garg, the Managing Director of Kalpaz Publications, New Delhi and his complete editorial and production team for the full cooperation to bring the book out so elegantly and brilliantly.

Editors

Dr S. Chelliah and
Dr Bijender Singh

Contributors

Dr S. Chelliah is Professor, Head, and Chairperson of School of English and Foreign Languages, Madurai Kamaraj University, Madurai (Tamil Nadu). He has produced seventeen PhD scholars, more than 176 MPhil scholars, and 104 MA projects. He has published six books and 272 papers at various national and international journals. He has served as chief guest/guest and speaker/special invitee at various national and international seminars and conferences; and also served as an evaluator/adjudicator for more than thirty PhD dissertations at various universities. He has served as Dean for curriculum development of Madurai Kamaraj University, Director for Board of Studies Section, Director for Spoken English Institute of Madurai Kamaraj University, Coordinator for CBCS Wing, Liaison Officer for SC/ST Cell of Madurai Kamaraj University, and member of Board of Studies for both UG and PG departments of Pondicherry University, Manonmaniam Sundaranar University, Bharathidasan University, Bharathiar University, and Gandhigram Rural Institute; and as an examiner of various colleges/universities for both PG and MPhil levels, and also coordinator for UGC Remedial Coaching Scheme for SC/ST/OBC and minority categories.

Dr Bijender Singh (MA, MPhil, PhD, UGC-NET, U-SET, M-SET, HP-SET, H-TET) is an English lecturer, editor, and writer from Haryana. He has earned his first PhD from USA on Shashi Deshpande and he has submitted his second PhD thesis on V.S. Naipaul in 2018. He has also done Sanskrit Honours (Shastri), Art and Crafts Teacher Course, and Multi-Purpose Health Worker (Male) Course. He has been the proud recipient of the Ambedkar Sahitya Ratna Award, Editorial Excellence Award, and Dr B.R. Ambedkar National Award. He is the Editor-in-Chief of *The Expression: An International Multidisciplinary e-Journal*. He writes in English, Hindi, and Haryanvi. He has written a few essays, some short-stories, and many Hindi lyrics, ghazals, nazms, and English poems. He has published many articles in peer-reviewed national and international journals, seminar and conference proceedings, and edited anthologies. Many research papers/articles have been written and published on his poetry books. He has written/published around two dozen books. Few of his books are available at the Princeton University Library, USA and the Library of Congress, Washington DC, USA.

Harish Mangalam is the Founder Member and General Secretary of the Gujarati Dalit Sahitya Akademi, Ahmedabad. He was an Additional Collector in the Government of Gujarat. He has published 14 books in different genres and apart from these books; he has 30 edited anthologies to his credit. He has received 12 literary awards from various organisations including Gujarat Sahitya Akademi, Government of Gujarat, Gandhinagar and Gujarati Sahitya Parishad, Ahmedabad. He has successfully organised national and international seminars/conference under the banner of Gujarati Dalit Sahitya Akademi, Ahmedabad. Since 20 years, he is the editor of *Hayati* quarterly – a mouthorgan of the Gujarati Dalit Sahitya Akademi. As a general secretary of the Gujarati Dalit Sahitya Akademi, he has published 110 titles of Gujarati Dalit Literature in Gujarati, Hindi, English and Sanskrit etc. He has presented his scholarly papers and delivered speeches on Dalit Literature in different universities and organisations all over India, including at the prestigious Indian Institute of Advanced Studies, Shimla. He is a leading figure among all the Dalit authors because of his commitment to raise Dalits' issues through his Dalit literary creations and field work of 'Annadhamm Yojana'.

Dr Ashok Verma is Associate Professor in the Department of English, Bhagat Phool Singh Mahila Vishwavidyalaya, Khanpur Kalan (Haryana). His areas of interest include Translation Studies and Marginal Writings. He has published sixteen research papers and presented papers in more than twenty seminars/conferences including one in Germany and another in Norway.

Dr Shikha Saxena is Professor and Head of Department of Humanities in Maharaja Agrasen Institute of Technology (Affiliated to GGSIPU, New Delhi). She is a poet, an ELT expert and short story writer. She has published more than 25 papers in various national and international journals. Her areas of interest are Gender Studies, Indian Writing in English and Literature of Marginality.

Dr Rumana Ashraf (MA, PhD) presently works as an Associate Professor in the Department of English in Government College for Women, Kashmir. She has obtained MA and PhD degree from the University of Kashmir. She has authored a book entitled "Margaret Atwood's Fiction: Self and Society." She has been teaching graduate and post-graduate students and has teaching experience of eighteen years. Dr Rumana has participated in many national and international conferences. She has authored two books and her research papers are published in many journals. Her areas of interest are Feminism, Kashmiri Literature, Ecocriticism and Translation Studies.

Dr C. Ramya (MBA, MA, MPhil, PhD) presently works as an Assistant Professor of English in E.M.G. Yadava Women's College, Madurai, Tamil Nadu, India. She has completed her master's degree in English, master's degree in Business Administration, master of philosophy in English and holds her doctorate degree in English. She has five years of teaching experience and she has published more than 40 research papers in peer-reviewed international journals. Her areas of interest are Psychoanalysis, Spiritual Studies and Literature.

Dr Suruchi Sharma (MA, PhD, UGC-NET) is an Assistant Professor in RKSD College, Kaithal, Haryana. She has done her PG from KMV College, Jalandhar, Punjab. She has been awarded PhD in English on Khaled Hosseini. She has presented her papers in many national and international seminars and conferences. Her papers have been published in many national and international journals and seminar/conference proceedings and several edited anthologies.

K.M. Keerthika (MA, MPhil) is a full-time PhD Research Scholar in the Department of English and Comparative Literature working on the topic entitled "Women's Stoicism and Self Identity in the Select Novels of Bharati Mukherjee, Chitra Banerjee and Jhumpa Lahiri: A Psychospiritual Approach" for her PhD thesis. She has been an outstanding student of MA English at Lady Doak College, MPhil English at S.F.R. College, Sivakasi. She has published 3 papers in international peer-reviewed UGC approved journals and attended one international conference on literary theory and also presented a paper in a national conference. She has published three articles in a national journal and seven articles in an international journal of peer review with impact factor. Among them some of her articles focus on her area of research and also on Dalit Literature.

Guni Vats is PhD Scholar at the University of Lucknow. She has completed her MA in English Literature from Central University of Rajasthan and she has earned her Honours in English Literature from the University of Delhi. She is a keen reader, budding researcher and an enthusiastic writer who takes immense pleasure in looking at diverse aspects of life from a psychoanalytical bent. She loves to experiment with themes, subjects and writing styles. She is keen to research on Indian women writers and carves a niche for them in the predominantly masculine world. Some of her works have been published in edited anthologies and journals.

N. Kaushi Reddy (MA, MPhil) is a full-time PhD Research Scholar in the Department of English & Comparative Literature, Madurai Kamaraj University, Madurai working on the topic entitled "Thematic Concerns and Stylistic Devices as Projected in the Fictional World of Bharati Mukherjee: An Evaluation" for her PhD thesis. She has been an outstanding student of MA (English) at Cauvery College for Women, Trichy and MPhil (English) at Bharathidasan University, Trichy. She has attended one international conference and a national seminar on translation. She has presented one paper in a national conference and has published five articles in an international journal of peer review with impact factor which focus on her research area and also on Dalit Literature.

Dr Kusum Kanger (MA, MPhil, PhD, UGC-NET) is an Assistant Professor in BAR Janta College Kaul, Kaithal, Haryana. She has earned her MPhil from Kurukshetra University, Kurukshetra. She has been awarded her doctoral degree on Angela Carter and Bapsi Sidhwa from NIMS University, Jaipur. She has presented and published her papers in many national and international seminars and conferences. Her papers have been published in many national and international journals and edited anthologies.

Ramanuj Mahato currently works as an Assistant Professor and Head in the Department of English at Magrahat College, under Calcutta University, Kolkata. He formerly taught at Chitta Mahato Memorial College under Sidho-Kanho-Birsha University, Purulia (W.B). With excellent academic background, he did his MA from Banaras Hindu University, Varanasi and he has qualified in UGC-NET thrice. He has already published his papers in many national and international journals as well as books from reputed publishers like Authorspress and Kalpaz Publications, New Delhi. His areas of interest are Cultural Studies, Indian English Writing, Dalit Literature, Diasporic Literature, Post-colonial Literature and Contemporary Literature

N. Padmapriyadhshini (MA, MPhil) pursuing her PhD under the guidance and supervision of Dr S. Chelliah, Professor, Head and Chairperson, Department of English, Madurai Kamaraj University, Madurai. Her research work focuses on complexities in human relationships and identity crisis. She has attended four international conferences and presented four papers out of which three papers have been published. She has published one article in an international journal of peer review with impact factor. She participated in two workshops, one on the social evils in literatures and another regarding the usage of online materials for research.

Rekha Batta is a PhD Research Scholar in the Department of English and Cultural Studies at Panjab University, Chandigarh. She has five year teaching experience as as an Assistant Professor of English at Shree Atam Vallabh Jain College, Ludhiana, Punjab and as Teaching Assistant in English at Punjab Agricultural University, Ludhiana, Punjab. She has presented scholarly papers in International Conferences and has also published research papers in national and international journals. Her area of interest is Native American Studies, Post-Colonial Literature and Subaltern Studies.

Anup Barman is at present an Assistant Teacher of English at Dalla Chandramohan Vidyamandir (H.S), Malda, West Bengal. He completed his Master of Arts in English from the University of Gour Banga in 2012. He also obtained his degree of Bachelor of Education from the University of Gour Banga in 2013. He is an independent scholar. He has participated in several national seminars and has a few publications to his credit. His areas of interest are Post-colonial Studies, ELT and Subaltern Studies.

Sabuj Sarkar is at present an Assistant Professor of English at University of Gour Banga, Malda, West Bengal. He is also currently engaged in doctoral research in the University of Burdwan, Department of English and Cultural Studies. He has published various papers in different international and national journals and anthologies. He has also presented several papers in national and international seminars. His areas of interest are postcolonial studies, folk studies and cultural studies.

Shikha Khandpur is a PhD Research Scholar in the Department of English at the University of Jammu. She is working under the guidance of Prof. Satnam Kaur. She completed her MPhil degree in the year 2018 during which she worked on the subject of conflict zones in India, and is currently working in the field of Gender Studies.

Dr Parveen Bala is an Assistant Professor in JECRC University. She has been into teaching for over a decade. She bags half a dozen of international papers published in peer-reviewed journals and has attended many workshops and seminars held in India. Her area of specialisation is Indian and Contemporary Literature.

Dr Vijaylakshmi currently heads the Department at JECRC University. She has been into teaching for the last 13 years with a total of 12 international papers to her credit. She has also authored a book with the title *Verbal and Visual Elements in William Blake's Songs of Innocence and Experience*. She began her career with ICFAI Business School, Hyderabad and has been into academics since 2005. She is also a member of the Editorial Board for two of the renowned journals viz. *International Journal of Languages and Literatures* and *International Multilingual Journal of Contemporary*

Research from American Research Institute for Policy Development, America.

Dr Sumitra Singh is an Assistant Professor at Amity University, Noida. She has delivered her lectures as a visiting professor in different universities in Australia, England and Singapore. She is the editor of *International Research Journal of Humanities, Engineering and Pharmaceutical Sciences.* She holds PhD in Afro-American Literature. She has presented research papers/articles in around seventy national and international conferences, seminars, and workshops. She has published many papers in various national and international journals and edited anthologies. She is also associated with various Community Outreach Activities.

Disha Sharma ((MA, SET) is a PhD Scholar in the Department of English from the University of Jammu. She has completed her MPhil and Master's degree from the same University. She two books to her credit out of which one is fiction and another is a valuable translation of Dogri Folktales into English. She has published various research papers in International journals and recently initiated to deliver in edited anthologies. She is presently writing paper on Bengali Culture. Her areas of interest are Dalit literature, Marxist classism, Gender Studies and Fat studies.

S. Divya Bharathi is a full-time PhD Research Scholar in the Department of English and Comparative Literature working on the topic entitled "Projection of Social Justice and Human Values in Select Novels of Mulk Raj Anand and Bhabani Bhattacharya: A Thematic Evaluation" for her PhD thesis. She has been an outstanding student of MA (English) at MKU College, Madurai, MPhil (English) at Madurai Kamaraj University, Madurai. She has published 3 papers in international peer reviewed UGC approved journals and attended one international conference at Thiruvalluvar University, Vellore.

Dr Budhanath Pratihast is an Assistant Professor of English in Bihar Institute of Law, Patna. He has done PhD in English Literature from Patna University. His articles have been published in few national, international journal and edited anthologies. His areas of interest are Indian Writing in English, Diasporic Literature and English Language Teaching.

S.F. Filomine White Sheela (MA, MPhil) is a part-time PhD English Scholar-cum-Guest Lecturer (English) with 3 years of teaching experience in the Department of English & Comparative Literature at Madurai Kamaraj University. She is one among the pioneering qualitative researchers pursuing her PhD Research programme with a special focus on Feminism and Diaspora in the intersection of Indian Fiction. Filomine White Sheela has attended 5 International Conferences and 2 National Conferences also. Her 15 articles have been published in UGC approved, peer reviewed, and multidisciplinary journals with ideal impact factor.

Sumedha Bhandari (MA, MPhil) is pursuing her PhD under the guidance of Dr Tejinder Kaur, Professor (Retd.), Department of English, Punjabi University, Patiala. Her research work focuses on the articulations of land ethic in the contemporary narrative of literary discourse. She has presented papers in five international and 15 national conferences. She has published numerous articles in national and international peer-reviewed journals. She has authored two books also. Presently, she works as an Assistant Professor in the Department of Agricultural Journalism, Languages and Culture at Punjab Agricultural University, Ludhiana. Her core areas of interest are Afro-American Literature, African Literature, Indian Writing in English, Postcolonial Studies and Ecocriticism. She is a member of the Editorial Board of *Literary Voice*, a peer-reviewed journal of national repute that has been running for more than one decade.

Anupama Rai (MA, NET) is a full-time PhD Research Scholar in the Department of English, Banaras Hindu University, Varanasi. Her research work focuses on the representation of feminine and female subjectivity and space in the select fictional work of Anjana Appachana, Chitra Banerjee Divakaruni and Uma Parameswaran. She had attended two international seminars and presented her papers there. She has published two research papers in international journal of peer review with impact factor. She has attended a two-month research workshop organized on the behalf of CSDS. Her areas of interest are cultural studies, gender studies and post-colonial studies.

Abirami P. (MA, MPhil) is a full-time PhD Research Scholar in the Department of English & Comparative Literature, Madurai Kamaraj University, Madurai, Tamil Nadu. She has published her papers in reputed national and international journals. Her areas of interest are Indian Fiction, Indian Drama, Gender Studies and Indian Writing in English.

A.P. Pavithra Bhuvaneshwari (MA, MPhil) is a Guest Lecturer in the Department of English and Comparative Literature of Madurai Kamaraj University and a part-time PhD scholar of Madurai Kamaraj University under the guidance of Dr C. Ramya, Assistant Professor, Department of English, E.M.G. Yadava College, Thirupalai, Madurai. She has been an outstanding student of MA (English) at DDE/MKU, Madurai and MPhil (English) at Madurai Kamaraj University, Madurai. She has published one research paper in an international conference and also published two articles in an international journal of peer review with impact factor.

Dr S. Jayanthi is working as an Assistant Professor of English at Sri S. Ramasamy Naidu Memorial College, Sattur. She has ten years of teaching experience. Her areas of interest are Indian Literature, Diaspora Literature, African American Literature, Subaltern and Literatures of Marginality and English Language Teaching. She has presented more than 30 papers and has published 25 papers. She has acted as a resource person and has delivered guest lecture is a member of the Board of Studies. She is the coordinator and contributor for the Practical English, a set of four books, published by Bloomsbury Publishers. The books are an attempt at self reliance, which guide the students to learn the language inductively. These books are written under the guidance of Professor Krishnaswamy, Former Professor of English, EFLU, Hyderabad.

Dr Arti Chandel is an Assistant Professor in English. She has been teaching English Literature and Language to the students at the graduate and post-graduate level in various Government Colleges of Himachal Pradesh since 2006. Presently, she is working at Govt. Degree College Sihunta, Chamba (Himachal Pradesh). She has been actively and passionately involved in research, presenting papers at international and national conferences and seminars on English Language Teaching, Diaspora, Ecocriticism and Ecofeminism and Symbolism; and contributing research papers to a number of international refereed journals and books on Indian English writers. Her areas of interest are: Indian English Literature, Postmodernist literature, Diaspora Writings, Subaltern Studies and English Language Teaching. She has reviewed more than a dozen books and is also Associate Editor of the Bi-annual international refereed journal *Poetcrit*.

Dr P. Bala Shanmuga Devi, Associate Professor of English, A.P.C. Mahalaxmi College for Women, Tuticorin, Tamil Nadu is an avid reader who has converted her hobby into a profession. Twenty-two years of teaching experience lies to her credit, yet she chooses to call herself only as a 'learner'. Her area of interest in research lies in literary theories and in Indian Writing in English. Indian mythology and ethos have been of primary interest to her on which she reads and researches a lot. She has published thirty research papers, a few poems and one book. She is also a creative writer by choice and hopes to publish her collection of short stories in the near future.

Dr B. Manivannan (MA, MPhil, BEd, PhD) is an Associate Professor in English in V.O. Chidambaram College, Thoothukudi. He is Tamil poet, author, translator, soft skill trainer and environmentalist. His doctoral thesis is on Irish poetry in English under the guidance of Dr Balachandran, *Kavignar* Bala, Formerly Convener, Tamil Advisory Board, Sahitya

Akademi. His areas of specialization are Poetry, Drama, Literary and Communication Theories. He has edited a book titled *Studies in Indian English Poetry: From Aurobindo to Laksmi Kanna.* He has published his articles in many national and international journals and edited anthologies. He is one of the Preliminary Panel Advisers, Award Committee, Sahitya Akademi, Govt. of India. He is the Chairman, P.G. English Examination Board, M.S. University, Tirunelveli, University nominee, P.G. Board of Studies, Sadakatullah Appa College, Tirunelveli, Member, P.G. Board of Studies, M.S. University, Tirunelveli, Member of Editorial Board in *Outreach: Multidisciplinary Research Journal.* His Poems and Short Stories have been published in Tamil Magazines. He has received Loyola Literary Media Award (2014) and Kavi Venthar Award (2015) for being the best poet among more than 300 poets in Tamil Nadu in 2014, conferred by Anantha Jothy Literary Circle and Meera Publishers.

Chapter - 1

Subalternity, Marginality and Untouchability as Projected in the Current Literary Scenario

Dr S. Chelliah and
Dr Bijender Singh

The accouchement of humankind is processed by God in the same way. Everyone in the world is born from the womb of the mother. In the world garden, God has created numerous varieties of flowers, which are different in colour, sizes, petals, fragrances and beauty, but each and every flower created by God has the unique status and is kept under the common concept 'flowers'. Likewise, human beings, who are created by God, may vary in colour, height, size and other attitudes but they come under the common concept 'humankind'. Since, all humans are born in the same way possessing common red blood, breathing common air and surviving on the basis on human approach depending each other. Humankind deserves equal rights to survive and exist in the world.

But the history from ancient period teaches the human kind a particular thing (i.e.) even from the primitive age humans are not treated equally. There exist a hierarchical position among them that is the leader and the followers, and the king and the followers. Later, when years passed by, the two way-divisions further divided into many communities and each of these communities had leaders and the followers, and further arose the diversity among these communities and these group of people themselves compiled the set of norms to protect themselves.

Certain groups of people face discrimination, segregation and injustice by other hegemonic group, who self-centeredly and egocentrically secured their position for their future generation by not minding about the needs of feelings, self-respect and dignity. These groups of people made a stereotype of vision in degradation by pointing out their specific race, skin colour and their choice of lifestyle by holding different beliefs and ideals of their own. The degraded and suppressed communities and the group of people brought into the prison of "subalternity", "marginality", and "untouchability".

The word "subaltern" has its origin from the Latin word "subalternus" in which "sub" means "under" and "alternus" means "every other". This word literally means, a British military term used for junior officer who is second of rank and means "subordinate". In other words, it also means of inferior rank. Italian Marxist theoretician Antonio Gramsci (1891-1937) used the term "subaltern" for the first time, outside the non-military sense and as a part of Marxist theory during 1920s. Gramsci is a noteworthy figure whose notions on subalternity are being read by the people across the world. He had to go to jail many times and he wrote around thirty notebooks.

He got imprisoned several times and he authored around thirty notebooks and wrote more than 3000 pages of history. His book *Prison Notebooks* was a series of essays which were written between 1929 and 1935. These essays cover a wide range of topics such as religion, the French Revolution, fascism, civil society, Fordism, folklore and high and low culture.

As a proletariat, Gramsci refers to the word "subaltern" to any person who belongs to an inferior rank of any race, class, religion, ethnicity, and gender. This term used by Antonio Gramsci denotes all the working classes of the world. The subalterns live at the lower level or rank in the social, political and other spheres.

The subaltern groups of people are low ranking in a social, political and other hierarchy, who are considered to be poor living under a dictatorship. In the view of western world, the concept of subaltern refers to the person who is politically, economically and socially inferior and it is evidenced through Eugene O'Neill's play *The Hairy Ape*. The protagonist of the play Yank is considered to be the subaltern, who senses that he belongs to the world controlled by the rich. Yank is a subaltern whose humanity is regressed by industrialization into a machine that humans are programmed to do one task. As a proletariat, Yank is the subject of "subalternity", where he entraps himself into the deeply and rigid bourgeois class and finally, he dies in the crush of the Ape which represents the highly predominating highest working classes. As a subaltern, Yank's inability to think, not only reveals his regression to a lower animal form, but also the inability and unbalances to adapt and survive himself in the world of class frustrations.

This describes the lamentation of Yank, which he is talking to himself, that once he was as strong as steel, but now Yank realises that he is no longer as powerful as he once was. The darkness emerges as a result of confusion that Yank sees devoid of himself. He does not find any scope or hope of his future. He is unable to see what's ahead and he was totally smashed by the high societal class as a working labour.

The concept subalternity", when it arrives in the Indian way of thinking, according to Gayatri Chakravorty Spivak, a postcolonial theorist, calls herself "a practical Marxist feminist deconstructionist". Spivak says that subalterns are those people who live at the bottom of the society and live in the Third world countries. Their rights are infringed by some ruling people and the people are divided on the basis of caste, class, gender, race, community and religion.

It is impossible for them to speak as they are divided by gender, class, caste, race, region and religion. In India, the subalterns are low caste people, whose voices are muted. They are called 'untouchables'. The low-caste subalterns are behind the prison of untouchability. The literal meaning of untouchability is to consider someone inferior and put him at the lower level of animals. These people are considered unpolluted and even their touch can defile the people. They are kept at a distance from the mainstream and they remain socially and politically ostracised. Their touch is contaminated or polluting a higher caste people. Those people or their community is despised, degraded section of people. The untouchable in India is found occupying the bottom most places in the society subjected to various social, cultural and other kinds of disabilities and exploitation. These people are called Dalits. The term 'Dalit' represents the group of people who are the sufferers of existential crisis. These marginalised people are the product of Hindu caste system. Following the caste norms and rules, the untouchables were subjected to all forms of oppression socially, economically, politically, culturally and religiously.

The emergence of Dalit literature in recent times brought forth many writers, who unmask the "Dalit consciousness" through their autobiographical narratives such as Omprakash Valmiki's *Joothan*, Sheoraj Singh Bechain's *My Childhood on My Shoulders*, Hazari's *Untouchable: The Autobiography of Indian Outcaste,* Laxman Bapu Mane's *Upara: An Outsider,* Vasant Moon's *Growing up Untouchable in India*, Balbir Madhopuri's *Changiya Rukh: Against the Night*, Susmita Bhave's *Pan on Fiery*, Gaikwad's *The Branded: Uchalya*, Bama's *Karukku*, Urmila Pawar's *The Weave of My Life* and Baby Kamble's *The Prisons We Broke*. Through these autobiographies, they bring forth the sufferings and pains that revolve around Dalits' life as a voiceless worm toasted on the heat of casteism in India. It is witnessed through Omprakash Valmiki's *Joothan* which is an autobiographical narrative of his untouchable's life. Om Prakash Valmiki in his autobiographical narrative describes his own life growing up as an untouchable in a village in Uttar Pradesh in the newly independent India of the 1950's. Valmiki's early life begins in an account of the individual struggle by a Dalit boy from the sweeper caste Chuhra. The word "Joothan" literally means left- over from meal and also in another sense, it also means unsuitable/unfit for consumption by another person. Thus, the Dalits have been mandatorily kept under control to eat "Joothan" for their livelihood.

The painful sufferings as a marginalized experience by Valmiki are that Tyagi Brahmins of the upper caste will not address them by their names. This Brahmin insults them by saying, "It was alright to touch cows and stray dogs but touching a Chuhra inflicted instant "pollution" on the Tyagis" (Valmiki 12).

Valmiki's family worked hard for managing to get two decent meals a day for the entire family. As a downtrodden caste, these Chuhras were not paid for their labour instead; they were beaten up and brutally abused. They were forced to eat joothan to fill up their empty stomachs. The treatment of the upper-caste people with the Dalits remains very bad. They abuse them. Valmiki has to clean the whole school at the orders of his headmaster just because he was born in a sweeper class.

Another autobiography Laxman Gaikwad's *The Branded* depicts how all the people of Gaikwad's community were given a brand of 'thieves' and they were mercilessly beaten by the police. Police would not spare even the children, women and the old people of the family. These people were not allowed to go to another place. Nobody would give them any work and they were forced to take the profession of thievery. The children would remain hungry at times and to get food was the biggest challenge for them.

Basically, women are considered to be subaltern. Especially, Dalit women are encountered as a woman, Dalit woman and as an untouchable woman. These women are triply marginalised. It is evidenced through the work of P. Sivakami's *The Grip of Change.* The Dalit women are considered to be Dalit among Dalits. They have to walk through the thorns of casteism in search of some fruit of freedom. The lives of Dalit women are unresistingly traumatic and their physic, psyche, actions, souls, words and emotions are always marginalised. *The Grip of Change* (2006) is the English translation of *Pazhiyana Kazhithalum* (1989), the first full length novel by P. Sivakami.

The protagonist of the story is Thangam; a young Dalit widow, is talked through the novel through various sufferings, such as caste, hierarchy, vulnerability of woman and triple violence – social, economic and patriarchal, faced by her in the novel. Through the character Thangam, P. Sivakami became a strong voice for the Dalit women's exploitation. Thangam is an agricultural labourer who was abandoned and denied of her husband's share of land by the brothers of her husband for her being childless. She could get her share of property only if she could satisfy the lust of her brothers-in-law. She was unable to save her honour from the brutal hands of caste hierarchy. Being a Dalit woman, she faces bodily violence not only at domestic level but outside her home at the cruel claws of upper caste men. Dalit women are interiorised to the position of mere toys in the trap of her own group and outside of her group. Instead of protecting Thangam, her brothers-in-law seized the opportunity to exploit her sexually.

> After my husband's death…My husband's brother's tried to force me, but I never gave in. They would not give me my Husband's land, but wanted me to be the whore for them. (7)

The novel as a whole projects Thangam in an exhausted and wretched state of an outcaste woman from beginning to end. She is never a fighter but always a victim of the society.

In case of African-American people, they are also considered to be subalterns because they are racially, politically and socially inferior and discriminated. They were marginalised and treaded as slaves. And this witnessed through the slave narratives of many black African-American authors, such as Harriet Beecher Stowe, W.E.B. DuBois, Toni Morrison, Maya Angelou, Booker T. Washington, Gwendolyn Brooks, Alice Walker and Loraine Hansberry. Through their works, they describe the cruelties of life faced by them under slavery as subalterns. It is remarkably unmasked through the work *The Interesting Narrative of the Life of Olaudah Equiano or Gustavus Vassa*, he shares out his one of the first major slave autobiographies. He writes his slavery painful circumstance as he is kidnapped from his homeland Africa when Equiano was only eleven-year-old and sold into slavery first in Africa. As Equiano admits himself in his narratives:

> The first object which saluted my eyes when I arrived in the coast was sea, and a slaveship, which was then riding at anchor and waiting for its Cargo. The filled me with astonishment, which was soon connected with terror, when I was soon carried on the board. I was now persuaded

that I had gotten into the world of bad spirits, and they were going to kill me. (Equiano 48).

Equiano faced the hardships and the terrors of being packed and trapped into slavery. Equiano sustained and subjected to severe terrors and whippings in the slavery where countless Africans tightly packed in this journeying to a life of cruel servitude. Equiano and his masses had to remain starved and the European slave traders' behaviour was not good towards them.

The African-American women are doubly marginalised as a woman and a slave. The women writers carve the sufferings and feelings of Afro-American women in their works, such as Toni Morrison, Alice Walker, and Maya Angelou and other writers. They bring the realistic image of Afro-American woman and their brutal pains in their life.

To conclude, it is further understood that the concept of subaltern is sandwiched between the concept of marginality and untouchability. It is unearthed through O'Neill's play that protagonist Yank as a middleclass poverty stricken proletariat is marginalized behind the conventions of bourgeois class and Yank is a person of untouchable according to the higher class woman Milred. Valmiki's *Joothan* and P. Sivakami's *The Grip of Change* portray the life of Dalits as untouchables and voiceless subalterns, who are marginalised socially, economically, politically. Likewise, African-Americans who are racially subalterns are treated as slaves and marginalized severely in all their basic needs in their life. Thus, the concept of subalternity, marginality and untouchability plays the major role in the life of subalterns.

Works Cited

Ambedkar, B.R *The Untouchables: Who Were They and Why Were They Become Untouchables?* (1948). New Delhi: Prestige Books, 1998. Print.

Aston, N.M. *Dalit Literature and African Literature*. New Delhi: Prestige Books, 2001. Print.

Braun, Joachim Von and Franz W. Gatzweiler, (eds.). *Marginality: Addressing the Nexus of Poverty, Exclusion and Ecology*. New York & London: Springer, 2014. Print.

Equiano, Olaudah. *The Interesting Narrative of the Life of Olaudah Equiano, or, Gustavus Vassa, the African Peterborough.* Ontario: Broadview Press, 2001. Print.

Rajkumar. *Dalit Literature and Criticism, Literary/Cultural Theory*. New Delhi: Orient Black Swan, 2019. Print.

Sivakami. P. *The Grip of Change*. New Delhi: Orient Blackswan Private Ltd. 2009. Print.

Valmiki, Omprakash. *Joothan: A Dalit's Life.* New Delhi: Columbia University Press, 2003. Print.

Chapter - 2

An Appraisal of Marginality in Select Dalit Short Stories

Harish Mangalam

First of all, I would like to clarify the various nomenclatures of the Marginal literature. We know this new stream of literature by 'Marginal literature', 'Dalit Literature', 'Subaltern literature', '*Bahujan* literature', and 'Progressive literature too.' All these terms are inclusive. Even though, there may be some differences of opinion regarding its nomenclature. Differences always invite good debate, intelligent discourse and after such churning, we get butter. Shapes of the bottle are changed, but the contents remain the same. Some people and even some writers of *'Lalit'* literature, show their displeasure and oppose to use the 'Dalit' word for literature, they believe that it is cast-base name which is ridiculous. Because their belief is false as 'Dalit' word is an adjective and not at all on any caste-base. Than what is wrong in using this word for literature? Why it should be opposed and that too by *'Lalit'* writers? We understand that a layman can oppose it, but how one being a writer can oppose it? Should we mean that they don't understand the meaning of 'Dalit' word? The answer is 'No, not at all.' Then their approach is not scientific. Their approach is shaky and baseless. Instead of changing the word 'Dalit,' why they don't think to change their brutal, ill-minded and rotten mentality? The definition of 'Dalit' word is very clear and broad as it should be, 'The Dalit literature means apart from any castes and creeds and those who are downtrodden.' They all are Dalit means 'crushed', 'segregated', 'suppressed', 'oppressed', 'repressed', 'women', 'untouchables', 'tribes', 'bonded labourers', 'child labour', 'stooge', 'slaves', and LGBTTQQIAAP (lesbian, gay, bisexual, transgender, queer, questioning, intersex, asexual, ally, pansexual) etc. We may name them marginalised people and their literature is Marginalised Literature.

The marginalised literature's subject, excellence and the language world has challenged to understand its many creations with a new angle. Marginalised literature is for emancipation of the community of the sections as mentioned above. The marginalised literature started to bring forth the social oriented writers and to patronize them. Against *varnashram* system, patriarchy, unscientific ancient scriptures, rotten traditional customs, exploitation, untouchability and atrocities, the marginalised literature has manifested its anger, not only anger but blew a clarion to up-root the deeply rooted high and low caste distinction. In the marginalised literature, there is an extensive narration of the conditions of socially, educationally, politically, economically and culturally exploited. From the sociological point of view, it helps to understand the complicated society based on *varnavyavstha.* It makes inevitable to redefine the prevalent principles. The question of discriminatory caste system is associated with identity which has become distinction for a so-called *savarna* class to continue to be hegemonic power in the Indian-Hindu society. How the Marginalised writer protests to all these questions and how their style of creations is differed from the traditional style. They have been victims of caste system. So, psychologically the marginalised people, in particular in rural India, were accepting their status as a slave since their birth and they believing that this social condition was their destiny. Then the ideology of Dr Babasaheb Ambedkar awakened and now a day, there is a great change in that mentality of upper castes people. They believe that we are also human beings as others and self-respect is generated. In the contemporary world of literature, it is considered as a modern and post-modern literary age, but I firmly believe that when 80% of the total population is from marginalised sections, therefore, this period should be considered as an age of Marginalised literature or Dalit literature, and so on.

Still caste system in Indian-Hindu society is intact, because the traditional people are accustomed to see the social system with the historical and religious sight and it is very difficult to annihilate *varnavyavstha* based on caste distinction, In India, to deny caste system means to destroy all the structures of deeply rooted hegemony of *brahminism.* It has become steady and permanent. How the marginalised literature looks at these questions and how it seeks political change? – To rethink on such questions socially and politically as well as religiously is an unavoidable. In the post-modern period, there is a social change, but instead of annihilation of castes, it has been changing the form of discrimination of castes. Over and above, our political elections in our country are completely based on castes which have become an obvious reality.

The expelled and neglected people of India have been systematically deprived of their constitutional rights, natural rights as the religious based social system has caused inhuman treatment of discrimination and untouchability is co-related with an elusive reality likewise, purity, karma, hell and heaven etc. and adhered to watertight compartments of castes barriers dividing man between man. Rabindranath Tagore said, "Sabar upar Manush – tabar upar kainahi" (above everything there is a man and above a man, there is nothing.) Since ages, *varnashravyavstha,* untouchability and graded caste system has made lagged far behind our nation in comparison to the progress of the other nations of the world.

The first and foremost, Gautama Buddha blown a clarion against caste system. At that time, there was humanity in the centre of 'Jain' and 'Buddha' religion. Both the religions imbibed a doctrine of equality. *Buddha* resisted *brahiminism* and raged a combat against violence and sacrificial rite *(yagna).* He firmly said that 'one cannot be illustrious by taking birth in Brahman family and one cannot be of low family by taking birth in Shudra should equally be respectable.' Buddha equated male-female and all the castes. This was the first great revolt against *Brahmans.*

> Buddha said with a firm determination:
> Na uchcha vaslo hoti, na uchcha hoti Brahmano
> Kamanna vaslo hoti, kamanna hoti Brahmano.

which means nobody is a *Shudra* by birth, nobody is a *Brahman* by birth. It was totally against God's speech *"Chaturvarnya maya srushti"* (I have created a four-fold society). *Buddha* resisted against religious ceremonies and rites, blind faith and violence. He defied the *Vedas* and said it is false knowledge. He associated two expelled peoples namely 'Suneet' and 'Prakruti' in 'Buddhist Monk Association' (Bhikshu Sangh). Thereafter, so many social reformists, sages and seers came and gone, but the iron walls of *Varnashram* and inhuman high and low discriminatory castes system is intact as it was prevailing in ancient period!! Following the ideology of the first Mahatma of our nation, Jyotiba Phule, was the first educational trainer to women and he educated Savitribai, the great dignitary of the world and Dr Babasaheb Ambedkar, the great emancipator of the untouchables of India, E.V. Ramasamy Periyar, the great revolutionary. The young educated and well-awakened litterateurs have started to further forward the war-chariot of Dr Babasaheb Ambedkar by creating marginalised literature (or Ambedkarite literature) inscribing sharpened words like an arrow with acidic language from their quiver.

I have selected a few profound short stories very relevant to the subject. There are many kinds of Marginalization, albeit I have given top priority to the severely marginalised sections of the Indian-Hindu society. The gravity of their exploitation, oppression, suppression, repression and ostracism by the hegemony powers is much more rather than any other classes of the society. The selected short stories are from Marathi, Hindi and Gujarati etc.

In the Marathi short story "A Curse of Caste", the prolific writer Baburao Bagul has depicted the macabre dance of Indian-Hindu caste discriminatory society. Baburao Bagul had to resume his duty so he went there. The people of Indian-Hindu society believes in *Varnashram* system created by *Manu* in his *Manusmriti* strictly on the bases of high and low castes, i.e. *Savarnas,* the so called upper castes and the *Shudras* the lowest rung of the society. So, whenever you go in rural India, the orthodox and rigid fellow would first ask your caste and sub-caste asking question to you like, "What caste you belong to?" immediately following the second question, "What is your sub-caste?" Asking such questions, what is the magic left behind it and knowing your caste, what the secret of it is hidden? After knowing your caste and sub-caste, they would decide how to speak, behave and show gesture too! Unless and until they know your caste, they would not feel comfortable. Here, everything is related with the castes totally based on religion. A *Savarna* man Ramchandran knew that Baburao Bagul belongs to a Chamar caste, the untouchable, suddenly Baburao Bagul was assaulted by so-called *Savarnas* (upper castes) fellows including Ramchandran. Baburao Bagul was persistently beaten up like anything. Because of severe thrashing on his forehead, blood was flowing. Baburao Bagul observed silence and he didn't do vengeance. At that time, his heart was full of topsy-turvy. But his companion named Kashinath, shown his displeasure against his silence and not resisting for his self- protection. Kashinath surprised and said to Baburao Bagul, "No, when they were beating you pitilessly and you remained silent? The writer is a skilful archer, so he released an arrow from his quiver very coldly and replied: "They were not beating upme, they were beating up Manu!"-and ends the short story. Because, *Manu*had accorded a sanction to such cruel inhumanity through the *Manusmriti.* He created *Varnaashram* system based on *brahminism* which is totally unscientific and inhuman. So, *Manu* is solely responsible for such social pollutions, better to say social crime. This is a unique punch of the story, gains its peak of the heights in the world of short story writings. The short story is an obvious example of artistic piece with the writer's proficiency, not only in the world of marginalised literature, but in the world of whole literature. The writer has fully controlled himself and from the artistic point of view, nothing is loud in delineation of short story.

I would like to mention here one very pathetic and barbaric incident of the gruesome dance of discrimination and ostracism caused by the Indian-Hindu society based on *brahiminism.* The killing occurred late night on October 20th in Maharashtra state, the native place of Baburao Bagul, the writer of this short story: The Dalit farmer named Samjay (ii) hiswife Jayshree Jadhav, 30 years and their 21 years old son Sunil Jadhav were found murdered outside their home in their 1.5 are *bajra* field. The bodies had been chopped. The body of a young Sunil Jadhav had been chopped into at least zero pieces, his head been split in two and the killer tried to stuff all the parts down the bore-well. Over and above, the mainstream media played anti-social and merciless role and completely suppressed the news. This shameless and brutal incident shows us how our society is rotten!

"Chat of Chaturi Chamar" is one of the best marginalised short stories by B. L. Nayer. In this short story, Chandan Chaube, belongs to so called upper caste runs his lorry of *Chat*. This lorry stand is nearer to *Tiwari* society. That means most of the people come to this lorry to eat *Chat* are of higher caste. While eating *Chat,* the people chit-chat of anything, "Now a day, there is no untouchability. There is a great change in the society. See, how the Hindus have been changed. Photos of Ram and Dr B.R. Ambedkar, both are kept altogether on the stage on occasion of kite-flying day, Hindu leaders Brother, now what more do you want? In Banaras, Hindus ate *puri* at the house of the Dalits. Low and high caste discrimination has been completely eradicated. Really, now the *Ramrajya* is in existence." The writer B.L. Nayer has beautifully woven day-to-day talks of the laymen who do not know ground reality of the society. Such baseless, unreasonable, silly and imagined trivial talks of the local people, heard by Chandan Chaube around his stand point of the lorry of *Chat.* There was always a heavy rush of the people those who use to come to eat *Chat.* He himself being alone, was unable to cope up with the catering of *Chat* to all the customers speedily. So, he called one of his friends from his native place for assistance. He sent a telegram to Chaturi Chamar to come immediately. After all, Chandan Chaube engaged his friend Chaturi Chamar. It is naked truth of the Indian-Hindu wicked society that nobody would like to take *Chat* from the untouchables. And it happens, what it would have to be happened. Chandan Chaube was completely misguided by day-to-day hearing of talks of trivial matters and unreal chit-chat of the people which were elusive for him. Chaturi Chamar was apprehended and didn't agree to sell *Chat.* Chaturi Chamar who comes from rural India, had bitter self-experiences of ugly society and untouchability. Various thoughts of fear caught his mind. Chandan Chaube became angry upon him and said:

> Chaturi, you are a rustic fellow. Now the time has already been changed. Now nobody is high or low by caste in the society. All are equal. When our leaders take meals with the people of backward community, when they eat *puri* from the house of the Dalits, then would not their devotees follow them? As per leaders say, the local people use to follow them. The society is not separate from such leaders. Both are dependent on each other. And this is not a village, this is a city. Here, the peoples are living. They have least concern with such matters. Chaturi, you don't afraid of anything, you can do this without any fear! Yet his internal soul was not ready to believe Chandan Chaube's say. Eventually, Chandan Chaube held the shoulder of Chautri Chamar and dragged him to lorry. He showed the boards written as 'Chat of Chaube' and 'Seller Chandan Chaube.' He added, "Nowhere Chamar is written on your forehead. How the people will dream of you that you are caste by Chamar? Chaturi, it is getting delay, be fearless.

But Chaturi being a Chamar, an untouchable, started feeling perception of destitute (inferiority complex). He was embraced by whirl wind thoughts, "If customers will see a new man like me, then they will definitely enquire and ask about me. Then what will I reply? Till what period, may I hide about my caste? One day, it will have to be revealed. I will not do such wrong." He himself thought to change the names of the boards. Instead going towards the society of *Tiwari,* straight forwardly he went to the shop of painter and got the boards repainted as 'Chaturi Chamar' after erasing out the words 'Chandan Chaube'. We all know very well what would have happened then? It happened what was expected in the four-fold stratified Indian-Hindu society. The *Savarnas* or upper castes people of Tiwari society shocked and astonished to read the name of 'Chaturi Chamar' in place of 'Chandan Chaube!' Some of the peoples, showed disgust and sense of disgrace, some were grumbling and running away! Some young people came nearer to lorry and started raving with abuses! Openly started to threaten and said to Chaturi Chamar, "To-day is the first day, so we are not disturbing you but if you will come tomorrow, we will make your condition worst. And at the end of the story, helpless Chaturi Chamar narrated and brought forward the whole incident into notice of Chandan Chaube. Ultimately, Chandan Chaube also came to understand the reality of the society. He himself realised that nothing has been changed in the society and discrimination is intact. At once, Chandan Chaube could not decide. But after some time of his deep engrossed silence and with his gloomy face, he told to Chaturi Chamar, "Chaturi, now you go back to your native village and do some labour, yet your time has not come to sell Chat!" The short story ends here with the torment satire on the discriminatory Indian-Hindu society and heightening great excellence of tactful art of the marginalised writer. Even in the age of science and technology, not a single pebble of the fort of *Varnashram* has been crumble down. Even to-day, it is intact. *Varnashram* system based untouchability is an obstacle and has blocked all the paths of development of the marginalised community. Here, we should mention the brutal, cruel, inhuman, cannibalistic incident recently occurred in the village, Mota Samadhiyala, of Una Taluka (Gujarat), is nothing but a well-planned attack on Dalits by communal minded so-called upper castes people, i.e. Hindus under the guise of *'Gau-Raksha.'*

If we observe minutely, the society of Hindu-India has not yet been reformed scientifically. The mentality and tendency has now become canker. Here, I would like to mention some very relevant lines of poem by Dr Babasaheb Ambedkar:

> No one personnel with other personnel
> But a Dalit meeting with so-called upper caste
> Take place just like
> Meeting with other nation.

Hindi short story "The Trespasser" has been written in Hindi, the title is 'Ghuspethiya' by very well-known writer Omprakash Valmiki. He has created an excellent short story and represented the painful condition of the segregated people of Hindu India. In Hindu-India, the Dalits are treated as if they are trespassers. 'Trespasser' means to enter in the land of other country illegally. At the time of Kargil War, some people trespassed from Pakistan to India and we call them as trespassers in political term. At that time, if Indian Army man kills the Army man of Pakistan Army man or Pakistan Army man kills Indian Army man, we call it murder of human being in humanitarian term. As such, in Hindu-India, the Dalits are treated as trespassers in political term and not in humanitarian term. In this Dalit short story, 'The Trespasser', the character named Sudhakar Soankar is a Dalit student. He has taken admission in Medical faculty. While commuting in the bus, some Brahman students beaten up him very ruthlessly. Some Hindu students kicked up brutally. One Brahman student named Mishra became angry and said, "If any student who belongs to Chamar caste, please stand up!" When Sudhakar Sonkar didn't stand up on his seat, one student named Pranav Mishra pulled his hairs and dragged him with cruelty. When Sudhakar Sonkar replied, "I am not a Chamar, I am Sonkar" Then Pranav

Mishra slapped him on his face and said, "You may be Chamar or Sonkar, but you are not a Brahman, that is enough!!"See, the influence of *Manusmriti.* Whatever provisions have been made for the upliftment of the downtrodden community by Dr Babasaheb Ambedkar in our constitution becomes useless as it is totally in the hands of implementers. All the students were joking and Sudhakar Sonkar was just like half-dead. Because of atrocities and inhuman treatment caused by Hindus students, Sudhakar Sonkar committed suicide. Such deaths of Medical and Engineering students of Dalits, simply become an advertisement. Not only Hindu students harass the Dalit students but teachers, professors and principals also harass the Dalit students and they prove themselves real Dronacharyas. Even the Dalit students tender their representations to the Dean, the Dean didn't initiate any action against the Hindu students. Instead initiating any action against guilty students, he went on saying on loss occurred to the upper caste students due to reservation! Here, an intelligent reader finds out the root cause of irritation to the Hindu students. The Dean said, "Admissions of the Dalit students in Medical faculty are just like the trespassers!!"

One essay titled "Untouchability or injustice" by Dr Babasaheb Ambedkar, has remarked that injustice caused by the Hindu students to the Dalit students is not a question, but how the so-called upper caste students come to know that the Dalits are separate community?! How they come to know that the Dalits are untouchables? Dr Babasaheb Ambedkar has raised a very important question that if the Dalits are Hindu, then why their dead bodies not allowed in the same crematorium?! In his another very important essay, 'Their wishes are laws unto us', he has quoted one case of a Dalit caste by a Domnamed Naubinin Kolkata- He was accused for the theft of a goat. But he was proved to be innocent. Then he lodged a case against the complainant for his defamation. At that time, that judge said, "How it could be a case of defamation to a Dalit?" Dr Babasaheb Ambedkar observed with a great surprise that "how the judge came to know that a Dalit do not have any kind of social status and respect!" Dr Babasaheb Ambedkar himself thought in his mind and replied to his own question that "It is due to Manuvadi-ideology." Dr B.R. Ambedkar was of the firm opinion that Hindu's mentality has not been changed and day by day, it has been deteriorated. He has written one another important essay, "Problem of Discrimination" in which he has categorically depicted reality of our society:

Rights of citizen means
Not the rights of the Dalits
The Government of the people means
Not the Government of the Dalits

Equal rights means
Not the rights of the Dalits
Equal opportunities means
Not the opportunities to the Dalits
That separation makes
This is an obstacle for their development.

Gujarati short story "The Flame" is 'Zol' ("The Flame" P. 113) by Harish Mangalam has been published in his Short story collection *Light of Darkness* translated by Dr Rupalee Burke into English. *Light of Darkness* has also been translated into German as 'Aus Demzwielicht' by Stephanie Kreiner and Helmuth Niederlie.

Dr M.B. Gaijan, a very well-known critic has unfolded all the aspects of the short story and focused on some salient issues are as under:

> "The Gujarati Dalit short story 'Zol' ("The Flame" 113) by well-known writer Harish Mangalam, is highly symbolical and suggestive. It does not only present injustice committed on Dalits of Gujarat, but Dalits victimized across the country. The writer has used autobiographical style. The protagonist suffers from eczema. Eczema is a kind of skin disease that creates great trouble to the patient. In this short story, cruelty is caused on Dalits and Dalits get the wound like eczema. This wound is unbearable to them. ("The Flame" P. 23)

The protagonist is telling that he used many medicines, tablets and creams, but none worked. He thinks, "What didn't the doctors treat it carefully? Why was eczema so difficult to cure an age when fatal diseases like cancer were conquered and heart-valves were replaced so easily?" ("The Flame" P. 111). The writer skillfully presents cruelty caused to Dalits on the base of caste nausea. He further said, "The doctor had told me that it would take some time before it was cured because it had been there since long...almost forty-five years have passed since then..." ("The Flame" P. 113).

The protagonist said the eczema based on castes nausea and cruelty is not that product of this time, century old issue that is. This short story is highly symbolical. Dalits are born with this sort of unbearable, even not immediate totally curable stigma. As a citizen of democratic India, the protagonist can't bear the cruelty. It indicates the protagonist's protest. "It continued itching, he scratched, applied cream, but the itching just wouldn't subside. It made him restless...His entire existence had blended with eczema." ("The Flame" P. 113).

Whenever cruelty is committed on Dalits, anywhere in India, he strongly protested. Because of his extremist thoughts and action, his friends warned him that fatal consequences would come. For the social change, different ideologies are discussed, like, 'Art and Ideology', 'Art and Reality', 'Materialism', 'Equality', etc. ("The Flame" P. 116). With his friends, he tries to find out solution, emancipation from this eczema like caste-based cruelty. He is unable to explain his wife about the issue of eczema. Because, there is no solution to remove it forever.

When the protagonist is meeting to his friends, he speaks loudly about his wound, others remain silent. Later on, they have replied one by one. Each one was victimized by the injustice and cruelty at different places and time. One got sore in 981, at that time in Gujarat, *'Anti Reservation Stir'* took place and many Dalits suffered. Another told him about Jetalpur incident, that is the small village of suffered because he got marriage with a so-called *Savarna* girl. Thus, each has wound. Each has suffering. To come out from the disease, they go to the expert of this disease. The expert is no more. But his inspiring statue is there.

> "This is the statue of a world famous physician, an authority on eczema... he had discovered the cure for eczema...but...this extremely caring and industrious doctor died under mysterious circumstances...! That is why, this disease has gone out of hand now." ("The Flame" P. 116)

> Then they all went to the statue of the doctor, Dr B.R. Ambedkar, End of the short story is highly suggestive, "A tremor shook the statue. There was a deafening explosion and a flame leapt up. The tongues of fire licked the air hungrily. The heaven glowed fiercely like hot sphere" ("The Flame" P. 115).

The short story creates unique impression because of them and writer's style. The writer has made experiment in the short story. Simply he mentions the series of incidents of atrocities on the marginalised community and applies elision of narration of incidents. He satires on M.K. Gandhi using ironical words like *'Aandhi'* (Dust-storm), *'Paandhi'* (Surname) and *'Gandhi'* (M.K. Gandhi). Because M.K. Gandhi believed in *'Varnashram system'* and simultaneously he said, "Untouchability is a black daunt on our fore-head' – both the statements are contradictory." ("The Flame" P 115). He was a politician. He didn't want to invite displeasure from Hindus, so played dual policy. He was not firm and committed as Dr B.R. Ambedkar. That is why, here in the short story, the writer mentions the statue of Dr B.R. Ambedkar and not of M.K. Gandhi. The writer prefers revolutionary and committed personality to mention here for the total welfare, upliftment and emancipation of marginal community of India.

In the contemporary period, halo of our country is worsened day by day. The religion based politics has stifled the dissent voice on the name of nationalism. Then the responsibilities of the artists in every fields becomes much more to have the liberty of expression. In such days, the condition of marginal community becomes very frightful. So, the marginal litterateurs have to make their pen more powerful against such social pollutions.

Work Cited

Gupta, Ramanikaa. *Dalit Kahani Sanchayan.* New Delhi: Sahitya Akademi, 2017.Print.

https://theprint.in/opinion/you-dont-look-dalit-and-other-things-upper-castes-must-stop-saying-to-dalits-immediately/263424/

Malsatar, Kanti. *Pachis Choka Dodhso*. Ahmedabad: Gujarati Dalit Sahitya Akademi, 2011. Print.

Mangalam, Harish. *Light of Darkness*. Ahmedabad: Yash Publications, 2012. Print.

Sharma, Pradeep K. *Dalit Politics and Literature.* New Delhi: Shipra Publications, 2006. Print.

Tulsiram. "Dalit Sahitya Ka Mool Swaroop Buddha Sahitya Se Utpan Hai." *Dalit Asmita*, Quarterly. New Delhi: Vol.1, Indian Institute of Dalit Studies, 2010. Print.

Chapter - 3

Negotiating Marginality through Female Body: Revisiting Marginal Women Characters in Krishna Sobti's *Zindaginama*

Dr Ashok Verma

The concept of marginality has to be perceived along the marginality-centrality dyad. Be it the dalits, the tribals, women or any particular ethnic group, they are marginal because they are in one way or the other not at the helm of affairs. In other words, they are not in the mainstream and as such, are doomed to be at the receiving end ever at the hands of the group that holds the centre. Naturally then, the latter would wield power over them pushing them back to the wall and thus, forcing them to a marginal position. However, there are instances when the so called marginal groups evolve new strategies for survival and in a given situation are able not only to register their presence but negotiate and resist marginality as well.

Marginality is embedded in the functioning of the prevailing power structures. These power structures may operate along the planes of gender, class or caste, their operation divides the society into two groups: the oppressor and the oppressed which can be expressed in terms of the binaries of self and other. The group that holds the central position would wield power over the peripheral group. This exercise of power is done mainly through two forms i.e. repression and hegemony. While repression and coercion represent the direct, physical manifestation of power, the hegemonic power is exercised surreptitiously through promotion of the ideology of the dominant group. This form of power is more complicated and therefore it is not easy to decipher its working by the unwitting oppressed who end up perpetrating the dominant power structures without even coming to realize the subtlety of operation of power.

"Where there is power, there is resistance," says Michel Foucault (95). The marginal subject who otherwise remains perpetually in a state of oppression at the hands of the dominant group, comes to locate fissures in the seemingly impervious structures of power and comes out with potential resistance. Interestingly, the same means of power which help the oppressor to oppress becomes potent tools of resistance as well. This duplicity is inherent to the concept of power.

When applied to the feminist position, this marginality-centrality dyad is largely perceived through the man-woman relationship in a patriarchal set up wherein a woman is seen primarily as a womb, a body. As such, the female body becomes the site of oppression at the hands of the patriarchs. Iris Young, a feminist, opines that female embodiment plays a significant role in her oppression. She, in her essay "Throwing Like a Girl," focuses on "the situatedness of the woman's actual bodily movement and orientation to its surroundings and its world" (143). Thus, women's failure to use the potential of their bodies fully, is not because they lack physical power but due to their being situated in a milieu that discourages them to take too much of space and approach physical activity tentatively and uncertainly. Young concludes that "at the root of those modalities is the fact that the woman lives her body as object as well as subject. The source of this is that patriarchal society defines woman as object, as a mere body, and that in sexist society women are in fact frequently regarded by others as objects and mere bodies" (155). And yet woman is also a subject, and, thus, cannot think of herself as a mere bodily object. This dichotomy between the two perceptions rends apart a woman's psyche. She can never be sure of herself, or what Young calls "cannot be in unity with herself" (ibid) and is always in a state of flux.

In her essay "Gender, Body and Everyday Life," Meenakshi Thapar too refers to the masculine projection of woman as primarily a body and not an individual which reduces woman's possibilities and potentials considerably. Thapar clearly perceives a complex power play behind this projection:

> ...even when the woman is viewed as a charming, beautiful body admired and applauded for her flawless beauty, ...the person remains perceived only as a body and not much more. This 'objectification' of the female body is clearly linked to sexuality to the extent that it is the woman's body as a sex object that takes precedence over everything else...Sexuality, gender, and the body, in a complex interplay of dominant forces, are clearly at the root of women's oppression in

contemporary society through the objectification of female form in everyday life. (33)

Marilyn Frye, a radical feminist critic says that "total power is unconditional access; total powerlessness is being unconditionally accessible" (103). As such, one possible way to resist against male power is to deny them access to women bodies, emotional support, domestic labour and so forth. She suggests that by controlling access, they can begin to assert control over power.

This paper seeks to analyse the 'marginal' women characters in Krishna Sobti's *Zindaginama* (1979). The choice of the text as well as the characters is specific in the sense that there are no overt feminist concerns. The novel which has no particular hero or heroine but people in general, is a novel of epic dimensions deeply imbued in the culture of the rural, pre-partition Punjab. The canvas of the novel is so panoramic that the reader feels transported in an altogether different world – a world which is so different from the modern, contemporary world and yet is so complete, so enchanting; it presents a culture which is all-accepting and all-embracing. Various characters from diverse social, religious and economical backgrounds come to jostle with one another to enrich the texture of the novel. On the surface, the novel offers a harmonious picture of life where the both the genders have internalized their ideologically promoted hegemonic images and as such are apparently content with their roles. Similarly, women characters exhibit no discontent in their subservient status to their male counterparts. No woman in the novel feels perturbed due to her marginalized status or her secondary position to man. In fact, this novel may be read as a counter argument to the feminist stance as it depicts a society wherein no such dissatisfaction is noticed.

However, the novel is fraught with instances of power play within the four walls of the household. This struggle for the power gets reflected in some of the clashes wherein the two wives of a man; or those of two brothers; or the mother-in-law and daughter-in-law are seen fighting for supremacy in the household. Nachchhatra Kaur sharing her condition with Kashiram; the fight between Sajad Bibi and Begam Bibi; Rasooli and her mother-in-law; Goma and Bholi etc. illustrate this point clearly. For obtaining this goal, they would go to any extent. They would feign illness, accuse of maltreatment and quarrel with the rival. There are dramatic scenes between women who wish to exercise control over the household. To quote one example, Rasooli trains Begum Bibi in the art of taming the mother-in-law: "Learn from me. Do as I did. Just stare at her fearlessly once. Once the shame in your gaze is gone, half the battle is won.... Instead of grumbling and whining, raise your voice and speak your mind aloud without hesitation. That's it; the battle is yours. Your writ will run!" (128-129).

These 'marginal' characters may be blissfully ignorant of the finer nuances of the feminist theory; they seem to apply it in their lives, nonetheless. One such instance is their being aware that by denying access to their bodies, they can upset the male dominance. It is interesting to note that this inter-gender conflict between has intra-gender overtones. The purpose of these 'insignificant' women characters is not to subdue the husband but through the husband, other women of the household. For instance, Rasooli denies her husband the access to her body to resist against her mother-in-law. She keeps him away from her for a few days and remains firm on her decision despite physical violence on his part. This persistent resistance on her part bears fruit as the husband acknowledges her viewpoint and starts favouring her in familial matters. Her case is a clear instance that by overcoming one's fears regarding physical violence, even a 'weak' woman can effectively counter the physical prowess of her husband. The subtle maneuverings of one's sexuality is worth noticing in the advice of Rasooli to Begam Bibi:

> Ache away! But don't let him touch you. Listen to me. On one hand, I would fight with auntie. On the other, I would go and sleep in *her* room only. My frustrated husband would bang the utensils, shoo the dogs loudly. But I would pretend not to hear. One day when I went to give him food, he grabbed my plait and said, 'Listen, bibi, fall in line or you'll suffer!' I shoved him aside and said, 'Look here, she's your mother, and my aunt. But if she wants to be the cruel mother-in-law, the battle's neither mine nor yours. Let me deal with her. And remove your cot from the house. Sleep with your father at the well, and I will sleep in peace with my sweet ma-in-law!'
>
> Beguma Bharjaaee, on hearing this, my husband saw red, dragged me by my hair and threw me down! I neither cried nor moaned. Got up, brushed my clothes, and calmly said, "You, mother and son, be cruel together. The good Lord will dry up your wells. Turn the seeds in the soil to rot. Put worms in standing crops." Rasooli started laughing. Beguma Bharjaaee, that was the day. To this day it is as if someone has done black magic on him. Pulling me close, he cajoled, 'Na na Rasooliye, don't curse my crops! I promise you, whatever Bebe may say or do, your man is always with you!' (130).

Rasooli may not have typically feminist interests behind resorting to this kind of resistance, but she has successfully located gaps in the dominant power structures and having done that, she is able to subvert not only the male authority over her, but the female authority of her mother-in-law as well.

Thus, the same body which has been an agent of woman's confinement becomes the harbinger of liberation from oppression when put to use smartly. This awareness of one's body, and its powers makes even the 'marginal' characters negotiate their marginal status and earn themselves a kind of centrality. Even if it is in the houshold and does not have any larger implications, it is putting theory into practice nonetheless.

Works Cited

Foucault, Michel. *The History of Sexuality: An Introduction*. Trans. Robert Hurley. New York: Vintage, 1979.

Frye, Marilyn. *The Politics of Reality: Essays in Feminist Theory.* California: The Crossing Press, 1983.

Sobti, Krishna. *Zindaginama*. Trans. Neer Kanwal Mani. New Delhi: Harper Collins, 2016.

Thapar, Meenakshi. "Gender, Body and Everyday Life." *Social Scientist.* 23.7 (July-Sept. 1995): 32-58.

Young, Iris Marion. *Throwing Like a Girl and Other Essays in Feminist Philosophy and Social Theory*, Bloomington IN: Indiana University Press, 1990.

Chapter - 4

Displacement and Marginalization of Santhals in Hansda Sowvendra Shekhar's *The Adivasi Will Not Dance*

Dr Shikha Saxena

Fag end of twentieth century has witness several movements for different motives and objectives. Dalit protests, farmers' rallies, women's candle-marches and Tribals' rebellions have sprung in news time to time. These people put their demands and rights in front of the society or the government. They raised voice against injustice, inequality, unemployment, discrimination and many more serious matters. This way, both Feminist literature and Dalit literature talk about almost the same kind of problems of the marginalised. In present context, Tribal literature, imbued with Tribal consciousness, is emerging in India and has become much interesting discourse in literature and criticism. A new kind of discourse emerged on the scene that dealt with deprivation, displacement and exploitation of tribal people. Hansda Sowvendra Shekhar's story collection *The Adivasi Will Not Dance* deals with the displacement of Tribals particularly Santhal community. This story collection depict that India is emerging as a developing country. H.S. Shekhar's present work is a documentary of Santhal Adivasis.

The first opening story "They Eat Meat" gives us glimpses of cross-cultural interaction. As Panmujhi and her family have to migrate to Vadodra due to the transfer of her husband from Bhubaneshwar. The first encounter came in the form of food habits (as they were from Santhal community). They have to change their food habits as:

> They may have to stop eating quite a few things we take for granted, Like what Jhapan? 'Er...for me, people do not eat meat here. No fish,

no chicken, no mutton, not even eggs'. Oh! Don't worry, Jhi. There are people who eat meat. While they do sell meat and eggs in some places, these things are not easily available. People here do not like to mix with those who eat meat and eggs. It is like that. (pp. 4-5)

People are even hesitant in giving their house 'on rent' to families; certain castes and creeds who 'eat meat'. Biran Kumang Soren encounters the problem of accommodation as he belongs to a tribal community:

> 'Er...Mr Soren, I hope you won't mind my asking this...Will you?'
> 'No, Sir, Not at all,' Biran Kumang said tensely, 'Please ask.'
> 'Er...Isn't Soren a tribal surname? Please I just want to know. For information's sake.'
> 'Yes, Sir,' Biran Kumang answered. We are tribals, Santhal. (p. 5)

According to the common belief people who eat meat are considered to be impure. As Vadodra is a Hindu city and people here do not eat non-vegetarian food. And the people who eat all this are considered to be impure. Hence Muslims and Christians do not stand a chance here. They have separate areas where they live – cities within city and separate *Bastis* are for Muslims and Christians. Even he was asked to hide his identity. He has to change his food habits and hide his real identity to get lodging as people here are biased. To quote the incident:

> 'You see Mr Soren...people may want to know about you. They are always curious. If they ask you where you're from, please will you just tell them that you are from Jharkhand? Just that much, nothing more. Better still, can you tell them that you've been transferred from Bubaneshwar? Mentioning a well known city clears the air quicker. You understand, don't you?' (p. 7).

Not only food habits but migration within country is considered as intrusion. Although the entire country is governed by one constitution and the rights of its citizens are equal yet narrow mindsets do not accept 'migrants' from other states. Locals feel insecure as they treat migrants from other states as 'intruders'. To quote from the story "Eating with the Enemy":

> Sulochna launched her own attack, 'So is this your father's tree? You Bihari's! You think this is your father's land. This is our land. Don't forget, you all are outsiders here. I am a daughter of this land and all the tree here belong to us.' (p. 68).

Moreover *adivasis* are not considered as a part of society. Most of the time *adivasis* are treated as 'untouchables'. One day Panmu Jhi made tea for workers and served them in steel cups and asked Sulochna, the maid to collect the cups after the workers had finished drinking and wash the cups themselves. Sulochna shrunk back in horror, 'But Didi she told Jhi, they are Adivasis' (p. 65).

Besides Marginalization there are no healthcare facilities in 'Tribal Areas'. In the story "Getting Even" the doctor comments, 'Hospital is the only important govt.-run health-care facility for miles in the godforsaker district in the Santhal Pargana. Other than me, there is one lady doctor for the female OPD, the female ward and the labor room…' (p.43). Glimpses of flesh-trade and human trafficking we find in "Eating with the Enemy" and "Merely a Whore." To quote from the text:

> 'These people are taking revenge on us because they sold our daughter in Delhi and we rescued her and brought her back….', the man continued. 'And this they do. They bring Santhal girls from villages on the pretext of giving them education and training and work and sell them away. My wife is also from that family,' the man said, 'but she did not like what they do...I am a simple man, sir. I do mehnat-mazdoori and somehow feed my family. Those people are rich. They make money out of selling girls (pp. 54-55).

Young girls even the teenagers are bought and married off to elderly men. Subhadra in the story "Eating with the Enemy" got married to a Marwari from Rairangpur town in Odisha who was much older than him. Mathabhangi, the teenager daughter of Sulochna, was ravaged by Babu, an elderly man who kept Mohini as a mistress in his house.

Talamai as depicted in the story "November is the Month of Migrations" is a Santali woman. She also migrates to earn her livelihood. On her way back to her home she was asked to do 'some work' for a jawan of railway protection force in lieu of 'bread pakora' and some money. In the dark corner of *Koyla Road* she stoop down to the desire of the jawan of Railway Protection Force. He not only exploits the woman but also makes some derogatory remarks.

In the story 'Merely a Whore' is a vivid description of the Lakhipur town where the men work for hours in coal mines to feed their families and women eat out of 'sweat and semen' of men. Entire township is engrossed with flesh trade. Young innocent girls were sent to flesh trade, "Sona had been brought to Jharna di by a supplier along with other girls; some from Bengal and Bihar, two from Nepal and three from Bangladesh" (p.148).

The entire story is full of description of flesh trade and how the young girls are exploited in flesh trade. Law and order situation in entire Santhal

Pargana is quite alarming. All such atrocities and inhuman practices are there as law and order is very weak. To quote the words of doctor:

> We have not been summoned to the court yet. Court decisions take time. May be it will take a year or two-perhaps more-before we are called. In the meanwhile, in the Santhal Pargana, so many Santhal girls will have been sold, so many Santhal boys implicated on false charges, so many FIRs filed in police stations, just for warring parties to get even with each other. (p. 57)

Another story in the collection "Baso-Jhi" is the representative of miserable life of a Santhal woman. The society is engulfed by many superstitions. It is the pathetic story of a woman who is baselessly declared as a dahni-witch. She used to lead a happy wedlock till the untimely death of her husband. After the death she bore the yolk of ploughing, feeding her two sons which later on turned her out from the house and later on when her grandson passed away due to diarrhea, the daughters-in-law got a golden chance to blame that she is a dahni (witch) and ate her child. The story highlights prevailing superstitions in the society. To quote from the text:

> Once the child died, and the yelling rose in intensity, the daughters-in-law lost no moment in declaring that their mother-in-law was responsible for child's death. What had she done? Why were they blaming her?' Tell us what you are up to inside your hut?' her sons asked. Which evil gods do you worship, and how many children do you need for your sacrifices?'(p. 127).

Basanti was stunned. Such questions could only mean one thing. But her sons – her own sons! – calling her a witch. She felt utterly helpless, much more than when she had been widowed. Desolate, she watched her sons ransack her one-room hut. Her utensils, her clothes, her clay pots, her tin-box, everything was thrown out. Not satisfied with all the damage he'd caused to his mother's hut and heart, the younger son grabbed Basanti by the hair and threw her to the ground. Then he kicked her in the abdomen. The old women screamed in pain and grief.

Later on when she was serving as helping in Soren Babu's household chorus, she eave-drops again that she is a dahni. She leaves stealthily the house of Soren Babu leaving an indelible mark on everybody's heart. To quote from the text:

> They went to the corner where Baso-Jhi used to sleep. The folding cot was set upright. On it were neatly arranged the clothes and other articles – a comb, oil, sal twigs for cleaning teeth, soap –t hat Baso-Jhi

> had received from the Soren family. Her rubber chappals were neatly arranged under the cot but Baso-Jhi herself, and her bundle, were gone. (p. 129)

The story "Desire, Divination, Death" is a very moving story where the pathetic state of tribal families has been depicted vividly. Subhashini the main protagonist is a widow and the mother of three siblings – Parul, Nilmoni and Kunaram. Kunaram was the apple of their eyes. The three of them – Subhashini, the mother became the sole breadwinner; Parul and Nilmoni became mothers to their baby brother. One day Subhashini has to leave for her job and when she was on her way with the Jalebis in her hands she had a premonition of his son's death:

> 'Yo..Kunnu? A preoccupied Subhashini halted at this sudden call. She turned around. No, it wasn't Kunaram, although the voice seemed very familiar. A sick looking boy, almost the same age as her son, clad only in a dirty gamcha, was staring at her with hungry eyes. Who is this?...Her tears had dried and her heart was racing. She knew that misfortune sometimes assumes human form and begs for alms…' (p. 140)

The last story "The Adivasi Will Not Dance" is the outcry of miserable situation of Santhals: their exploitation, their land snatching, their predicament and finally exhibition by political leaders at different official functions. The story is full of descriptions of cunning practices by big business tycoons who have grabbed their land for mining coal from that area. To quote the words from the text that reveals the bereaved story of all native Santhali's:

> "At that time, our Santhal Pargana was not broken up into so many districts. Today, all diku, Bihari and all, they have broken up our Santhal Pargana for their own benefits." (p. 177)

Moreover as they have become poor villagers, they can't send their children to good schools. Children are deprived of modern education. We find a final heart cry in the following words,

> "All our certificates and shields, what did they give us? Diku children go to schools and colleges, get education, jobs. What do we Santhals get? We Santhals can sing and dance, and we are good at our art. Yet, what has our art given us? Displacement, tuberculosis" (p. 178).
>
> The Santhal leader mourns the final predicament:
>
> "Our music, our dance, our songs are sacred to us Santhals. But hunger and poverty has driven us to sell what is sacred to us….be it an athletic

meet, some inauguration, or any function organised by someone high and mighty-in the name of Adivasi culture and Jharkhandi culture, it is necessary to make Adivasis dance. Even Bihari and Bengali and Odia people say that Jharkhand is theirs'. They call their culture and music superior to those of us Adivasi. Why don't they get their women to sing and dance in open grounds in the name of Jharkhandi culture? For every benefit in job, in education, in whatever, the diku are quick to call Jharkhand their own-let the Adivasi go to hell. But when it comes to displaying Jharkhand culture, the onus of singing and dancing is upon the Adivasi alone." (p. 179).

Throughout the story we find the pain of displacement from their native land. Their land have been grabbed by big businessmen who will make a power-plant there and the coal deep-delved under their field will be used in the thermal plant as fuel. When he heard the slogan of 'Mera Bharat Mahan' he wondered:

"Which great nation displaces thousands of its people from their homes and livelihoods to produce electricity for cities and factories? And jobs? What jobs? An Adivasi farmer's job is to farm. Which other job should be made to do? Become a servant in some billionaire's factory built on land that used to belong to that very Adivasi just a week earlier?" (p. 179)

The speech by the leader of the dance troupe seems to be a 'clarion call'.

"Johar, Rashtrapati-babu. We are very proud and happy that you have come to our Santhal Pargana and we are also very proud that we have been asked to sing and dance before you and welcome you to our place. We will sing and dance before you but tell us, do we have a reason to sing and dance? Do we have a reason to be happy? You will start building the power plant, but this plant will be the end of us all, the end of all Adivasi. These men sitting beside you, have told you that this power plant will change our fortunes, but these same men have forced us out of our homes and villages. We have nowhere to go, nowhere to grow our crops. How can this power plant be good for us? And how can we Adivasis dance and be happy? Unless we are given back our homes and land, we will not sing and dance. We Adivasis will not dance. The Adivasis will not-" (p.187)

The text has a context in current political scenario. We read in newspaper the news of Mao attacks and mine blast but if we try to understand the problem in the light of current descriptions of emotional bereavement, physical exploitation and mass displacement and exploitation of Adivasis clan, we will be able to solve the problems in a practical way.

The entire narrative of Hansda can be interpreted in a different context where there is no glorification and justification of any of the party rather he as one of the member of Santhalis tried to create an awareness of the displaced and exploited Santhals. He is successful in presenting the reality 'as it is.'

The current narrative is also important as a piece of artistic expression and proves 'pen is mightier than sword'. They are powerless in front of powerful people; there are weak in front of land grabbers, no one is there to address their grievances, but through this artistic expression masses can hear their voice; felt the pain of displacement; understand the agony of losing everything. Work of art can break all the boundaries. Santhalis were stuffed in jails when they tried to demonstrate in front of constitutional administrators and ministers. Canes were charged if they did not yield but the power of pen is above all boundaries.

The current story collection is very important as a piece of literature that gives us an authentic account of Santhals and their exploitation. To quote the words of Himal Southasian:

> "The Adivasi Will Not Dance" represents a collection of little histories that are contributing to the character of India as a developing, diverse and evolving nation. The language of this book is truly polyphonous with multiple traditions and varied realities co-existing between English, Santhali, Bengali and Hindi tempos and cadences...Shekhar's work in this volume is a tribute to lives of struggle and Marginalization, carefully avoiding the exotic or self-pitying tone. His craft is suffused by love for his people that reminds readers of Baba Nagajurna's poetry-familiar and distant, angry and lyrical."

The entire text is marked for typical words like *kadahis, katoris, lungi, saya, gamcha, police –wallah, bread pakora* and some typical Hindi expression like '*Achchha, theek hai, chai piyoge* adds to the local colour. The setting of this story collection is the squalid towns of Jharkhand.

Thus, "The Adiwasi Will Not Dance" is a mature, passionate, and intense socio-political book of stories where Hansda treated the harsh realities in a threadbare manner and established himself as one of the most important contemporary writers.

Works Cited

Dutta, Sudipta. "Who is Hansda Sowvendra?" August 19, 2017.

Shekhar, Hansda Sowvendra. "The Adivasi Will Not Dance". New Delhi: Speaking Tiger Publishing, 2017.

The Hindu. Delhi. "Interview: Hansda Sowvendra Shekhar on the Ban on His Book" August, 2017, Scroll.in.

https://scroll.in/article/909655/my-life-others-lives-and-lives-of-trees-where-hansda-sowvendra-shekhar-s-new-novel-came-from

Chapter - 5

Women's Search for Selfhood: Marginalised Women in Margaret Atwood's Select Novels

Dr Rumana Ashraf

Margaret Elenor Atwood is much prolific novelist, poet, essayist, and environment critic. She was born on 18 November, 1939 at Ottawa in Canada. She has written many works but her novel *Surfacing*, *Handman's Tale, Oryx and Crake, Lady Oracle, The Edible Woman* and *The Blind Assassin* etc. are well-known works. She has written on the marginalised status of the women in the patriarchal set up of the society. She tries her hand at writing when she was merely five years old and she took it more seriously in her teen age. Her novel *The Handmaid's Tale* (1985) revolves around the sexual slavery of the women. Her novel *The Blind Assassin* (2000) is a memoir of an old Canadian woman. Her novel *The Edible Woman* (1969) and *Surfacing* (1972) also deal with one or the other aspect of a woman.

Margaret Atwood's novel *Surfacing* (1972) deals with the notions of separation, gendered identity and women's problems in the society. In this novel the central protagonists returns to her hometown so that she may find her missing father.

Marital bond brings many problems to women as men consider it their birthright to keep control over women. Marriage increases the problems of women as they feel helpless to perform many duties altogether. The men's expectations remain high from women. David openly insults Anna. Her only identity was that she was David's wife. Their relationships demonstrate the present condition of relationships of the couple and the total degradation and lack of understanding. Anna's artificiality is clear from her morning make-up. The narrator of the novel *Surfacing* thinks that her mother has been the victim of the society. Her mother hated doctors as they took her as a tool of their experiments:

> She [the mother] hated hospitals and doctors; she must have been afraid they would experiment on her, keep her alive as long as they could with tubes and needles even though it was what they call terminal, in the head it always is; and in fact that's what they did. (*Surfacing* 17)

Hossein and Amani observe about this novel:

> Margaret Atwood's *Surfacing* is about such relations which have their roots in the Enlightenment view of 'reason.' It celebrates, among other things, the attempt to 'surface' from the 'lake' of such relations of power which have 'submerged' the feminine and the natural. (Hossein and Amani 9).

Lady Oracle (1976) is a parody of gothic romance and the fairy tale tradition. The novel has been written in the flashback technique. It revolves around a central female protagonist Joan Foster who has passion for writing romantic novels and this is the way she escapes from her problems. She has been narrated as an overweight girl in her childhood whose mother criticises her. She starts having relationships with a performance artist.

Atwood has portrayed the acute hunger for identity in the female characters of her novels. Her novel *Lady Oracle* depicts the protagonist Joan Foster's search for identity and harmony in her life. Joan's inner and outer worlds are quite different and her development remains the focal point of this novel. George Wood Cock also opines, "The novel is an account of a rite de passage, a story "of self-realisation and hence of life realisation" (Woodcock 25). Joan wants that the positions of women should change in the present patriarchal and man dominated society.

According to Atwood, women are merely considered as tools to consume and extent the progeny. She has used the female body as a dominant factor to use and discard for men but women crave for power and identity. Margaret Atwood has narrated the astute depiction of female body in the novel *Lady Oracle*. The female protagonist Joan Foster is "torn between unconscious feminist questions and the stereotypical answers which society provides" (Humm 127). In the novel Diana's statue of Ephesus has been used as a symbol of the essence of feminine identity. In this context Molly Hite thinks it as "a paradigm of patriarchally controlled female body" (Hite 135).

Atwood's novel *The Handmaid's Tale* is a pathetic tale of women whose lives are not much better than slaves or animals. The description "women tied up or chained or with dog collars around their necks, women hanging from trees,...women being raped, beaten up, killed" (*HT* 128) presents the moving pictures of the women. The women are considered just a tool for sexual enjoyment. In this novel, a Handmaid has no idea where her husband and daughter are. Handmaid is sent to Fred's house so that she may bear a child for him.

This novel depicts how the women are deprived of their identity as they have no right to keep their names. The name is the identity of a person but the women are deprived of their identity. The names of these women are deliberately obliterated and erased from the memory by keeping them under some kind of psychological treatment. In this novel the memory of handmaid's daughter is very weak. That's why she feels, "My name isn't Offred, I have another name, which nobody uses now because it's forbidden....I keep the knowledge of this name like something hidden, some treasure I'll come back to dig up, one day. I think of this name as buried" (*HT* 94).

The names of the handmaids are put on the names of their commanders to whom they are presenting themselves as a child bearer. Their names are on the basis on the commanders as for Fred 'Offred', for Oglen 'Ofglen', for Warren 'Ofwarren', and so on. Thus, the lives of these handmaids are depended on their commanders.

There are different categories of women. The first category can be called handmaid. These women's role is much substantial and Aunts control the handmaids. The second type of women are wives of the elite class commanders. The third type of women are Marthas who are negligent women who cannot give birth to children and work as housemaids. The fourth type of women are 'unwomen' i.e. who cannot serve their commanders and are old. These also cannot produce children and these women clean the nuclear toxic waste due to the old age. The fifth type of women are upper class 'econowives' who enjoy full freedom. These women are fertile.

The men of the Gilead are all fertile and only women can be barren or infertile. Handmaids have no right to allow with other handmaids. They must remain silent and perform their respective tasks which are assigned to them. The handmaids remain without feelings and passion in their lives. They have to curb their inner feelings, desires and dreams. The conversation with another handmaid is considered a kind of rebellion. Thus, in Gilead talking with another handmaid is a crime that's why Atwood writes, "There is a lot that doesn't bear thinking about. Thinking can hurt your chances" (*HT* 17).

The women's dress codes are also restricted in this novel. Men have liberty to wear any clothes according to their choice but women are not allowed to wear colourful dresses. Handmaids are given red garments with white wings so that they may not be able to see other people or the other people may not see their faces. Atwood writes in the novel, "Everything except the wings around my face is red: the color of blood....The white wings too are prescribed issue; they are to keep us from seeing, but also from being seen" (*HT* 18). The housemaids are allowed to wear green gowns "Martha's dress, which is dull green, like a surgeon's gown of the time before" (*HT* 19).

Commanders' wives are given blue gowns and they are told to maintain gardens and attend some functions, "The blue-clad wives of the commanders preside over their homes and gardens, and attend public functions such as the Prayvaganzas, Salvaging and childbirth" (Freibert 281). Aunts are given brown color dress. 'Econowives' wear blue, green, and red gowns. Gray garments are for the 'unwoman', "The gray-clad Unwoman, those who refuse to cooperate with the system, work in the colonies, cleaning up the city ghettoes, toxic dumps" (Freibert 281). There is no future of the women in Gilead.

Margaret Atwood has discussed in this novel that the women's position is not good. The women are kept under strict patriarchal pressures. The handmaids are given only three chances and if they fail to get pregnant. If a woman does not get pregnant in three chances, she is declared as an unchaste woman. Arti Sahu observes about this novel:

> Atwood through this novel shows her opposition against patriarchal monopolization over women. She questions the issue as to why men are given the power to subdue the women along with the other contemporary issues like pornography, power politics, abortions, rape and toxic waste etc. in the novel. Through *The Handmaid's Tale,* Atwood poses questions of female oppression and their marginalization in almost all totalitarian states. (Sahu 6).

Her novel *Cat's Eye* (1988) is a coming-of-age novel that depicts the story of a girl named Elaine and her search for identity in the world. Elain is an eight years old girl who moves to Toronto when her family moves there because her father gets a job as a professor. She faces problems in her school and she is bullied by a girl named Cordelia. There are some turns in the plot. Earlier Cordelia bullies Elain but later Elain starts mocking Cordelia. The novel depicts her affair and the problems of her life in this novel.

The Robber Bride (1993) is set in Toronto, Canada. The novel opens with three women Rose, Charis and Tony who get together in a month so that they may dine together. The novel has theme how women are used only for sexual pleasures. They are expected to do all the household work, take care of the children also.

Her novel *Hag-Seed* (2016) is retelling of William Shakespeare's *The Tempest* (1711). Miranda is Felix's daughter and Nadia is his wife in the novel. Miranda dies at the age of three. She takes keen interest in her father's staging of *The Tempest*.

Thus, from all these novels, it is clear that Margaret Atwood's novels deal with the contemporary issues or the state of women in the phalocentric society. The women of her novels seem to be struggling for the identity and meaning in their lives. It has been rightly stated, "After all, Atwood's narrative focuses specially on men's domination of women by means of other women" (Hammer 39).

Works Cited

Atwood, Margaret. *Surfacing*. 1972. London: Virago, 2011. Print.

—. *The Handmaid's Tale*. 1985. London: Vintage Books, 2010. Print.

Hammer, Barbe Stephanie. "The World As it Will Be? Female Satire and the Technology of Power in *The Handmaid's Tale*". *Modern Language Studies*. Spring.1990: 39-49. Print.

Maggie Humm, "Going through the Green Channel: Margaret Atwood and Body Boundaries." *Contemporary Women Writers*. Manchester: Manchester University Press, 1980. Print.

Molly Hite, *The Other Side of the Story*. Ithaca and London: Cornell University Press, 1989. Print.

Freibert, M. Lucy. "Control and Creativity: The Politics of Risk in Margaret Atwood's *The Handmaid's Tale*." Ed. Judith McCombs. *Critical Essays on Margaret Atwood*. 1988. 280-91. Print.

Pirnajmuddin, Hossein and Omid Amani. "Margaret Atwood's *Surfacing* as a Critique of the Enlightenment Reason." *CS Cananda: Studies in Literature and Language*. Vol. 3, No. 2, 2011, PP. 6-10.

Sahu, Aarti. "Portrayal of Marginalized Women in Atwood's *The Handmaid's Tale*." *Language in India*. Vol. 16:5. May 2016. 1-7.

Woodcock, George. "Surfacing to Survive: Notes of the Recent Atwood." *Ariel*, Vol. 4 No. 3. July, 1973.

Chaper - 6

Social Stratification, a Savage: A Comparative Analysis of Dr Ambedkar and Mulk Raj Anand

Dr C. Ramya

> *Caste is a state of mind. It is a disease of mind. The teachings of the Hindu religion are the root cause of this disease. We practice casteism and we observe untouchability because we are enjoined to do so by the Hindu religion. A bitter thing cannot be made sweet. The taste of anything can be changed. But poison cannot be changed into nectar. (Ambedkar 135)*

The social organization of the Indo-Aryans, based on the theory of *Chaturvarnya*, can be called a very logical idea or innocent principle to run the society perfectly to fulfill daily requirements of the people. The people of the society were divided into four classes namely Brahmin (Priests), Kshatriyas (Soldiers), Vaishyas (Traders) and Shudras (Menials). Babasaheb Dr Ambedkar insists that it goes further and crafts the principle of 'graded inequality' which sows the seeds of inequality in the society. It has been labelled as impossible for the Shudras to rise above the ignominable and disabled condition of them as this *Chaturvarnya*'s 'graded incquality' is not just notional but legal and penal also.

Dr Ambedkar explicitly unveils the actual history of social stratification in his W*ho were the Shudras?* elucidating the aboriginal communities of Indian people as the Shudras were one of the Aryan Communities of the Solar race and it was the clearly evident in the history that the Aryan society exhibited only three Varnas namely Brahmins, Kshatriyas and Vaishyas, and the Shudras never formed a separate Varna but ranked as a part of the Kshatriya Varna in the Indo-Aryan Society. On account of the constant and unabating rivalry between the Shudra kings and the Brahmins in which the

Brahmins were put through a reign of terror and tyranny, thereby, creating a persistent loathing and abhorrent attitude towards the Shudra king in the minds of the Brahmins and hence they refused to perform the *upanayana* of the Shudras. *Upanayana*, being one of the prominent and important traditional rites of Hinduism, marks the acceptance of a student by a teacher (a Guru). This *samskara* is denied by the Brahmins to the Shudras and thus, they became socially degraded and fell below the rank of the Vaishyas who were actually Kshatriyas. Thus, they came to be known as Shudras or the fourth *varna*.

While there were so many socialists, anti-socialists, politicians, orthodox Hindus and other classes of Hindus proclaim that Dr Ambedkar has not shown any respect for Hindu's sacred scriptures. Dr Ambedkar assuredly confesses that he has used every detail of the information about *Chaturvarnya* and as a historian; he has documented every minute details that he mentioned in *Who were the Shudras?*. In order to discover who the Shudras were, one must explore the origin of the *Chaturvarnya* in the Indo-Aryan society. The ninetieth Hymn of the Tenth Mandala of the *Rig Veda* says:

> Purusha has a thousand heads, a thousand eyes, a thousand feet. On every side enveloping the earth he overpassed (it) by a space of ten fingers. (*WWTS* 21)

'Purusha Sukta' is a Hymn of the *Rig Veda* that is dedicated to the Purusha, the "Cosmic Being" who is both immanent in the manifested world and yet, it transcendent to it. It has been written in the *Rig Veda*:

> Purusha himself is this whole (universe), whatever has been and whatever shall be. He is the Lord of immortality, since (or when) by food he expands. (*WWTS* 21)

Such is the greatness of 'Purusha' that all existence is a quarter to him and three-fourth of him is that which is immortal in the sky. The reason why Dr Ambedkar gives a detailed explanation of 'Purusha' is that 'Purusha Sukta', is the theory of the origin of the universe and, is the cosmogony. It is not only justifying the creation of the universe but also the social organization has been aroused from the body of this Great Creator. The four classes namely, the Brahmins or Priests, Kshatriyas or Soldiers, Vaishyas or traders and the Shudras or Menials are born from the mouth, arms, thighs and feet respectively.

Astonishingly, 'Purusha Sukta' not being a mere cosmogony but it is a divine injunction which prescribed the formation of the society on the basis of the *Chaturvarnya*. It became the ideal of the Indo-Aryan society which doesn't just concern itself with the origin of the classes but propounds wisely as the theology was created by God. Babasaheb Ambedkar writes:

> The equation of the different classes to different parts of the body is not a matter of accident. It is deliberate. The idea behind this plan seems to be to discover a formula which will solve two problems, one of fixing the functions of the four classes and the other of fixing the functions of the four classes and the other of fixing the gradation of the four classes after a preconceived plan. (*WWTS* 35)

Brahmin, as prescribed in 'Purusha Sukta', is born from the mouth of the creator. Mouth being the noblest part of the anatomy, the Brahmin becomes the noblest of all the four classes. Being noblest, he has been given a stalwart of the noblest function i.e. teaching, the resourcefulness of knowledge and learning. Arms being below the mouth and consequently, the Kshatriya who were said to be born out of the arms of the creator, are given the order of precedence next below the Brahmin and is preordained to fight, the profession which is ranked next to knowledge-bearing. Hence, the Kshatriyas' profession was to be soldiers. The traders and industrialists are ranked below the warriors and thus, the Vaishyas are given an order preceding the Kshatriyas whose function is assigned to be trading and they are said to be born out of the thigh of the creator, the port of the body below the arms. The feet form the lowest part of the human frame and are considered ignoble. 'Purusha Sukta' preaches that the Shudras are borne out of the feet of the creator. Accordingly, the Shudras are given the function of being menial and the filthiest of all the functions.

Mulk Raj Anand, one of the pioneers of Indo-Anglian fiction, depicts this sensitive portrayal of an Individual, Bakha, by penetrating through the grim realities of the social life in India. Bakha, the protagonist of the novel *Untouchable*, is a member of the lowest caste in India – the street- sweepers and Latrine cleaners. Being a young adolescent boy, Bakha has got the natural instinct and drives of having fun and entertainment but all his natural instincts are considered a luxury or an offence just because he belongs to the class of untouchables who are ordained in the sacred literature of Hindus as *Avarnas*, which means those who have no *Varna* or class. Bakha is often called not just by his name but is followed by any of the unparliamentarily words such as:

> "Ohe! Bakhya! Ohe Bakhya! Ohe, scoundrel of a sweeper's son! Come and clean a latrine for me." (*U* 22)

Even his father bellows:

"Are you up? Get up, you illegally begotten." (*U* 21)

Babasaheb Ambedkar doubts and puts forth a logical and judicious question:

> Social classes existed in all societies. The Indo-Aryans were no exception. Nevertheless, no theology has ever thought it necessary to explain how classes arise. Why then did the Purusha Sukta make the explanation of the origin of the social classes its primary concern? (*WWTS* 30).

The civil status of the Shudra, the worst system of pains and penalties to which the Shudra is subjected by the Brahminic law-givers, the Brahmanic theory of the status of the Shudras are adequately quoted from various manuscripts of Vedas, the sacred literature of the Hindus. Here are a few examples. According to 'Kathaka Samhita' (xxxi.2) and the 'Maitrayani Samhita' (iv. 1.3; i.8.3), "A Shudra should not be allowed to milk the cow whose milk is used for *Agnihotra*" (*WWTS* 48).

There are so many statements in different Hindu religious books also. It has been written in the 'Aitareya Brahmana' (vii. 29.4) and the 'Panchavimsa Brahmana' (vi.1.11) that "Shudra is a servant of another (and cannot be anything else)" (WWTS 48) and the 'Apastamba Dharma' Sutra says, "If a student and a Shudra woman merely look at each other, the recitation of the Veda must be interrupted" (WWTS 51).

Mulk Raj Anand, through the character of Sohini in *Untouchable*, tries to give his audience a clear picture of the pain that an untouchable underwent in his life in pre-Independent India. Sohini, a fair-complexioned girl faces humility in every moment of her life. Even her daily routines to live a day is a challenging one; for instance, Gulabo, a washerwoman slams and swears at Sohini as she comes forward to fetch water:

> "Bitch! Prostitute! Wanton! And your mother hardly dead..."
> "There is no one to give you water here! There are so many of us ahead of you".
> "Aribitch!.... Aren't you ashamed of showing your teeth to me in the presence of Men, Prostitute?" (U 35)
> "You annoy me with your silence. Eater of dung and drinker of Urine! Bitch of a sweeper!" (U 36)

Such horrendous life is the lives of the untouchable women as portrayed by Mulk Raj Anand.

The 'Vasishtha Dharma Sutra' promotes what may be eaten and what may not been eaten. It has been written in it that the food given by a doctor, a hunter, a woman of bad character, a mace-bearer, a thief, an abhisasta, a eunuch (or) a low-caste person, a miser, a prisoner, a sick man, a soma plant seller, a carpenter, a washer man, a dealer in spirituous liquor, a detective, an usurer, (or) a cobbler. It is also further written, "If a Brahmin dies with the food of a Shudra in his stomach, he will become a village pig in his next life or be born in the family of that Shudra" (*WWTS* 52).

The peak of remorse is felt when the 'Apastamba Dharma Sutra' quotes even the procedure of how the people of the classes should salute other people. It goes on stressing:

> A Brahmin shall salute stretching forward his right arm on a level with his ear, a Kshatriya holding it on a level with the breast, a Vaishya holding it on a level with the waist, a Shudra holding it low (and) stretching forward the joined hands. (*WWTS* 53)

Mulk Raj Anand's portrayal of the harrowing realties of the untouchables' life is honestly spine-chilling and the gruesome atrocities experienced by the Shudras leaves us dumbstruck and unimaginable when Bakha was puts into a heinous humility just because he accidentally touched an upper-class Hindu. The twice-born upper class Hindu explodes:

> "Keep to the side of the road, Ohe low-caste vermin! Why don't you call, you Swine, and announce your approach! Do you know you have touched me and defiled me, cock-eyed son of a bow-legged scorpion! Now I will have to go and take a bath to purify myself....Don't you know, you brute, that you must not touch me!" (*U* 64)

Thus, Dr Ambedkar's *Who were the Shudras?* unveils the gruesome social stratification that prevailed in pre-Independence India and Mulk Raj Anand, indeed, attempts a social metaphor exploring the holistic array of discriminated nation that followed the divine ordination of 'Purusha Sukta' for centuries. When 'Purusha Sukta' makes the *Chaturvarnya* a sacred institution, "would it not have been possible for the author of 'Purusha Sukta' to say that the different classes were born from the different mouths of the Purusha and such a conception could not have been much difficult as the 'Purusha' of 'Purusha Sukta' has one thousand heads, enough to assign one species of creation to one of his head" grumbles Dr Ambedkar and stresses that it is deliberate as the sacred literature has been designed and created by the Brahmins and all the rights have been retained to them so that they may sustain their superiority over the non-Brahmins.

Works Cited

Ambedkar, B.R. *Castes in India: their mechanism, Genesis and Development*. Jalandhar: Bheem Patrika Publications, 1977. Print.

—. *Who were the Shudras*. New Delhi: Samyak Prakashan, 2011. Print.

Anand, Mulk Raj. *Untouchable*. New Delhi: Arnold-Heinemann Publishers, 1981. Print.

Chapter - 7

Marginalized Status of Women and the Breaking of the Barriers: A Study of Kamala Das' Poetry

Dr Suruchi Sharma

Kamala Das is the exponent of feminine sensibility, especially the sensibility of the modern middle class woman in Indian society. For centuries together, the Indian woman has been regarded as a door mat or a child-bearing machine .Woman has been a prisoner within the four walls of her own house. She is caged in the mould of Sita and Savitri. Kamala Das is a rebel, an iconoclast. She has revolted against the hush-hush prudery and conventionalism of the Indian society in its attitude towards woman, love and sex. She has projected a different kind of pictures of a woman. She has depicted in her poems the patriarchal pressures of the society on women. Her poetry presents the marginalised status of women but simultaneously, she has broken the barriers which are made by men for women so that they may remain under their dominion. According to her, woman is a vibrant human being, in sobbing with emotions and pulsating with passion. According to her, 'to be loved to madness is the greatest desire of a woman'.

Kamala Das was born on 31 March 1934 in Malabar, Kerala. Her real name was Madhavikutti and Kamala Das is her pseudonym. She embraced Islam in 1999 and she became Kamala Suraiyya. She wrote in Malayalam and English. She got married in 1949 when she was merely fifteen years old and her marriage remained a failure. She got Kerala Sahitya Akademi Award in 1969. She is best known for the protest poetry. She died on 31 May 2009 in a hospital in Pune. Her autobiography *My Story* was published in 1976. In the same year, she published a novel also. The title of the novel is *Alphabet of Lust*. Moreover, she wrote some poetry collections and few essays also. Kamala Das had poetry in her blood. Her poems are highly autobiographical. In her autobiography, *My Story*, she remarks:

> Poets cannot close their shops like shopmen and return home. Their shop is their mind and as long as they carry it with them they feel the pressures and torments. A poet's raw material is not stone or clay, it is her personality. (Das 165)

The most striking feature of Das' poetry is its elemental force and intensity of passion, as says Parthasarthy, "her poems seem to boil over". There is very little of Ezekiel's conscious craftsmanship or of the breezy comic irony of Ramanujan. The strength of her poetry emanates from her powerful personality. Courage and honesty are the strength of her character and also her poetry. She is essentially a poet of love, of sexual love. Dr Devinder Kohli compares her with the Australian poet Judith Wright, "Like Judith Wright, whose skills and range are wider Das is primarily a poet of love."

Parathasarthy remarks "She is the only Indian woman poet who has written honestly without shame of her desires". She has been a controversial figure due to the frank and open depiction of sex and lust in her poetry. Jaikrishnan Nair writes about it:

> The modern English poetry with all its aggressiveness and boldness begins and culminates in Kamala Das. No other feminist poets in India could achieve the absolute rebellious dimensions of Kamala Das in her poetry. In fact, Kamala Das makes a poetic revolt by way of introspectively pondering upon the unfortunate state of existence in which Indian women conduct themselves. (Nair 128)

She has depicted her sexual encounters, her family and relationships with her husband and how society reacts to her. In the man-dominated society everything is decided for woman by man. Kamala Das has written in that time when women were just kept in the houses and they were not considered the part of the social and political set up.

Her poem "An Introduction" is a beautiful poem of her poetic credo (faith):

> I met a man, loved him Call him not any man
> He is every man
> Who wants a woman just as I am every
> Woman who seeks love. "An Introduction"

She writes that she is proud of being an Indian. Her critics, friends and cousins advise her not to write in English. She prefers to write only in

English that is half English and half Indian and it seems to be a funny language but it gives her pleasure. Her language is as important as is cawing to a crow and roaring to a lion. She writes:

> I am Indian, very brown, born in Malabar,
> I speak three languages, write in
> Two, dream in one.
> .... Why not leave
> Me alone, critics, friends, visiting cousins,
> Every one of you? Why not let me speak in
> Any language I like? The language I speak,
> Becomes mine, its distortions, its queernesses
> All mine, mine alone. ("An Introduction")

Kamala Das describes her childhood experiences also and the changes that occurred in her body in adolescence. She tells her experience how she became a grown up woman and she was married with a man by her parents:

> I was child, and later they
> Told me I grew, for I became tall, my limbs
> Swelled and one or two places sprouted hair. ("An Introduction")

Kamala Das was a different type of woman and she did not want to live a life of a traditional woman. She wanted freedom in her life. That's why she starts living her life according to her own will. Bijay Kumar Das writes about Kamala Das' life of revolt in these words:

> As she deals with the conflict between passivity and rebellion against the male-oriented universe, her tussle with love, sex, lust, womanhood, has most usually centred itself upon her relations with her husband or with the other men in her life. (Das 44).

After her marriage, Kamala Das revolts against the womanliness. She wore her brother's trousers and got her hair trimmed. She is always pressurized to become a woman and behave like a woman and behave like a wife. She is told to be busy in the household activities and she is not allowed to look outside from the window. It is advised to her:

> Dress in sarees, be girl
> Be wife, they said. Be embroiderer, be cook,
> Be a quarreller with servants. Fit in. Oh,
> Belong, cried the categorizers. Don't sit
> On walls or peep in through our lace-draped windows.
> Be Amy, or be Kamala. Or, better
> Still, be Madhavikutty. ("An Introduction")

She is directed not to think over the matters of men and she should learn to bear the pain of a woman i.e. pain is inseparable part of a woman's life. She talks about the endless carnal desires of men and the unfulfilled quest of love of a woman. Kamala Das writes how she would revolt and drink at midnight and break all the social taboos and patriarchal norms.

It is I who drink lonely
Drinks at twelve, midnight, in hotels of strange towns,
It is I who laugh, it is I who make love
And then, feel shame, it is I who lie dying
With a rattle in my throat. I am sinner,
I am saint. I am the beloved and the
Betrayed. ("An Introduction")

Her poem "The Dance of the Eunuchs" was published in her poetry collection *Summer in Calcutta* in 1965. In this poem, Kamala Das talks about the summer when eunuchs came to dance and their anklets would do jingling sound under a gulmohur tree. Their voices were harsh and their theme was melancholic. Their limbs were thin and dry. Even the crows on the tress were silent. Then a thunder came followed by lightening and rain which filled the earth with the smell of urine of lizards and mice.

Kamala Das' poem "The Looking Glass" deals with another theme of the marginalised status of women. There are twenty-four lines in this poem. The poem has been written in a simple language. The poet has aroused some erotic images in this poem. The beginning of the poem depicts it in these lines:

Getting a man to love you is easy
Only be honest about your wants as
Woman. ("The Looking Glass")

In this poem, she advises a woman to stand in front of mirror with her lover. She says that if a woman looks in the looking glass of her heart, she will find that she desires sexual enjoyment as much as a man. In this way, the lover will know that he is stronger than her and her beloved is softer and younger. She advises her to admire her lover's body. She advises her to give everything:

Gift him all,
Gift him what makes you woman, the scent of
Long hair, the musk of sweat between the breasts,
The warm shock of menstrual blood, and all your
Endless female hungers. ("The Looking Glass")

The poem tells the importance of man in woman's life. Das writes that it is very difficult to live without a man. She writes that the life partner becomes your life and without him your life become dull and drab.

Kamla Das' another poem "The Sunshine Cat" also has been taken from *Summer in Calcutta.* The poem depicts the difference between love and lust. It is a confessional poem and the poet speaks about those people who loved Kamala Das. She describes her husband a selfish, coward and a ruthless watcher. She started having extra-marital affairs with those people who were much younger to her. She frankly speaks about her sexual encounters with many people. She tells that her young lovers flatly refused to love her. They said frankly:

> ...they said, each of
> Them, I do not love, I cannot love, it is not
> In my nature of love, but can be kind to you. ("The Sunshine Cat")

When she came to her consciousness and recalls those moments, she starts shedding tears about thinking of those lovers who never loved her and just utilized her. When her husband came to know about her secret affairs with many people, he would keep her locked in a book of room.

One day her husband locked her in winter in the same room and when he returned in the evening, he found that she had become half-dead due to severe cold and she was of no use for a man i.e. she had lost all sexual desires:

> He returned to take her out, she was a cold and
> Half dead woman, now of no use at all to men. ("The Sunshine Cat")

Kamala Das' poem "My Grandmother's House" is another confessional poem which was published in 1999. In this poem, she speaks that it was her grandmother's house where she received love. Kamala Das was too young to read the books at that time and the snaked moved among books. Now her grandmother is no more and the house is surrounded by silence and unhappiness. The poet thinks many times to visit her grandmother's house. She addresses her husband that once I was very happy in my grandmother's house and now I am searching love at strangers' door. The ending of the poem clearly depicts it:

> ... I who have lost
> My way and beg now at strangers' doors to
> Receive love, at least in small change? ("The Sunshine Cat")

Kamala Das has written a poem titled "The Freaks" in which she has talks about her husband who is in a hurry for the physical intimacy. He has only sexual desires and there is no lovc or emotional attachment for her.

But, they only wander, tripping
Idly over puddles of
Desire… ("The Freaks")

The poet shows that she does not like her husband's sun-burnt face, her dark-cavern face and her uneven teeth.

…Who can
Help us who have lived so long
And have failed in love? ("The Freaks")

She is pining for the true love and emotional attachment from her husband but in fact, there is no such kind of relationship between them. She called her heart an empty cistern. She calls that she is abnormal and is much different from other people.

The poet tells that she has lived many years of married life but she could not establish healthy relationship with her husband. She wanted to get real love but she could get that love neither from her husband nor from her lovers. She remains hungry for love. He silence and loneliness stings her like a snake and that's why she calls herself a 'freak'. In order to hide her freakiness, she shows her flamboyant lust time to time.

Her poem "In Love" is about the heat of emotions. She compares her husband's mouth to the blazing sun. Her husband would reach to her like a carnivorous plant. She is sad to see that she has no place in his heart:

Where is room, excuse or even
Need for love, for isn't each
Embrace a complete thing a finished. ("In Love")

She falsely tries to show that she is also sexually mad. She tells that there is no any room for their love and there is only a complete physical attachment only. When he kisses me, I ignore his advances because I think that there is no pure love in these activities. The bodies seem to be communicating in the poem and the heart is silent. She is not happy in the physical involvement but she does so in order to make her husband happy. Her husband is unable to understand her feelings and she had to subdue her emotions.

The silence in the poem speaks not about the silence of the room; it is the silence of the heart. When the poet looks at the crows flying, she feels that their wings have been smeared with poison. It is a psychological fact when a person is sad; he feels sadness in the surroundings also.

This skin-communicated
Thing that I dare not yet in
His presence calls our love. ("In Love")

Kamala Das' poem "My Mother at Sixty-six" is about the fear of loss of her mother. It is about the mother-daughter relationships. The poet was going to Cochin Airport with her mother and her mother's face was half-open. She was looking like a corpse at that moment. The poet compares her mother's face to a late winter's moon. She was very said at heart but she did not want to expresses her hidden emotions of fear and insecurity without her mother and that's why she bids adieu to her mother smilingly.

But all I said was, see you soon, Amma,
All I did was smile and smile and
Smile... ("My Mother at Sixty-six")

In the poem "The Stone Age" the poet addresses her husband directly and she blames her husband for not loving her. In the opening lines she calls her husband an emotionless, stonehearted and impassive person. He takes decisions of every step of her life and she is given no right to decide about her life. He has kept her in the web of marriage and entrapped her. He shows that he is kind but in fact, he is stern. The poet writes in the beginning of the poem:

Fond husband, ancient settler in the mind,
Old fat spider, weaving webs of the bewilderment,
Be kind. You turn me into a bird of stone, a granite
Dove, you build round me a shabby room. ("The Stone Age")

She thinks that her husband has made her a bird of stone or granite dove. She holds her husband responsible for the shattering her dreams. When he reads books, he disturbs his sleeps. She keeps hidden her sexual desires and she calls these extramarital affairs like the drains She keeps her relationships with another lover who lives around forty steps away from her house. She is seen by his neighbour how she comes line rain. Kamala Das writes how her husband keeps full control on her body. He does not love her and he sleeps on her breast. She calls the life so short and to get love is so difficult.

To conclude, it can be stated that Kamala Das' personal life remained much tumultuous and devoid of love. Her husband did not love her and tortured her. Sometimes, she would also think to commit suicide. She writes in her autobiography how once she sent a servant to the chemist shop so that she may take pills and commit suicide but she remained unsuccessful in her effort as all the chemists refused to give him pills without doctor's prescription:

> One day, being able it no longer, I sent the cook to chemist's shop for a dozen tablets of barbiturates. No chemist would give them without doctor's prescription. The cook, on his return, empty-handed, told me with tears in his eyes, that he too would take tablets if I decided to kill myself. (Das, *My Story* 103).

Works Cited

Das, Bijay Kumar. *Modern Indian English Poetry*. Bareilly: Prakash Book Depot, 1992. Print.

Das, Kamala. *Summer in Calcutta*. New Delhi: Everest Press, 1965. Print.

—.*Only the Soul Knows How to Sing*. Kottayam: DC Books, 1996. Print.

—. *The Descendants*. Calcutta: Writer's Workshop: 1967. Print.

—. *Old Playhouse and Other Poems*. Madras: Orient Longman Ltd., 1973. Print.

—. *My Story*. New Delhi: Sterling Publishers Pvt. Ltd, 1976. Print.

Nair, Jaikrishnan. "The Onset of poetic Rebellion: An Explication of Kamala Das's 'An Introduction". *Indian Writing in English*. New Delhi: Atlantic Publishers & Distributors, 1999. Print.

Chapter - 8

Shifting Attitude of Immigrant Women in Bharati Mukherjee's Select Fiction: An Analysis

K.M. Keerthika

There is no chance of the welfare of the world unless the condition of women is improved. It is not possible for a bird to fly on one wing.

– Swami Vivekananda

True to the words of Swami Vivekananda, the condition of women doesn't changes; and women are still considered as the subject of man's violence. Generally, it was hidden between the walls of houses, but nowadays the violence is perpetrated on woman, which almost becomes as a source of pride.

The woman in the world is not a true woman either because she has been corrupted for centuries. She believes that they are equal to man and they are under the protection of their loved ones, she feels that she came out of man's rib, not from their feet or head, but from the side.

In the modern world the qualities of women change. There was a quite difference between traditional and modern women. The reason laid behind these changes are their freedom for education, less social boundaries and the liberty provided for them from their family. Many women writers started to express their feelings to the society through their writings. There were many women writers who express the life of immigrants in the form of novel.

Bharati Mukherjee is one such writer who beautifully portrays the life of the immigrants in the American land. Through her fiction she tries to focuses on the life and attitude of the women which change because of cultural shock, domination and conflicts faced in their life in the foreign land.

Mukherjee's marriage to someone outside her culture changed her life, and she moved to Canada with her husband where she underwent racism and alienation. Immigrant experiences in Canada and the US has influenced her to portray the life of women in her novels. Like Mukherjee, her protagonists also suffer because of immigration, and they feel difficult to create an individual identity. So to attain their liberty, they try to get rid of the male dominated society and they change their attitude and try to become the role models for many other immigrant women. Mukherjee in an interview stated her views for the immigrant women:

> We immigrants have fascinating tales to relate. Many of us have lived in newly independent or emerging countries which are placed by civil and religious conflicts...When we uproot ourselves from those countries and come here, either by choice or out of necessity we suddenly must know about 200 years of American history and learn to adapt to American society. (Interview)

Mukherjee's fiction focuses on the concept of migration, expatriates experience of alienation, position of new immigrants, Indian women and their struggle. She presents the shifting attitude of women when they travel from their home land to the alien land.

When people move on to the unknown land, they feel as if they are outsiders. They try to recreate themselves into a new personality and bring out a new attitude in the place they are going to survive. They create a new self and change themselves by adapting to the situations which makes them to forget their own culture. This makes them feel that their home is not a foreign land.

Indian women are assumed as a sign of prestige. To maintain the reputation of family, they are forced to maintain the rules and regulations, chain of customs and traditions because they are considered responsible person for the growth and welfare of the family. Men want their wife to be traditional and follow the ancestral values in their life whereas women want to lead a life full of freedom.

Mukherjee depicts the life of the protagonist in a shifting attitude. The protagonists remains shy, loving, caring and religious until they remain themselves, and their attitude slightly changes when they long for their freedom under the male dominated society. They transform themselves as bold, intelligent and smart women which can be seen in the works of Bharati Mukherjee.

In the novel *Jasmine*, Mukherjee portrays the life of Jyoti, born in a small town and migrated to America. She faces various adverse circumstances as an immigrant and tries to adjust and adapt the painful situation. Likewise in the novel *Wife*, Dimple lives in the fantasy world where she faces obstacles and she tries o overcome that by making a decision of her own. In the novel *Desirable Daughters*, Tara gets stuck between Indian traditions and Western life-style. In the novel *Tree Bride*, Tara has been transformed to aggressive or independent woman who leads her life on own. In the novel *Tiger's Daughter* the protagonist leads a confused and frustrated life due to several problems and finally, she takes a violent demonstration.

Mukherjee believes that the change of attitude happens because of crossing multiple borders of language, history, race, time. In the novel *Wife*, Dimple is a middle-class Hindu Brahmin, she is a mature woman character but she rebels for her freedom and to attain that, she even kills her husband.

As a teenager, she leads an imaginary life where she keeps herself away from the realities of life. In India women have to respect their parents when it comes to marriage, girls have to obey their parents for their marriage. In the novel *Wife*, Dimple believes that marriage can change her entire life with full of freedom and happiness, but all her belief was broken into pieces. She feels like a prisoner under the supervision of her mother-in-law. She feels suffocated to stay over there. At one point of time she got excited when she came to know that she is going to migrate to America with her husband. But her excitement disappeared when she comes to know that she is pregnant. Women considered pregnancy as blessing but she considered it as an obstacle. She even kills a pregnant mouse which indicates her unwillingness in her pregnancy. She tries to terminate her pregnancy.

> She had skipped rope until her legs grew numb and her stomach burned; then she had poured water from the heavy bucket over her head, shoulders, over the tight little curve of her stomach. She had poured until the last of the blood washed of her legs; then she had collapsed. (*Wife* 42).

After her migration to America, she feels lonely and does not get any consolation. Dimple tries to maintain balance between her home land and foreign land and wants to be a perfect wife like Sita, who stands as an icon of purity, patience and sacrifice. But Dimple was gradually shifted to the depressed condition. She feels that Amit never gives her permission to adapt the openness and modernity of America. This made her to fall in love with Milt Glasser. Her relation with him becomes deeper and she makes physical relationship with him. This shows her change of attitude which got highly influenced by the American life style.

Dimple doesn't even feel guilty for betraying her husband and violating the duty of a wife. She feels oscillated between the moral values of her native land and the values of the new land. Without understanding her, Amit advises her: "You must go out, make friends, do something constructive, not to stay at home and think about Calcutta (*Wife* 111). She becomes emotionally disturbed and blames Amit for her unhappy life. So she decided to kill him, she takes her kitchen knife and stabs him madly seven times in his neck.

> She sneaked upon on him and chose a spot, her favourite spot. Just under the hairline, where the mole was getting larger and browner, and she drew an imaginary line of kisses because she did not want him to think she was the impulsive, foolish sort who acted like a maniac just because the husband was suffering from insomnia. She touched the mole very lightly and let her fingers draw a circle around detectable spot, then she brought her right hand up and with the knife stabbed the magical circle once, twice, seven times. (*Wife* 212-213).

As an Indian woman, her act of murder is quite different to an ideal wife. She wants to be an ideal wife like Sita, but her fate turns her life upside down and she becomes as murderer who kills her husband. The change within Dimple happened only because of the high expectation to be free from the bondage of male dominated society, which made her to do so.

Women are cherished under a social structure; they lead a life according to the wishes of the others. The Hindu Indian tradition imprints in the hearts and minds of the women that women should obey her husband, undergo suffering. Mukherjee's women protagonist Jyoti in the novel *Jasmine* faces lot of suffering in the society and violated Indian tradition.

Jasmine is the story of a rural Punjabi girl; she was courageous enough and stands against the oppression of women in the male dominated society. By marrying Prakash, Jyoti comes out of the male dominated village. As free minded man Prakash gives all freedom to Jyoti and named her as Jasmine. After the death of Prakash, she decided to travel to America. She tries to lead a balance life between modernism and tradition. Through her travel, the attitude of Jasmine changes according to the situation.

During her travel she faced lot of difficulties, she was raped by Half-Face, but she murdered Half-Face. She feels herself as Lord Yama, after killing him. The incident changes her entire life. Through this she learns to fight against any situation. By suppressing her own Indianess, she tries her best to adapt the American traditions. Jasmine's journey from place to place indicates her strong determination to establish herself in the American mode of life. Taylor named her as 'Jase'. Taylor and his wife help Jasmine to adjust the new society.

When Jasmine comes to Iowa, she starts her new life with Bud and changed her identity as 'Jane'. But Jasmine was not happy over there. She tries to fulfil his needs and sacrificed all her individuality but Bud never understands her feelings. She keeps on changing her attitude and identity and changes her name as Jyoti, Jasmine, Jase and finally Jane. Jyoti evolves as a village girl of Hasnapur, transforms to 'Jasmine' after her marriage and then becomes 'Jase' in the alien land and further changes to 'Jane' and finally becomes Iowa woman. She has undergone many changes and accepted each change as a new challenge of her life and shifted her role according to each transformation. Indira talks about the explicit manner of Jasmine as:

> "Jasmine blooms from being a different alien with forged documents into adventurous Jase living only for the present. The tugging between the opposing forces does not intimidate her rather it excites her. Amidst the other immigrant domestics who hang suspended between the two worlds, Jasmine feels proud that she is getting rooted in the world".(Indira 86)

Jasmine fights against her fate and superstitions. She becomes a unique being with the help of others she created her own life. She becomes highly adaptive and her ability to adapt to circumstances to make her successful in all situations. Through the life circumstances Jasmine emerged as a great warrior.

Desirable Daughters is beautifully woven, thoughtful and intelligent story of three Calcutta-born Brahmin upper-class sisters renowned for their beauty, wealth, and privileged position in society. In an interview with Bill Moyers, Mukherjee explains why she named her book *Desirable Daughters,* "because in Hindu societies, especially in overprotected patriarchal families like mine, daughters are not at all desirable. They are trouble". (Moyers) But these three sisters are beautiful well-educated and very desirous to live their lives according to their choice and want to come out from the conventional role assigned to women in the orthodox Indian society. Padma and Parvati marry against the wish of their father. But Tara was not that much courageous like her sisters, so she obeyed her father's word.

After her marriage she migrated to San Francisco. She tries to show herself as a typical Indian wife. She tries to balance herself between the existing tradition and expectations of her husband and for the welfare of the family. But at one point of time, she gets fed up and gradually becomes tired to perform her domestic duties and she longed for her freedom. She gradually moved on to American lifestyle. She started calling her husband by his name. An ideal Hindu woman has no permission to utter her husband's name. Tara shifted her attitude from a traditional woman to modern woman.

> ...His American friends call him Bish...I, of course, as a good Hindu wife-to-be, could not utter any of his names to his face. But we're progressive people: after crossing the dark waters to California I called him Bishu, then Bish. (*Desirable Daughters* 23)

Tara at one point of time divorced Bish and moved on to a new life style. She met Andy and develops sexual relationship with him. As she believes that she has become American, she doesn't feel guilty about her relationship with Andy. As a modern woman, she breaks the taboos of her traditional Indian society. She tugs between two selves and two identities. As she is torn between dual pulls of her attitude, she is intensely aware of her difference. She says:

> I am not the only blue-jeaned woman with a Pashmina shawl around my shoulders and broken-down running shoes on my feet. I am not the only Indian on the block. All the same, I stand out, I'm convinced. I don't belong here, despite my political leanings; worse, I don't want to belong. (*Desirable Daughters* 79).

She could not come out of her Indian tradition. She gains her inspiration through the life of her great grant mother Tara Lata. She realized the fact that being remain as traditional women can remain as a freedom fighter in a male dominated society, so she finally realizes that, as she possesses American and Indian selves, she try to merge in selves to rebuilt her own self.

Mukherjee's affinity to Indian soil and culture is rooted in her fiction. She foregrounds the transformation of her characters as a result of immigration in her works. She portrays the tension of women in the society. Her characters undergo transformation from one culture, people, identity or place to another new social, political, cultural and geographical milieu. In the patriarchy society, woman has no rights to shape her life as she wishes. Men determine the fate of women, take all domestic decisions and decide what is good or bad for them. Women have no identity of their own.

They are considered as puppets in the hands of men. Women are treated as dolls without any feelings and emotions. As Mukherjee crossed geographical barriers and national identity, she displays sympathy and understanding of women under the male-dominated society and she beautifully brings out how they overcome such barriers.

Works Cited

Indira, S. "Jasmine: An Odyssey of Unhousement and Exhousement in Commonwealth Writing". *A Study in Expatriate Experience*. Ed. R.K. Dhawan and L.S.R. Krishna Sastri. New Delhi: Prestige Book, 1994. Print.

Moyers, Bill. *Bharati Mukherjee: Interview by Bill Moyer*. June 20, 2003. Web. June 1, 2019.

Mukherjee, Bharati. *Desirable Daughters*. New York: Theia, 2002.Print.

—. *Jasmine*. New York: Grove Weidenfeld, 1989. Print.

—. *Wife*. Boston: Houghton Miffin, 1975. Print.

—. Quoted in Sunday Review. *The Times of India*. Oct 1, 1989. Web. June 1, 2019.

Nayyar, Sanjeev. "The Status of Women in India". *E-Samskriti Culture Spirituality Travel*. Nov. 2000. Web. June 1, 2019.

Chapter - 9

Redefining Peripheries: Urbanization and Prostitution in Indian Literature

Guni Vats

> *I saw girls and women chewed up and spit out by the brothel system...ice used to physically break pre-pubescent girls and make them amenable to exploitation...mutilated bodies, bottles shoved up vaginas, scars of cigarette butts on breasts, repeated fractures, suicides and murders.*
>
> **– (*Ruchira Gupta ix-x*)**

Decades have witnessed women fighting for their basic human rights, demanding a society where they could be equal, be free of stereotype occupations, express themselves and probably step out of the kitchen to enjoy a fag of freedom. Present paper discusses just about the women who don't exhaust their lives in the kitchen, they step out in the public domain, a space carved by men for men and work in the fringes of the dominant patriarchal space overstepping every cautious ruling laid out for the women of virtue. These women who are prostituted and consumed every night untangle the neatly folded sections of urban space in India and unveil the filth of the hypocrite urbanism that rapes women every day and builds its development over the rotten bodies of consumed humanity.

Michel Foucault in his essay, "Of Other Spaces: Utopias and Heterotopias" marks that our era of space is marked by the juxtaposition of elements that carve the shape of a space. Structuralism could explain the desperation of elements, links and points trying to assume a sort of shape as an effort to interact with each other, establishing a relationship that either juxtaposes or gives them the space to coexist, thus defining what we could call a structure. A society could be understood taking its form in the very above mentioned fashion. Elements interact and form a net with time to create a space that assumes a structure and soon authors its own history.

The entanglement of time and space creates a hierarchy of space that is in its turn heterogeneous. These heterogeneous spaces then form binaries and the division happens along the culturally constructed lines of perceived notions: external and internal space, public and private space, material and cultural space, male dominant and female dominant space. Foucault explains that the era of nineteenth century onwards belongs to the arrangement of points and places in a space such as trees, lamp posts, beds etc. This arrangement marks the characteristic of a space. Precisely how the building in Manto's *The Hundred-Candle-Power Bulb* that was once an elite office becomes the shelter of a prostitute and the home in Chughtai's *The Housewife* transforms a woman of loose character to a housewife. Through short stories, my paper tries to understand how a space declares its virtue based on time and experiences and how the elements communicate to brand a space its character. Space that exists in the patriarchal structure, a heterotopia that abides and reverses the expectation of the conventional external space and thus labeled, and its residents treated as mere points of the network and not flesh and blood.

The quality of a space depends on its entanglement with time. Time's movement could be lateral or circular, vertical or horizontal. Time elapsed in decades brand its character and so does time that goes by as age and also the vertical division of time that witness's night from day and evening from morning. An urban park in India bustles with activities in morning and evening, it becomes the place of fitness for enthusiasts, place for business for hawkers, place for solace for the tormented, place for introspection for the busy and place for interaction for the occupied. It offers its visitors whatever comfort they come looking for. The same park offers shade to the traveler under its trees in the scorching sun of unrelenting summers and warmth to the mothers and their children looking for an afternoon nap in the freezing winters. Often hawkers could be spotted resting on the benches after their long day stroll or children from the adjacent underprivileged dwellings enjoying open spaces that offer a relief from their cramped and overcrowded homes. The trees appear glee and provide shelter to the birds that come looking for their share of space. The same parks become the site for soliciting prostitutes as the sun sets. The glee trees shade the vulgarity and nudity from the upper class dwellings and witness the horrific dance of obscenity. Women solicit men under the trees and lamp posts and the benches and shrubs mourn the body penetration with the women that sell their bodies to earn a square meal.

> Although a grief had torn her to pieces, she still walked to the garden and stationed herself there. She had been coming here for many years

> to do business...she smiled at men...nobody asked her her price...time and men passed her by. (Bagul 32)

The trees that had played with the children now consume the wails of the women dying every moment they spend in the parks where men come to live a little more every morning. The lamp posts that act as the milestones for a lost soul and illuminate the future of few who cannot afford the luxury of electricity become the pick-up points for prostituted women as the night falls. The society living in high rise structures and travelling in expensive cars taunt the lamp posts of felicitating a business that taints the reputation of an urban city. A public space is created within the public space that mocks the regulations laid out in the morning conferences that swears by the protection of women and puts its women on display in the evenings. Space and place are complex ideas. While people pass through the geographical place, the space remains in the memories. The experience of a place carves a space and these experiences differ by the hour. Niranjana's short story, "The Last Customer" travels from a home to the streets to the drains to the school. Every establishment and relationship is mocked by the mute girl who cannot answer the society but by destroying herself and leaving her body to be eaten by the vulture, her last customer. The story questions every place and insults the urban public space for consuming a young mute girl but giving her a place to cover her rotting body. The story spans wide and far with the girl and dies with her, marking the death of a space that has no place for humanity in it:

> No one was willing to go beyond the intersection. The ceaseless expanse of buildings and the cool breeze over the plains brought along a foul odor...she stood below the deodar tree on the footpath...she reached the other end of the city and exited it...at the very edge of the city was a school, deserted by the night...a lonesome lamp-post in the middle...and then by night in the shrubs on the green grass, dying a couple of times every day...the municipal van would come by to pick up the corpse. (Niranjana 38-45)

The juxtaposition or superimposition of elements not only brand a space but create heterotopias that exist in reality but abide by or reverse the conventional structures in all their might. The twenty first century recognizes pleasure as the rule for creating spaces. Where families are formed to abide by the conventional norms of a society, brothels are formed on the outskirts to provide pleasure to the man, the creator of space. The elements of home interact differently in a brothel; the interaction decides the relationship between elements and people. The bed that witnesses consummation of a marriage or comforts the ailing child becomes the aid to rape in the brothel, a death bed for the unlucky few. Brothels thus become a structure where pleasure becomes the center and any play of the signifiers must culminate at the signification of pleasure, dominantly the pleasure of man. Kamala Das' short story, "A Doll for the Child Prostitute" questions the existence of the structure called home and the design of the interaction of elements that brands it so. Rukmani's home becomes a place that looted her of her innocence and raped her virginity, the place that insulted the father daughter relationship and forced her to the flesh trade. Whereas Ayee's brothel becomes the place where she plays and eats and learns the trades of life. She finds a loving father in a client, the inspector *sahib* who ultimately develops daughterly affection for her and supports her in the worst times. Not only the interaction of elements but the experience brands a space and decides the experiences of its inhabitants.

Michel Foucault deals with the idea of Utopia and Heterotopia precisely to the extent where a scientific and architectural explanation unveils the coexistence of spaces that are the other. Utopia is an ideal place that is devoid of all the wrongs of the real space. It is an illusion, a place where everyone would want to live but does not exist. Heterotopias on the other hand are real places but steering away from the reality of the real and conventional constructed space. If the real world be understood as the heterogeneous existence of many binary spaces that accommodates slight diversions to the rule of its structure, the structure would still be left with a few crevices and more prominent margins. Deconstruction and Post Modernism or Post Structuralism attempts to demolish the illusionary shape of the structure so as to realize the center that acts as the force of play that keeps the structure together. Structure of the real world depends on a systematic hegemonic exercise that creates an illusion and busies every point in the structure in attempt to reach and become the Utopian impossible. Amongst all the activities of the real world exists a parallel world that is strategically hidden from the eye of the conventional world and its inhabitants. Conscious attempts are made that the two spaces must interact the very least. This parallel world could be understood as the Heterotopia, the real space that exists away from the conventional space and in acceptance or rejection of the norms of the real world. Prisons, saunas, colonies, asylums, brothels are the few examples of heterotopias. The discussion of brothels as the extreme heterotopia is of utmost importance because the exploited elements of heterotopia are the innocent women who are victimized till the extent that they normalize the pain and loose all energy to fight the wrong.

The rights and wrongs of the real world don't exercise in the heterotopias per say. The human rights of a free citizen are not awarded to the murder victim convicted and punished in the prison. Brothels or the heterotopias of prostitution are strategically kept away from the eye of the real world. The elements of the two spaces are carefully avoided to interact and if they do so by accident, the residents are forced to pay for the compromised existence of the heterotopia. Utopia and Heterotopia converge at a point where both entertain the existence of a space that deviates from the real world. Many of the vices of the real world are absent from the heterotopia of brothels. This takes us back to the point of deviation of the two spaces. Where the real world fights for the abolition of racism, discrimination based on body types, homosexuality, freedom of expression and the stereotyped threats, heterotopias enjoy the freedom levied on them. The prostituted women are never shown cooking food or doing the household chores, they are encouraged to earn money, Manto's and Chughtai's prostituted protagonists are heard uttering bitter obscenities, the protagonists of Bibhutibhushan Bandopadhyay's *Heeng Kochuri* are shown enjoying smoking where they even take a jibe on the women of real world who are not allowed to smoke.

Every heterotopia is a structure in all its glory and every structure depends on the hegemonic dominant agencies to create a hierarchy. It is this hierarchy that facilitates binding the structure and ensuring that it rests on the center carefully constructed. Brothels are carefully carved in the same fashion. They exist as the hostels for prostituted women, run by women who were once the victim of the same trade and all ultimately answerable to the man who runs it all. The compromise of public and private space in the heterotopia enjoys its own definitions and interpretations of the external and the internal. The room of the brothel becomes a public place where a woman is forced to share her flesh as if that was a public property but her pain and disease becomes the personal matter and illegal mutilations and abortions are carried out in private. The external public space is controlled by the pimp who takes his share of making the flesh available and the inner quarters of the brothel, the stinky crammed rooms play the role of a *zenana*. The hegemonic structure of brothel ensures that the elements busy themselves in obeying by the order and thus ultimately concentrate on delivering the most pleasure. Among the prostituted women are the hierarchies of ones who look like the respectable women, the loose character women amongst the hoard that have no claim to the conventional character, the virgins, the amateur, the children, the experienced, the elder sisters, the co-sufferers and the opportunists. The respectable institutions of the real world are mocked in the heterotopias. Marriage is often mocked at or used as a metaphor in brothels, a respectable wedded woman as a taunt, voluptuousness as a sumptuous meal, colour as the proximity to the real world and virginity as the opportunity to more money.

> What is wrong in being dark?...I am dark, but every client asks for me…you wear underpants like girls of the upper classes…I would love to have a home of my own and a few children…but I don't want to have any man in my house. (Das 5-15)

Heterotopias are indeed formed by the interaction of elements but they don't exist alone. Heterotopias have a relation to all the remaining spaces. They perform two types of functions; heterotopia of illusion exposes every real space and the heterotopia of compensation creates a real space – a space that is the other. Brothel is thus the heterotopia of compensation. It does not reveal the crevices of the real space but forms a real space that is the other. This other space caters to the need that cannot be fulfilled in the real world. *The Hindu* covered a special story titled "A Tainted Tradition"; it unveils the four hundred year old tradition of prostitution in the Natpurwa village, seventy kilometer east of Lucknow. The village with a population of approximately five thousand seems like any other village from the outside but a brave interrogation led to the secret that every family swears by. The village still witnesses seventy five percent of its women being prostituted daily. "The men are used to eating off the women…they will not let their source of income dry out" reveals Chandralekha, a villager determined to free the village of the clutches of this oppressive tradition. The people don't have any other stable source of income and education is yet to see the light of day in the darkness of the village. Every woman is conveniently subjected to the life of prostitution when she comes of age and no man experiences the expected need to provide security to the women of the house. The expected roles of brothers and sons have dried out in the village where they unashamedly play pimps for their mothers and sisters. Their only explanation to being devoid of the emotion of any masculine possessiveness is that they have never known who their father is, this is what they have seen and that is why they exercise it without any hesitation. The heterotopia of compulsion, the real space but the other is carefully kept separate as it is in close proximity to the neighboring villages and cities and urban spaces feed the other space so that it bears the filth in it and not disturb the sanctity of the real world. The entire village is an appropriate example of a living heterotopia which is nurtured by the diplomats of the real world as they are often the customers of the village, the other.

The existence of heterotopias of compulsion depends on the luxury they provide without the hassles of the real world. The sex could be found in the space of the real world but there it comes with the obligations of the real space, whereas heterotopias provide pleasure in exchange of a few wads of currency notes. They are known to be the places that thrive in the darkness, where the faces of clients do not matter. Every man that comes looking for pleasure is but a customer and the only interaction appreciated is the exchange of sexual service for money. The business operates devoid of any emotion and responsibility. Since the heterotopia provides a space away from the real space, the customers enjoy no-interference from and no-surveillance of the real world. The masculinity of the real world takes an aggressive turn behind the dim lights of the other space and the consequences shame the very existence of humankind. Men feed off girls of the same age as their daughters, they get aggressive and subject the woman to inhumanity that probably derives from the frustration of the real world, the sex turn to lust turns to inhumanity turns to sadism which ultimately leaves the prey and predator empty of any human emotion. Masculinity exercised in this other space could not be understood by the definitions laid out by the intellectuals of the real world, it is the expression of self – destruction, self-hatred, self-loathing that finds an expression in the other space and leaves it tattered.

Prostitution and urbanization in India have been dealt with the intellectual capacity of reviewing and re-interpreting the margins of the patriarchal structure. My paper redefines the peripheries and revisits the margins. It realizes in its course that it is not a struggle of the margins to come to the center but the struggle of a structure, a heterotopia striving to interact with the real world. The structure needs a deeper understanding of its construction and careful deconstruction. The oldest profession has perhaps changed its face and in an attempt to fit in the space of the real world formed a space of its own, a space that lies at the point where binaries coincide and meanings are reconsidered. Foucault talks of mirror as a space that acts both as a Utopia and a Heterotopia. The mirror exists in the physical world yet the image is but a reflection. The image could be who you are or who you want to be, depending on its perception, thus agreeing to the two functions of heterotopias. Brothels could be seen as the mirror standing in between Utopia, Heterotopia and the Real Space. It is real yet virtual, public yet private, cultural yet material, a place run by women yet dominated by man, it is a professional place yet a personal abode. Urbanization has painted prostitution in new colors that camouflage well with the real world yet bleed to be freed. The spaces in urban areas are aggressively defined but it is the prostituted space that transcends all meanings, forms new meanings and hides behind the constructed spaces struggling to find a place in the gendered space!

Works Cited

Bagul, Baburao. "Woman of the Street." *River of Flesh and Other Stories*. Ed. Ruchira Gupta. New Delhi: Speaking Tiger, 2016, 31-37. Print.

Bandyopadhyay, Bibhutibhushan. "Heeng-Kochuri." *River of Flesh and Other Stories*. Ed. Ruchira Gupta. New Delhi: Speaking Tiger, 2016, 46-60. Print.

Chughtai, Ismat. "The Housewife." *River of Flesh and Other Stories*. Ed. Ruchira Gupta. New Delhi: Speaking Tiger, 2016, 205-220. Print.

Das, Kamala. "A Doll for the Child Prostitute." *River of Flesh and Other Stories*. Ed. Ruchira Gupta. New Delhi: Speaking Tiger, 2016, 1-30. Print.

Foucault, Michel. "Of Other Spaces: Utopias and Heterotopias." *Rethinking Architecture: A Reader in Cultural Theory*. Ed. Neil Leach. London: Routledge, 1997, 350-355. Print.

Gupta, Ruchira. ed. *River of Flesh and Other Stories*. New Delhi: Speaking Tiger, 2016. Print.

Kotiswaran, Prabha. Ed. *Sex Work*. New Delhi: Women Unlimited, 2011. Print.

Kumar, Raksha. "A Tainted Tradition." *The Hindu*. Editorial. 23.03.2013 (19:54 IST): n. pag. Web. 11 February 2017.

Manto, Saadat Hasan. "The Hundre-Candle-Power Bulb." *River of Flesh and Other Stories*. Ed. Ruchira Gupta. New Delhi: Speaking Tiger, 2016, 61-68. Print.

Niranjana. "The Last Customer." *River of Flesh and Other Stories*. Ed. Ruchira Gupta. New Delhi: Speaking Tiger, 2016, 38-45. Print.

Chapter - 10

Social Exclusion of Woman Characters in Select Novels of Bharati Mukherjee: A Brief Study

N. Kaushi Reddy

Literature has been the most powerful medium of stimulate the human emotions and thoughts through writings and it provides an opportunity of coddling life which was never known to us now and before. Through the writings of literature, we have the opportunity to mix their lives, social setup, and system of values, culture, creed, nature, behaviour, attitudes and life conditions.

In the process of social exclusion, certain groups of people or communities are excluded from various rights, privileges and opportunities which are meant only for some specific people or groups, and the weaker sections of the society are denied to these rights due to some factors which are the root causes of marginality.

Social exclusion or marginalization generally talks about social inequality in which discriminated or underprivileged people struggle to get benefitted of the facilities or the resources. They also have the desire to participate actively in the social life. In this way, socially and economically backward people remain at the fringe level of the society.

Many feminist writers such as Dorothy Richardson, Helen Cixous, Simon de Beauvoir, Kate Millet, Virginia Woolf and Angela Carter etc. focus on the gender inequality in which 'gender' is a word designed by society to honour men. It is neither biological built nor a creation of God; it is a creation of society. The journey of life for women remains much challenging and they are discriminated at different levels. They girl children are killed in the womb and the female infanticide has emerged as a main problem not only in India but across the globe.

Women are kept aside in all the domestic and social activities and they are generally kept in the house so that they may bring up their children, clean the house, cook the food and help in the agriculture etc. works. Apart from it, they have to serve the elders and satisfy the bodily hungers of their respective husband. They are considered inferior to men and they are neither given social rights nor the property rights. Women are kept aside from making the decision over their lives. Even their customs and traditions force them to do such things in the name of so called 'decorated culture'. Our male-dominated society never allows women to take part in the social, political and adventurous works like women.

Sherry B. Ortner, a sociologist, embellishes about the non-participation of women in the social activities. According to her, culture is more important than nature in every society and this is the main cause of marginalization. As a result, men expect that women may lag behind in all the social activities. Ortner says that universally, women are generally considered close to nature because their functions are, more or less, concerned with the natural process.

In India also, many women writers have contributed a lot in English literature and they have depicted the marginalised positions of women in their works. There are many names such as Kamala Markandeya, Nayantara Sahgal, Rama Mehta, Anita Desai, Kamala Das, Kiran Desai, Shashi Deshpande, Namita Gokhale, Arundhati Roy and Gita Mehta who have depicted the real position of women in their novels. Many female dalit and non-dalit writers have depicted how even the men of their families did not allow them to take part in many domestic matters in their semi-autobiographical or autobiographical works.

Women remain frustrated and feel inferior because of being girl in their father's home as well as their in-laws home. They are badly treated for dowry issues. Though a woman has the ability to take any decision for her future but she has no choice for thinking about her career. In that situation, women feel depressed and they take the step to commit suicide. Women view the world through the eyes which gives an image of constant threat, anger, anxiety, resistance, helplessness, fear and depression.

Wife, the second novel of Bharati Mukherjee published in 1875, is nothing but the story of a slightly neurotic and depressed young girl, Dimple Das Gupta who gets married with a neurosurgeon according to the desires of her father because he wanted to give her daughter's hand to a finically secure person. Amit Basu was an ordinary boy from a middle-class family and he fails to provide all the facilities to Dimple for which she has always dreamt.

Her husband was also not satisfied with Dimple due to many reasons. Dimple would see herself like Sita who was the ideal wife of Lord Rama who has given the fire ordeal to please her husband. Sita had to walk through the fire in order to prove her sanctity when she lived in Ashok Vatika after the event of her kidnapping by Demon King Ravana.

Arranged marriages, by means of the matrimonial advertisements, are become prominent. In the lives of girls matrimonial advertisements sometimes bring disasters in their life. They have to obey the male authority of the house. It is the reality that marriages are generally arranged by the male persons in the house. The girl should subsume her individual identity into the patriarchal dominance and social and cultural identity. Women are considered as properties in the hand of male dominated society.

Women are marginalized by their complexion also. Mrs Basu had some objections on the name of Dimple. She considered her as 'frivolous not having any serious purpose or value'. Mrs Ghosh, who is sister of Amit, personally feels that Dimple's complexion was even darker than they had seen in Dimple's photograph.

Mr Dasgupta advised his wife to try to make Dimple with white complexion. After two weeks, Mrs. Basu and Mrs. Ghosh agreed that Dimple was a satisfactory match. Dimple saw the Magazine title in which the couple was selecting 'their' colours, especially their bedroom colours. That was supposed to be the best part of getting married: being free and the way of expressing them. This represents the "freedom to express their own wish", but in Dimple's case, it was impossible in her mother-in-law's house. She pretends herself as a happy woman.

Dimple is having the habit of reading magazines and spending hours to writing the letters to editor. In that, she said "Marriage is the song of the road and we should all sing it" (27), otherwise the virtues of our culture will fall. Marriage alone teaches the virtues of sacrifice, responsibility and patience. According to Dimple, happiness is our only goal in the marriage and editor reply for that was "Our glorious culture is wither and fall off by the way-side" (27). They went to Manhattan for party, they met Vinod Khanna, and he done a business degree at NYU, then opened an import-export business. Jyoti introduced Vinod was doing well with his business. When Vinod Khanna offers a job for Dimple, Amit said, "One breadwinner in the family is quite enough" and Dimple cannot do simple Maths surely, she ruin your business. This situation reveals the male dominance and discouragement over the female empowerment.

One day, they have gone to party at Mullick's family. In that party, they served a drink and she was waiting for the permission from Amit. He said that she is free to take decision. She can uphold Bengali womanhood if she wishes but she felt unhappy to do such things in front of her husband. She knew very well about Amit, if she takes any drink in the party, Amit would definitely pass it to his mother and his mother would call Dimple's parents and she will accuse them of raising a dissipated daughter. As an Indian woman, it is her feminine duty to subdue her emotions and desires and take step according to her husband.

Dimple is not able to adjust in a foreign culture and the English environment. Mukherjee highlights the loss of sanity of Dimple as an attribute to her sense of alienation in American culture. Mukherjee deals with the complications that emerge from being thrown between two worlds. In the end of the novel, Dimple seems to be much frustrated and she murders her husband and eventually, she also commits suicide. Thus, Bharati Mukherjee's novel *Wife* did not win the heart of the readers because the heroine of the novel fails to adjust and assimilate in a new culture.

Bharati Mukherjee's another *Jasmine* (1989) is about a seventeen years old girl Jasmine who becomes widow in a young age. The novel tells her state of exile, her identity crisis, a sense of loss, the pangs of separation, and disorientation. Her journey of life is an excruciating tale of self-awareness, identity crisis and self-assertion. Jyoti tries her level best to assimilate and merge into a new world. *Jasmine often suffers dislocation. She tries to grab the opportunity to reinvent herself in the new world. Jasmine enjoys the assimilated status of immigration in the adopted homeland.*

Her marriage with Prakash Vijh provides her a bit relief. She gets love from him and they move to the United States of America. Thus, it was a complete transformation of a village girl who becomes the wife of an American man.

Prakash gives her much liberty and he changes her personality. He changes her name also so that she may be able to assert her own identity in America but there was something else in her destiny. Prakash is killed by a religious extremist in a bombing. Even after her husband's death, Jasmine takes decision to go Florida alone so that she may carry out her husband's plans.

In the novel *Jasmine*, Bharati Mukherjee has taken the theme of identity crisis of a widow who goes to Florida to fulfill her husband's dreams. She is the pivotal female character of this novel who keeps changing her names.

She has seen many transformations in her life. She puts different names for her such as *Jyoti, Jasmine, Jazzy, Jase and Jane at different places such as Hasnapur, Jalandhar, Florida, New York, Iowa and finally California.* She has her relationships with different men and she is free to take the decisions of her life after the death of her husband. She is forced to choose whether to stay out of loyalty or follow her heart. Prakashvijh, was killed by a bomb planted by Sukhwinder in the central bazaar of Jalandhar, her own escape on the occasion having been miraculous. Moreover, Jasmine was raped in the Flaming court motel in Florida by half Face. The table was turned; the rape victim transforms herself into an incarnation of the blood thirsty goddess kali, by slitting her own tongue. Jasmine is transformed to stab her aggressor half face to death. Thus, the novel narrates the trials and tribulation of Jasmine's life.

Bharati Mukherjee's novel *Desirable Daughters* is a tale of a bride named Tara Lata, the Tree Wife who is merely five years old. In Indian society, the patriarchal ideology and mindset deeply ingrained, and thus relegates the girl child to subordinate marginal position likewise orthodox religious beliefs and superstitions. Tara Lata's father marries his daughter to a tree just because he thinks that this is the only way he can save her daughter from exploitation of a man, "His daughter's true fate, the fate behind the horoscope, had now been revealed: a lifetime's virginity, a life without a husband to worship as god's proxy on earth, and thus, the despairing life of a woman doomed to be reincarnated" (14). This statement is the reflection of superstitious belief in horoscope. Tara Lata is headed towards her destiny. A Sanskrit scholar and a Brahmin, he decides to duly perform the ceremony, to a tree as bridegroom so that she can overcome the curse of widowhood. It is surmised that she is united with God, and now she is eternally doomed to be a married woman leading a life of purity, sainthood and lifelong virginity. Marriage of a child at the age of five is an infernal tradition, widely practiced in those days. Getting a child married to a tree to prevent a lifelong widowhood was another prevalent shortcoming of the patriarchal society.

The marriage system of Hindu community has a uniqueness of its own. Hindu marriage is not merely a union between a female and a male which is social sanction, sacred bond, and its religious, spiritual development and divine sacrament. On Wedding Night, a snake bites the bridegroom, so Tara made to protect the husband from poisonous snakebite for that she prescribed offerings to Goddess Manasha, is a Hindu folk goddess of snakes or the cobra deity of East Bengal, who causes or prevents snakebites. All rites had been faithfully observed by Tara. From the groom's party, an elder man came to oppose the rites which were performed by Tara: that is, "When the *stree-achar* rites were performed, some woman must have been unclean. You can deceive judges, but you cannot fool goddesses" (13). He offends; some of the women are being here as menstruating devotee. So that is the reason for the death of bridegroom. Tara's fiancé is killed by a snake on her wedding night, five-year old Tara Lata is spared the disrepute of life as "She was now not quite a widow, which for a Bengali Hindu woman, would be the most cursed state, but a woman who brings her family misfortune and death" (12). This is the impact of history, community, and religion upon a woman's identity.

This novel tells the story of three Bengali sisters who have different fate, though they were born alike in Calcutta. The protagonist says, "Sisters three we are … as like as blossoms on a tree. But we are not" (*Desirable Daughters* 21). Tara prefers to live separately from her husband so that she may assert her feminity and may be able to redefine her identity as a woman. She takes full enjoyment with Andy as she finds something new and scintillating in his company and all this was against the traditional Bengali norms, rituals and rules. She takes a divorce from Vish. Thus, the novel *Desirable Daughters* has parented the position of women in a marginal manner and this has presented a real picture of women in the world.

The society is framed against the women who do not spoke out against the patriarchal system of gender roles or any injustice. Women must have equal rights and they should be given equal opportunities so that they may not leave behind in any area of human development.

Women have equal participation in all the social and political issues but women are not treated with respect. Let the society be ready to accept the changes that are happened in society which are regarded to women. Only our constitutional provisions cannot put an end to the problems of women, even men should also give them equal status. In Modern world of science and technology, when the whole world has shrunk, women's status and their position should be enhanced. but the status and position of women is rather deteriorated. In conclusive remarks, Bharati Mukherjee has depicted the marginal women in her novels.

Works Cited

Mukherjee, Bharati. *Jasmine*. New Delhi: Virago Publications. 2014. Print.

—. *Desirable Daughters*. New Delhi: Rupa Publications. 2003. Print.

—. *Wife*. New Delhi: Penguin Books, 1990. Print.

Ortner, Sherry B. *Is female to Male As Nature is to Culture?* Stanford: Stanford University Press, 1974. Print.

Chapter - 11

Marginalised Status of Women in Anita Desai's Select Novels

Dr Kusum Kanger

Anita Desai was born in Mussoorie, Uttrakhand in 1937. She has been an Emerita John E. Buchard Professor of Humanity in the Massachusetts Institute of Technology. Her father D.N. Mazumdar was a businessman from Bengal. Her childhood name was Anita Mazumdar. Her earlier education was from Queen Mary's Higher Secondary School. She began her writing career since her childhood. She wrote her first story when she was merely nine years old. She completed her graduation from graduation from Miranda House from the University of Delhi. After that she completed her master degree in English literature. Her husband's name is Ashvin Desai. She had four children. She has been shortlisted for the booker prize three times.

Desai's first published novel was *Cry the Peacock* (1963). *Clear Light of Day* (1980) is her autobiographical novel. Her novel *In Custody* was adopted as a movie in the same name. She has written many novels on the basis of her experience. She has received the Sahitya Akademi Award in 1978 for her novel *Fire on the Mountain*. She has written many works. Anita Desai's novels tell about the depth of human life and the real essence of the things as she tells in an interview also, "All my writing is an effort to discover, to underline and convey the true significance of things" (IWP 348).

Cry, the Peacock is her first novel which was published in 1963. Maya is the central female protagonist of this story. Maya is daughter of Raisahib who is a prosperous advocate in Lucknow. Her childhood life was devoid of pleasure.

One day an astrologer told her that after the four years of marriage, a tragedy will happen with her and either she or her husband will die. After her marriage she thinks, "We had been married four years.... I knew the time had come. It was now to be either Gautama, or I" (*Cry, the Peacock* 43).

When Raisahib comes to know about this prophesy, he send albino out of town and orders other members and the servants of the family not to tell about it to Maya. The word 'fate' was banned in the house since that day, "The word had not been uttered in my presence nor 'astrology' nor 'palmistry'. Hush, he had carried in any such matters were mentioned" (*Cry, the Peacock* 75).

Gautama is Maya's husband whose characteristics resemble with Gautama Buddha who renounced the world. Gautama of this novel reminds us of ascetic Buddha while Maya reminds us to the materialistic pursuits of life. Gautama is realistic who lived in Delhi as a scholar and he is away from the materialistic world. Maya is a motherless child. Her brother Arjun has gone to America for making his career. Maya got everything from her father. Gautama is Raisahib's friend. He speaks in a logical and philosophical tone. He is not sensitive.

It was a mismatched marriage and the novel is based on the marital discord. The novel opens when they are in the fourth year of their marriage. Maya has to compromise in her life even after marriage. She remains always sad and does not try much to come out of her inner turmoil. When their pet dog Toto dies, Maya wants to perform the rituals of the dog but Gautama calls the vehicle of the municipal corporation and Maya becomes detached.

Maya feels much dismayed at the death of her pet dog Toto as she was emotionally attached with it because she was an issueless woman, "Childless woman do develop fanatic attachments to their pets" (*Cry, the Peacock* 10). She could not see the carcass of Toto that's why she rushes "to the tap to wash the vision from her eyes" (*Cry, the Peacock* 5). It was shocking and cataclysmic incidence for Maya but for Gautama it was merely a natural phenomenon. Gautama's family had a formal sort of environment.

> One did not speak of love, far less of affection. One spoke – they spoke – of discussions in parliament, of cases of bribery and corruption revealed in government, of newspaper editors accused of libel, and the trivial that followed, ... They had innumerable subjects to speak on (*Cry, the Peacock* 75).

She does not get physical relationship also according to her expectation. She thinks about one relief in her life and that is her ensuing death.

Her husband is cynical and uncooperative. If she had got her husband's support, she could have forgotten her dilemmas and problems. When Maya is with her family, she feels well but when she is alone, she feels broken. She remembers that a female is always used as doll in her parental home and then in her husband's home.

Maya was romantic visions in her life but her husband was neither romantic not loving. When there was rain, the peacock would cry and she would listen the crying of the peacocks. She would understand how these peacocks were calling their peahens. She compares her own state with the lives of peacocks. She is crying for love and life.

She was obsessed with the idea of her death. Suddenly, one day she thinks that her husband may also die after four years. Once she calls her husband Gautama at the terrace. Maya tells Gautama about the beauty of the moon and night. When Gautama comes near the corner of the terrace, she pushes him down from the terrace. In this way, she kills her husband. She thinks that Gautam was a loveless husband and he was devoid of passion. Maya's sister-in-law and mother-in-law take her to her paternal home at Lucknow. She is sent to a mental asylum and finally she dies.

The novel *Bye Bye Blackbird* has been written on the theme of migration. The people of London do not want to keep Indian immigrants in London. When these immigrants go to a foreign land, these people are not liked by the natives. The story revolves around three characters. Adit Sen, Sarah and Dev. Dev has recently come to London to do Advance Course of Economics. Dev feels personally humiliated in London.

Three types of bathrooms have been made in London: for gents, for ladies and for Asians. Dev feels much thwarted. Adit Sen tells his wife to leave London and go to India. Sarah does not agree initially but later she gives her consent to accompany him. Dev also thinks to do the same but at the end of the novel, it is seen that Dev accepts it as his destiny and somehow, he wants to be the part of London life in spite of all the problems and hurdles he faces there. Sarah makes arrangement for Dev before leaving to India.

Anita Desai's novel *In Custody* is about language. In this novel, she tells about the difference between Hindi and Urdu. The year the novel was published, the famous Urdu Shayar Faiz Ahmad Faiz was died. In this novel, Deven is a self-made man who is engaged in a job which he does not like. He is a Hindi professor in Mirpore in Lala Ram Lal College. This novel was shortlisted for the Booker Prize and this novel is about the search for self, meaning and identity.

The novel *Fire on the Mountain* was published in 1977. In this novel, Nanda Kaul is a university Vice Chancellor. Her daughter is Asha. Ila Das is her childhood friend and Ram Lal is her cook. Nanda Kaul is a widow and lives a solitary life in Kasauli Hills. She does not like to disclose her feelings. Except postman and her friend, Ila nobody visits her house. She has spent many years in the service of her husband, children and grandchildren. But now she does not let anyone intervene in her personal life. Suddenly, a responsibility of Raka, a granddaughter comes on her shoulder. Raka is born recluse like her.

Her novel *Fasting, Feasting* is set a small town in late 1970. There are two sisters Uma and Aruna who have brought up in a conventional environment. Uma takes interest in her studies. Uma's mother supports her brother in every decision. When Arun is born in the house, Uma is told to take care of her younger brother. Uma is not allowed to study further. When Uma grew young, her suitors rejected her every time. They take interest in her sister Aruna who was more beautiful than Uma. Ultimately, she is married with an old man. He also deserted her. Uma is married with a wealthy boy and starts living in Bombay. Uma's parents wanted Arun to study but they never allowed Uma for the same.

When day Uma's aunt takes her to the ashram and Uma lives in ashram happily. She spends a month there but her parents call her back. A doctor also gets ready to take her in the hospital as an assistant but her parents do not allow for it also because she was a girl and her parents were apprehensive about her safety. Uma's eyes are filled with dear to see her marginalised position even in her own family.

There is another girl, Anamika in this novel. She wanted to go to Oxford for further studies but her parents marry her in a wealthy family and her in-laws beat her. One day, a news comes that Anamika died by burning. It is not clear in the novel whether she dies by it was a suicide case or it was a murder.

Voices in the City novel is set in the city of Kolkata. The novel shows the changes that are taking place in the modern life and is creating conflict with the traditional life style. The novelist has clearly told the negative sides of Kolkata. The play is about four siblings – Arun, Monisha, Nirode and Amla. Arun goes to England for his studies. Monisha is a neurotic and she is married in a traditional family. She has no children. Her mother-in-law and sister-in-law make her do all the household work. Her Husband Jiban also does not try to understand her. She feels herself lonely and neglected after her marriage. She feels that nobody thinks about her life and dreams. She feels that she has been entrapped in marriage. She thinks about her existence in the world,

> Is this what life is then, my life? Only a conundrum that I shall brood over forever with passion and pain, never to arrive at a solution? Only a conundrum - is that, then, life? (*Voices in the City* 125)

She commits suicide by burning herself alive in the bathroom. When her siblings do not understand the reason of her neuroticism but later they come to know from Monisha's diary.

Amla and Lila, her aunt, talk about the circumstances under which Monisha and Jiban were tied in a nuptial knot:

> 'Did you meet him before they were married?'
>
> 'Yes. Your father asked me to visit his family and report, so I did. I met Jiban and his family before your parents did.'
>
> ...
>
> The old woman shrugged. 'I thought so too, but perhaps he thought, he was being sensible - that Monisha ought not to be encouraged in her morbid inclinations, and that it would be a good thing for her to be settled into such a stolid, unimaginative family as that, just sufficiently educated to accept her with tolerance. That is how mother excused its happening. (*Voices in the City* 199)

Nirode's life remains a constant struggle. He remains unsuccessful in his career. His mother wants to help him but he does not accept her help due to her relationships with Major Chaddha. He relates Kolkata with the goddess Kali who is a goddess of destruction.

Amla is the youngest daughter who also faces many problems in her life. Her job also does not give her satisfaction. When Amla finds her life dull and devoid of any interest, she feels sad. Her sister, Monisha's suicide gives her a shock. She does not feel satisfied while working for an advertisement firm. She starts making illustration for the Panchtantra stories. She finds the story of the Panchtantra much interesting.

Anita Desai's novel *Journey to Ithaca* is another novel that throws light on the women's personal life. Sophie is the main female protagonist of this novel who is quite different from her husband Matteo. Both are anxious to visit India but both of them have a different temperament. On the one hand, Sophie wants to come to India so that she may enjoy the natural landscape in India. She plans to visit Goa and Kashmir so that she may enjoy the beautiful scenery of these states, 'Why not? I want to go to Goa and eat shrimp. I want to go to Kashmir and live on a houseboat. And lie in the sun and shampoo my hair and eat omelettes all day' (*Journey to Ithaca* 47). Her husband Matteo wants to live in an ashram so that he may be able to learn the mysteries of human life.

> "I want to know why we are here"
> "I told you – to find India, to understand India, and the mystery that is at the heart of India."...
> "Couldn't we stay in our own country?"...
> "I told you, because here it is possible to understand the mystery. Over there is not."
> "Why not?"
> "Over there people don't even know there is a mystery. No one thinks about it. Here they do.
> There are people – great sages – to guide you. I need such a person."
> "And I? She put her hand to her chest. Don't I need you? Don't you need me?" (*Journey to Ithaca* 37-38)

Anita Desai's novel *Voices in the City* (1980) is about three families – Das, Ali and Mishra Family. There are four children in Das family – Bim, Tara, Baba and Raja. The novel has been written in four parts. Bim is central female protagonist of this novel. She is different from other women characters of the novel. She subverts the traditional model of the womanhood. She does not want to live her life like a traditional woman. Instead of being suppressed by men, she wants to emerge as a dominant woman character. She is against the marginalised position of the women.

Anita Desai is an unparallel Indian woman writer who writes about the every problem of a woman faces in the man-dominated society. She has depicted the suppressed characters but some of her characters are very bold also which has made her writing unique and interesting. Anita Desai's distinctness can be well-interpreted by her reader. Asnani also holds the views in this context:

> What distinguishes Anita Desai from other writers is her preoccupation with the individual and his inner world of sensibility – the chaos inside his mind….Desai is not interested in social or political probing, the outer weather, the physical geography, or the visible action. (5).

Works Cited

Asnani, Shyam M. Desai. "Theory and Practice of the Novel." *Indo-English Writers Series* 6, 5-16. 1985. Print.

Bande, Usha. *The Novels of Anita Desai.* New Delhi: Prestige, 1988. Print.

Desai, Anita. *Cry, the Peacock,* New Delhi: Orient, 1983. Print.

—. *Journey to Ithaca.* Great Britain: Vintage, 1998. Print.

—-. The Indian Writer's Problems." *Indo-English Writers Series* 6 (1985): 1-4. Print.

—. *Voices in the City.* New Delhi: Orient, 2001. Print.

—. *Women Writers. Quest*, 65, April-June, 1970. Print.

Interview by Yashodhara Dalmia. *The Times of India*. 29 April, 1979. Print.

Chapter - 12

(Re-)Defining the 'Marginal' Identity and 'Alternative Media' as a Voice of Democracy: Exemplifying Arundhati Roy's Fictional and Non-Fictional Works

Ramanuj Mahato

Arundhati Roy as a voice of "alternative media" (the term denotes to re-define such media which aim at challenging all forms of social economical as well as political domination and unfolds better alternatives to "true democracy" whose voice is often marginalised in respect of mainstream media) is the topic for present discussion. A new approach of writing which tends to merge various genres in Roy's writing highlights her unique identity as a social activist as well as a writer rather than a traditional literary artist. She emerges as political activist who stands as a true voice of marginalised media contrasted to mainstream media, concerning the hypocrisy and double standard of society and her later writing aims to unmask the fallacy of virtual democracy concerning the secrecy of rule as uttered by many contemporary writers in their story based fiction. She penetrates into the deeper aim of her writing incorporating directly the problems of political and social issues of post-independent India as well as international politics going so far from popular trend of 'Indianization' or 'diasporic sensibility' of Indian English Writing unlike her contemporaries. She presents anti-establishment aspect of society and her writing shows the complex relationship between mainstream and marginalised agencies in society. It is her conscious endeavour to unmask the reality. She actually blurs the genres of fiction and non-fiction with special hue of democratic writing overshadowing the tradition of Diasporic writing.

Now, in the era of globalization especially at the end of 19th century media play vital role for spreading information across the globe. The relationship between mass media and society seems to be unbreakable and solidified in the time being. Though the term 'media' unfold different level of interpretations regarding social change; and gradually a new branch of media emerges i.e. "alternative media", as R. Abel thought it to be 'indefinable' opposing the basic principle of 'mainstream media', constructed upon modern capitalism, commercial profit. Milzi Waltz in *Alternative and Activist Media* writes, "It describes media that are alternative to, or in opposition to, something else: mass-media products that are widely available and widely consumed" (Waltz, 2005 p. 04). Thus 'alternative media' mark societal change and responsibility as invariably employed with 'participation' with activist approach in political, economical and social point of view; it challenges so called established system or 'canon' of society and the term "alternative media" fundamentally refers to 'politically progressive, left-wing media that aim at challenging capitalism and corporate (media) power ...' (Downing, 2001, p. 88). It also denotes, according to Mitzi Waltz:

> ...those media that provide a different point of view from that usually expressed, that cater to communities not well served by the mass media, or that expressly advocate social change would meet this very basic definition. (Waltz, 2005, p. 04)

In fact, 'alternative media' is the voice of those marginalised group who are misinterpreted by mainstream media though this is considered that alternative media being small-scale at the same time non-profit agencies which are singly-owned and operated as self-imposed and collective way as aimed for radical social change. But 'alternative media' basically counter mainstream overview and assumptions. More specifically, alternative media suggests 'democratic forms of communication' that approaches towards the non-profitable, social enterprise having marginalized identity. Chris Atton argues in *Alternative Media*:

> Alternative media, I argue, are crucially about offering the means for democratic communication to people who are normally excluded from media production. They are to do with organizing media along lines that enable participation and reflexivity. (Atton p. 4).

Arundhati Roy is the noted author of three significant screenplays, eight works of non-fiction and a dozen essays and articles. As social activist and intellectual voice her impact on Indian society cannot be ignored. Embarking her struggling journey from Kerala to Delhi, her writing career begins with *The God of Small Things*, a revolutionary novel which is brilliantly structured projecting the social reality with autobiographical hues. But her conscious identity as an active citizen brings a significant transition in her writing career when she accepts political writing instead of novel writing and denying its aesthetic structure. Roy focuses more on activism representing the identity of the oppressed or marginalised individual or community as Alex Tickell observes that Roy is actually emphasizing her valid right to furnish "political claims in the 'alternative rhetorical site' of fiction and explore different kinds of political truth-telling." She intends to prove herself as a writer believing 'never simplify what is complicated or complicate what is simple' and views in "Come September":

> Fiction and non-fiction are only different technique of storytelling. For reasons I do not fully understand, fiction dances out of me. Non-fiction is wrenched out by the aching, broken world I wake up to every morning. (11).

In fact, she has a real soul of an activist which never flows in mainstream rather speaks off in favour of 'subaltern', meant as 'of inferior rank', is an important term adopted by Antonio Gramsci in his noteworthy work *Prison Notebooks* addressing those sections in society who are subject to surveillance as well as oppression of the dominant classes under the veil of surface progress. Developing a journalistic trend of writing she directly concentrates upon the fundamental problem of society both in India and outside of it along with the dark side of democracy and special emphasis on marginalized section. Her era consciousness is revealed not through her fictional and non-fictional writings rather her involvement in social media, web lectures, blogs, interviews, has successfully connected those marginalised groups or community that are constantly in war with mainstream voices, fighting for their democratic rights. Her writing emerges out in response to certain events and issues like massacres, pogroms, genocide, assassinations, death sentences, political corruption, and Hindu extremism. She also believes that two weeks after September 11, American government was solely responsible for "military and economic terrorism, insurgency, military dictatorship, religious *bigotry* and unimaginable genocide (outside America)."

She also thinks that the United States worked as paradigm of mainstream culture that dominated the Middle East countries by imposing chaos and furnishing the hell of sufferings. She has highlighted on several topics which have national interest such as India's connection with nuclear weapons, America's dominant policies upon India and Narmada Dam project but her emphasis is always on imparting voice to the marginal. Being a critic of neo-imperialism she remains a voice of protest of all legacy of cultural imperialism to advocate anti-globalization movement. But in the tradition of non-fiction writing she adds the individual talent of her latent aesthetic understanding of various ideas. She has never directly criticised a particular side rather creates literary observation by her impartial outlook.

In *The God of Small Things,* Ms Roy speaks about cultural dogmas, class conflicts, family tension, and love laws through a pair of twins in Kerala, India. On other hand, it is a tale about suicidal motifs and incest desire, speaks of the fall of the Compson family and some marginal issues are depicted to portray the reality of Indian society. Here Arundhati Roy also follows *écriture féminine* for experimenting and breaking away from traditions. It delineates actual emotion of the women. Actually this novel is authentically replete with Roy's early childhood memories and the trauma of marginalised Indian society in microcosmic view. Later she has temporarily ceased her fiction writing and concentrates upon non-fiction writing later changed her plan what she described "a terrible shift". Her entire energy gets directed fully towards social and global politics. She feels comfortable in her new social career. The change has occurred both in the perceptions as well as in the purpose of writing and the position of a writer in society. However, she marks a double shift while again being a writer of her recent work *The Ministry of Utmost Happiness* that exposes typically marginal world through references of dark stories of Indian history like Godhra riots, Kashmir insurgency and marginal character like, Anjum who is doubly marginalised being a Muslim as well as a transgender, reflect the true story of oppression of marginal individual or community.

In fact, Arundhati's journey towards "alternative media" has broadened her relation with internet access for reaching into the middle of problem. Whereas literature forgets its basic principle of aesthetic pleasure and gets connected with "internet media" Actually Roy unmasks her image as a social activist and projected her voice through the print media like blogs, interviews articles and electronic media. She criticises the 'blatant performances' of the mainstream media through the spontaneous involvement with social media. Henceforth "alternative media" speaks of the voice of the marginalised; it naturally fulfils purpose of Arundhati Roy and incites her to say against mass media in "Peace is War":

> *Unfortunately, mass media, through a combination of ignorance and design, has framed the whole argument as one between those who are pro-development and those who are anti-development...(75)*

Without circumscribing her writing career on so-called Indian English Literature and Indian theme of writing, she penetrates deeper into the world politics and contemporary issues. Her writing emerging from autobiographical hue reaches the significant level that makes her works universal. She blurs the genre of fiction and non-fiction. Roy also believes that these are two facets of a single coin but the primary focus lies on identifying the marginal issues in societies that need to be understood in reality.

In fact, she achieves a new milestone in the field democratic writing which makes her an iconic figure of "alternative media" which challenges the mainstream media with her activist approach and highlights the true realism of society by focusing real motif of life. Her presence in various social events, talk-show, interviews has corroborated her opinions, views that she has shared in her essays to mark the justice for those unprivileged section of the society. Unlike her diasporic contemporaries Arundhati Roy, according to Padmini Mongia, has highlighted "marketing myth" as an author and this approach has led her to deal the matter with social concern. She has always described social issues having the mask of stories rather than stories having the mask of issues. To her theme is vital that is principal target for a writer. She in this context says "Come September":

> *The theme of much of what I write, fiction as well as non-fiction, is the relationship between power and powerlessness and the endless, circular conflict they're engaged in. (11)*

Her non-fiction works like *The Algebra of Infinite Justice* focuses on the U.S. war policy against Afghanistan and the double standard attitude regarding the establishment of peace. According to her U.S. govt has legitimized terrorism by illegitimating "other". In her essay "The Cost of Living" Roy dares to discuss on two significant issues – the hypocrisy of Narmada dam projects and unorganized settlement policy of India. Thus she claims in "Ahimsa":

> The NBA (Narmada Bachau Andolan) believes that big Dams are obsolete. It believes there are more democratic, more local, more economically viable and environmentally sustainable ways of generating electricity and managing water systems. It is demanding more modernity not less. It is demanding more democracy, not less. (5)

Roy's *The End of Imagination* (1998) manifests India's initiative of testing nuclear weapons in Pokhran, Rajasthan. Wherein Roy's *Power Politics* is truly based on the theme of 'war on terrorism' and her view is very clear that war cannot end war. In another essay "An Ordinary Person's Guide to Empire" she talks about the war in Iraq and probes into the basic reality and truth behind any war:

> It's become clear that the War against Terror is not really about terror, and the War on Iraq not only about oil. It's about a superpower's self-destructive impulse towards supremacy, global hegemony. (94)

Field Notes on Democracy: *Listening to Grasshoppers* compiles a couple of essays where Roy seeks to explore the answer of the burning question "Is There Life After Democracy?" It is sharply critical to the mainstream culture and unveils the hypocrisy, weaknesses corporate greed and corruption in India's current model of government that dominate marginalized voice of Indian culture. "Most chilling of all", writes Chomsky in his review, "is that much of this grim portrait is all too familiar to the West." As Michel Hogan in his book "A Savage Capitalism" attacks on the ignorance in the chapter entitled as "A Cure of Historical Amnesia" depicts the limitation of 'alternative media' that tells the irony how little most people in the United States know the authentic history of U.S. relations in all aspects with Mexico and other Latin American countries; Roy similarly talks about this ignorance how the concept of democracy is supposed to be unknown to the mass. According to her, we know about virtual democracy which has nothing to be related with maximum benefit:

> The crisis in modern democracy is a profound one. Free elections, a free press, and an independent judiciary mean little when the free market has reduced them to commodities available on sale to the highest bidder. (215).

Like Noam Chomsky, Roy also enters into the deeper perspective of society and appreciating the magnitude and intensity of Chomsky, challenges the sun of American empire and criticises the role of mass (mainstream) media that support the power game of American authority. She also believes that Chomsky is not only brilliant but also heroic who "wants to destroy the very structure on which it rests" (51). Thus like a 'lady Chomsky' she raises the crucial issues of embedded structure of social hegemony. The Booker Prize winner and social activist, Arundhati Roy has asserted true definition of democracy in most of her writing through the identity of 'alternative media'. In this connection Roy emphatically asked an obvious question in "Public Power in the Age of Empire", "Is There Life after Democracy?" and she further adds:

> Are Democratic governments accountable to the people who elected them? And critically, is the public in democratic countries responsible for the actions of its sarkar? (210).

In fact, all her fictions and non-fictional works are based on actual problems regarding social justice having the outlook of propagandist literature. She not only identifies the issues and the causes of social problem but also offers realistic and feasible solutions. Her writing brilliantly touches the issues which really concern for our social equity and her spontaneous expression about the real picture of world in general and India in particular turns her as a democratic writer in per excellence. Analysing the entire perspective of Arundhati Roy's vision, it can be stated the she has marked out the seed of the problems and it gets developed through the branch of her fiction and non-fictional works. She has actually fictionalised her non-fictions and non-fictionalised her fiction. Murari Prasad in the book *Arundhati Roy: A Critical Perspective* opines that Roy's contribution lies in her own activist approach that arouses the consciousness of identity among the marginal community as well as the marginal characters created by her. At the same time according to Ashcroft, she also emphasizes her 'political resistance' that reflects her true concern for society.

In fact, Arundhati Roy probes deeper and brilliantly endeavours to project the relation between dominated and dominating group in society and her voice always represents the marginalised and their call for justice. Thus, her writing discovers the new motif through 'alternative media'. Hence Arundhati Roy writes in "Instant-Mix Imperial Democracy":

> We need to create a universe of alternative information. We need to support independent media like Democracy Now, Alternative Radio, South End Press. (122).

It asserts the role of critical media instead of participatory media and in the words of John Downing 'alternative media' is a kind radical media which "express an alternative vision to hegemonic politics, priorities and perspectives" (Downing, 2001,) and very naturally its suits the unique theme of Arundhati's writings and gives a penetrating view of marginal identities of those untraced, unfocussed and most uncovered stories that remain unnoticed and silenced behind the lance of mainstream culture.

Works Cited

Ahmed, Aijiz. *Reading Arundhati Roy Politically. Frontline.* 8 Aug, 1997.

Atton, Chris. *Alternative Media.* London: Sage Publications, 2002. Print.

—. *An Alternative Internet*. Edinburgh: Edinburgh University Press, 2004. Print.

Barry, Peter. *Beginning Theory: An Introduction Literary and Cultural Theory*. Manchester and New York: Manchester University Press, 1995. Print.

Beauvoir, Simone. *The Second Sex*. Trans. H.M. Parshley. New York: Knopf, 1952. Print.

Downing, John H. *Radical Media: Rebellious Communication and Social Movements*. Sage, London, 2001. Print.

Ferguson, Russell. "Introduction: Invisible Centre". *Out There: Marginalization and Contemporary Cultures*. R. Ferguson, Martha Gever, Trinh T. Minh-ha, and Cornel West, (Eds). Cambridge: The MIT Press, 1990. Print.

Gramsci, A. *Selections from the Prison Notebooks*. New York: International Publishers. 1971. Print.

Hamilton, James. *Alternative Media: Conceptual Difficulties, Critical Possibilities. Journal of Communication Inquiry*, 24, (2000): 357-378.

Helen Margetts, Peter John, Scott Hale, and Taha Yasseri. *Political Turbulence: How Social Media Shape Collective Action.* Princeton, NJ: Princeton University Press, 2016, 5.

Hogan, Michael. *Savage Capitalism and the Myth of Democracy: Latin America in the Third Millennium*. London, 2009. Print.

Roy, Arundhati. *The God of Small Things*. New Delhi: Penguin Books India, 2002. Print

—. *An Ordinary Person's Guide to Empire*. New Delhi: Penguin Books India, 2013. Print.

—. In an Interview with Alice Traux. "A Silver Thimble in Her Fist." *New York Times*. May 25 1997. Web.

— In an Interview with David Bersamian. "The Progressive". February 2007.

—. *Introduction. Listening to Grasshoppers*, xi. New Delhi: Penguin Books India, 2009. Print.

—."Winds, Rivers and Rain." The Salon Interview. Online.

—. "The Algebra of Infinite Justice." In *The Algebra of Infinite Justice.* London: Flamingo, 2002. Print.

—. "The End of Imagination." *The Algebra of Infinite Justice*. London: Flamingo, 2002. 1-38. Print

—. "The Greater Common Good." *The Algebra of Infinite Justice*. London: Flamingo, 2002. 39-166. Print.

—. "The Ladies have Feelings, So..." *The Algebra of Infinite Justice. London: Flamingo, 2002. 167- 212*. Print.

—. "War is Peace." *The Algebra of Infinite Justice*. London: Flamingo, 2002. 213-232. Print.

Tickell, Alex. *Arundhati Roy's The God of Small Things*. Abingdon: Routledge, 2007. (81- 110)& (103-109).

Chapter - 13

Rhetoric of Storytelling: Subverting the Colonial Ethos in "A Geronimo's Story"

Rekha Batta

Despite being the original inhabitants, Native Americans are one of the marginalized ethnic groups of the US. The persistent struggle of natives for recognition, livelihood, and land rights has raised questions about their treatment at the hands of the settler forces. A long period of colonialism, which now has taken a shape of paracolonialism, has tried to vanquish the culture and race of Native Americans in one form or another. The social injustices that natives have confronted from the first European contact are still in continuance with its political, legal, economic and social inequities. Nevertheless, the construed structures or models developed by mainstream American society are interrogated in the literature of Native American authors and Leslie Marmon Silko is one of the authors who have subverted the colonial ethos in the literary works.

Born in 1948 in Albuquerque, New Mexico, Silko is an accomplished Native American novelist, poet and essayist of mixed Laguna-Pueblo, Mexican and white ancestry. Her upbringing in Laguna-Pueblo culture has kept her intact with the cultural and traditional values of the tribe. Being raised by her grandmother and aunt, she has listened stories from them which are considered as a core part of the Laguna-Pueblos. Silko's association with the importance of storytelling has led her to combat the master narratives by delineating an active presence of natives on American lands. For Silko storytelling is not about telling bed time stories to small children; instead it integrates wider dimensions of telling (Yellow Woman 80). She is of view that storytelling keeps the memory of incidents alive which once happened to someone else. Johansen in "Narrative Power in Native American Fiction: Reflections of Leslie Marmon Silko's "Storyteller"

(1981)" contends that Silko's literary works have an inherent power to challenge the political and cultural hegemony of whites and reclaim the things which have been lost in the perpetual struggle. Her short story named "A Geronimo Story" which is collected in an anthology of Kenneth Rosen's *The Man to Send Rain Clouds: Contemporary Stories by American Indians* (1974) challenges the hegemonic discourse by highlighting the rhetorical tracks of native voices.

Set in 1880s, "A Geronimo Story" narrates an artistic version of the participation of Laguna Scouts in search for an Apache chief Geronimo. It was the time when newspapers and articles often ran sensational stories about the attempts of white settlers to protect themselves from raiding of the Apaches led by the legendary warrior Geronimo. Silko's great grandfather and his brother who got married in Laguna community and served in the Third Battalion had given the account of raids on the Apaches. Inspired from the historical events of raids, Silko has interwoven the rhetoric of oral and written stories though she has not given any clue about the historical event. The story begins with Andy, the first-person narrator who accompanies his uncle Siteye along with the white militia in search of Geronimo and other Apaches. They do not encounter Geronimo during the course of their search but the thinly disguised treatment that Laguna Regulars get with the US army in a campaign against Geronimo reveals the racist attitude of the whites for natives. However, Silko has efficiently delineated the superiority of the Lagunas by subverting the whole context of their search for Geronimo. This subversion shows the active presence of natives over the absence which Vizenor terms as 'survivance'.

The exploration of Geronimo in 'Pie Town' portrays a difference in motives of the US white army and the Laguna Regulars. The variation in their motive is portrayed through a dichotomy of bestiality and compassion. Andy, the narrator of the story, saddles and rides on horse with his uncle, Siteye in search of Geronimo. While he saddles the horse, he describes how he has traded the horse from Navajos by giving his mother's sewing machine instead of twenty dollars that Navajos asked for. The incident signifies the tribal ethics of humility and behavioural tradition of exchange which stands in stark opposition to the lack of solidarity exhibited in the dominant white American society. In addition, the scene indicates an importance of community among Native Americans which remains absent in the white society as they emphasize individualism. The tribal ethics of humility are weighed against the actions of whites in the story who are on hunt for men. The guns, rifles, revolvers are the technological advancements of the white society but these have been used to terrorize and vanish the colonized. In story, Major Littlecock takes the army near Apache campsite. The cavalry approaches him with cocked rifles and he himself holds a revolver which symbolizes their bestiality and stupidity as they could not find Geronimo on the site. The act of white cavalry and Major Littlecock challenges the contrived stereotype of savage by interrogating their civilized behaviour.

The story also denotes an inherent racism in the dominant white society which tries to suppress the voice of natives. When the Laguna Regulars reach the Pie Town and have dinner, Major Littlecock asks Captain to have dinner with the white people in separate dining room but rest of the native scouts are ordered to eat in the kitchen. "The scouts were eating in there, except for Captain who was invited to eat with the white people in the dining room" (Rosen 139). After having dinner when Mariano (one of the Laguna Regulars) inquires about the sleeping place, Captain tells Major Littlecock that they all can sleep in kitchen. However, Littlecock disagrees with him and apprises the native scouts to sleep in the horse's stable as women live inside the civilian quarters. His masculine racist voice expresses that army regulations do not allow them in the same space. Major Says, "I regret, Captain, that isn't possible. Army regulations on using civilian quarters – the women, you know what I mean" (141). Although Captain is a white man, and is allowed to sleep in the civilian quarter yet he also bears the racist front of white society as he is married to Laguna woman. He is often called by a pejorative term 'squaw man' by the white officers. However, he combats the white society by remaining indifferent to them. It can be observed from his callous behavior when he does not stand from his seat to pay respect to Major. It is not only Captain who resists the racist outlook of Major but Siteye also defies him and subverts his racism by using his native Laguna language. He confronts Major in words, "you are the one who has a desire for horses at night, Major, you sleep with them" and all native scouts start laughing at his statement. The statement acts what Vizenor terms "Shadow words" because these overturn "the terminal vernacular of manifest manners and the final vocabularies of dominance" (Vizenor 68). The sarcastic humorous comment challenges the racist attitude of Major as he does not understand the Laguna language of Siteye. In a confused state, he desires to learn the Laguna language but his confusion and anger at Siteye's remarks delineates the contrivance of native language which is a potent tool to combat the contrivance of the settler forces.

Silko in this story also indicates a fluid celerity between American patriotism and nationalism and a persistent expression of tribal cultural nationalism. It has been indicated in the story that Laguna scouts are the members of Native American military who want to protect their families and communities from genocidal violence. Geronimo who is under search in the story was a legendary warrior of the Apaches and was fighting against the invasion of the whites on native lands. In the whole story, he remains absent but his presence for white community is of utmost importance. After the treachery and massacre of Casa Grande in 1873, Geronimo had a fierce fight with Mexicans which led to hostilities and ruthless massacre of Apaches as the sole motive of the settler forces was to exterminate all Indians from their lands. The desire and hunger for the lands interrogates the hollow nationalism of the white Americans as their nation is built on a stolen land. Geronimo escaped with the Apaches in the southwest mountains where the Laguna Scouts along with Captain and Major Littlecock's militia are searching in the story. The presence of Laguna Scouts in helping the militia reveals their contriving motives as they are following them just because they have paid them. Mariano says, "I only came because they pay me. Next time they won't even able to pay me to come here" (141). Besides him, Siteye in a cynical manner mocks the white militia at their inability to find Geronimo. He says, "I'm sorry that the Apaches aren't around here. I can' think of a better place to wipe out. If we see them tomorrow we'll tell them to come here first" (142). The 'peaceful violence' inflicted upon natives by whites is subverted through the art of using words in an appropriate manner as Siteye believes that any man can act violently but he/she may not destroy his enemy with words (142). The white Americans believe that the military uniform upholds their dignity and shows their essence of patriotism. Major Littlecock asks the native scouts about their uniforms as they have been in Indian clothes. Nevertheless, Siteye boldly tells Major that they wear uniform in winters as "it's too hot for wool now" (140). The military uniform for natives is just a disguised look because it has been contrived by the settler forces to justify their violent actions. However, for natives it is nothing more than a piece of cloth which they use to protect their body.

Apart from it, Silko also tries to destabilize the image of rationality and intelligence being possessed by the whites. Russell Means in *Where White Men Fear to Tread* asserts that "rationality is a curse since it can cause humans to forget the natural order of things in ways other creatures do not" (Qtd. in Manifest Manners, xv). The proclamation of Means can be analyzed in the story as the suspicion of Geronimo's campsite shows the foolishness of Major's speculative mind because it turns out to be a sheep camp of Mexicans. Lagunas believe that knowledge of place and landscape is of an utmost significance to trace the lost way. Siteye tells Andy the importance of remembrance of place and landscape since it has played an important role in their survival. He describes how he once has forgotten his way to Big Bead Mesa and it is only by remembering the snake hole and following a snake to its hole that he reaches at the desired destination. Vizenor contends that "memories, visions and the shadows of heard stories are the paramount verities of a tribal presence" (Vizenor 56). While travelling along the edge of the lava, Siteye also explains that their ancestors had places in the lava caves which they kept full with food and water whenever they had been chased by any enemy. Thus natives use nature as a guiding spirit which helps them to tackle the difficult situations. On the other hand, Major's inability to relate himself with the landscape shows his callous and bull-headed drive.

With the profound insights of place and landscape, Silko has subverted power structure of the settler forces by prioritizing nature over power. The search and hunt for Geronimo, with the white militia becomes a moment of precious rarity to Siteye and Andy. The geographic terrain of the place shows harmonious relationship of natives with nature. Andy finds a stream and drinks from it. He describes water as precious and rare that shows his respect not only for his horse but also for water. The running water of stream symbolizes the emerging consciousness of the natives against whites and Geronimo's free will which is not captured by the white army. Besides this, hunting of deer by Andy and Siteye denotes their relationship with Laguna ceremonies but the tragic consequences of capturing and imprisoning natives delineate the imperial violence of the settler forces. The end of the story shows Siteye's protest against the violent forces as he says, "We sat there for a long time remembering the way, the beauty of our journey" (144). He nods his head gently and says to Andy, "You know that was a long way to go for deer hunting" (144). The denial of carrying out the original objective of colonial military portrays that Andy and Siteye are not interested in their vindictive and malicious goals but rather exploit it to undertake a traditional Laguna-Pueblo ceremony of hunting deer. Linda J. Krumholz asserts "Finally, spirituality redefines power. Insofar as power is located not in technological, economic, or military domination but in the spiritual realm" (73). Andy and Siteye return home with their rewards from the traditional deer hunt whereas the American military returns to the fort without achieving success though they had limitless supply of men and arms.

Thus by subverting the colonial inventions of the whites, Silko has resisted the contrivance of the white society by questioning the authentication of mainstream American society. The rhetoric of tribal consciousness interrogates the colonial dichotomies which have brought disruptions and imbalances in the native understanding of the world. The stabilization of the stereotypical and historically inaccurate images of Indians has given birth to cultural biasness and prejudice in the white society and Silko goes beyond the ethos of white confinement to show them their own 'fake images'.

Works Cited

Fitz, Brewster E. *Silko: Writing Storyteller and Medicine Woman*. Norman: University of Oklahoma Press, 2004. Print.

Jaskoski, Helen. *Leslie Marmon Silko: A Study of the Short Fiction*. New York: Twayne, 1998. Print.

Johansen, Ib. "Narrative Power in Native American Fiction: Reflections on Leslie Marmon Silko's "Storyteller" (1981)." *P.O.V.: A Danish Journal of Film Studies*, No. 18 (December 2004). Web. April 25, 2019.

Krumholz, Linda. "Native Designs: Silko's Storyteller and the Reader's Initiation." *Leslie Marmon Silko: A Collection of Critical Essays.* Barnett, Louise K., and James L. Thurston (ed.). Albuquerque: University of New Mexico Press, 1999. 63-86. Print.

Rosen, Kenneth. "A Geronimo's Story." *The Man to Send Rain Clouds: Contemporary Stories by American Indians*. New York: Viking Press, 1974. 128-144. Print.

Silko, Leslie Marmon. *Yellow Woman and a Beauty of the Spirit: Essays on Native American Life Today*. New York: Simon and Schuster, 1997. Print.

Vizenor, Gerald. Manifest Manners: Narratives on Postindian Survivance. USA: University of Nebraska Press, 1994. Print.

Chapter - 14

Evolution of Subaltern Consciousness of Women from 'Draupadi' of the *Mahabharata* to Mahasweta Devi's 'Draupadi': An Analysis

N. Padmapriyadharshini

India has a great tradition of respecting women as Goddess, rivers, trees, and great natural gorgeous things. The respect given to women and their deeds is evidenced through numerous ancient books. India is basically known for its high ancient tradition and all those prides are recorded in two great epics namely the *Ramayana* and *Mahabharata*. Both these epics give a clear understanding of man being respectful towards women. All the decisions taken by women were appreciated and they were considered the rule-setters in those times. India's greatest histories are totally based on women. Some great scholars have confessed that the two great epics are created only due to women. Men considered all the decisions taken by women whether it was good or negative. Starting from Kaikeye and Seetha in the *Ramayana* and from Satyavati to Draupadi in the *Mahabharata*, the decisions taken by women are accepted by men. Their decisions created epics in Indian tradition. The importance given to women in those days is totally evident through these cases. Not only these two epics, there are many Sanskrit and ancient Tamil literary works also in which women are given so much attention. Chaurvedi Badrinath writes about the role of women in the Mahabharata as:

> In the stories through which the *Mahabharata* speaks of life, women occupy a central place. In living what life brings to them, the women of the *Mahabharata* shows that the truth in which one must live is, however, not a simple thing: nor can there be any on the absolute

statement about it. Each one of them, in her own way, is a teacher to mankind as to what truth and goodness in their many dimensions are. (2010: 8).

Even though there are many women characters in two great Indian epics, the character of Draupadi of the *Mahabharata* is considered so much powerful and great. There are many controversies prevalent with this character for being the wife of five men at a time. But the words that came out of her mouth are considered very precious and everyone followed it without questioning back. Draupadi is the most respected and as well as most humiliated character in the story. Her pride lasts in Indian minds forever. She is always quoted as an example of courage and heroism. Mahasweta Devi has pictured Draupadi through her protagonist Dopdi Mehjen. Mahasweta Devi has reconstructed the character of Draupadi by twisting the situations against her but however at the end of the story, she voiced out the real strength in a woman. Mahasweta Devi has a habit of naming her characters from epic stories. In this story, she has chosen Draupadi's name and it is damn perfect. Mahasweta Devi, through *Draupadi* proved that the strength and fury of a humiliated woman is much furious than a hungry lion.

Mahasweta Devi was a Bengali writer, a social activist and a journalist. She earned great fame for her contribution to the growth of tribal people in India. She has written more than hundred novels and more than twenty short story collections, majority of them in Bengali. "Draupadi" is one of her short stories from her short story collection namely *Agnigarbha*. Though she was an English professor, she wrote many of her works in Bengali. Gayatri Chakravorty Spivak, a professor at Columbia University and a famous critic, have authored many books and also translated the works of Mahasweta Devi into English. So, in Gayatri's translation of Mahasweta Devi's short stories named *Breast Stories*, "Draupadi" is a famous short story that runs for about twenty pages.

"Draupadi" is a most powerful and extraordinary documentation of violence and harassments implied on the tribal women in West Bengal. The Dalit people living as tribals are subjected to many social issues such as caste and class untouchability. They also face many social, economic and political problems. The tribal women are considered double marginalized because they face gender and sexual oppression both in their homes and outside the home. Hence women belonging to subaltern community are considered 'subalterns' in the 'subaltern society' by Gayatri Chakravorty Spivak in one of her books. Through this story, Mahasweta

Devi has pictured the dark face of post-colonial government that denied rights for the tribes. Through this story, she has given justification to the claims of the so called 'local terrors' such as Naxalites. The suppressions and denial of rights made them to commit serious terrorist activities. This story was set in Naxalbari area of West Bengal during the peasant rebellion in 1967. The landless farmers and farm labourers started fighting against the feudal masters and the government that denied lands for them. Low wages from the Zamindars made the peasants to fight for their rights. Not only the peasants from the local tribes but also the migrants like Dopdi and her husband Dulna Majhi are forced to work for minimum wages. These people did not actually fight for more wages but for their survival. The post-colonial governmental system forced some brutal systems to eradicate Naxals by labelling them as local terrorists.

Dopdi Mejhen was the protagonist of this story and the incidents that happened around her are the part of the plot of the story. As she was projected as a Naxalite, the whole story is set in a gloomy power dominated environment. Naxalites were actually located in large numbers in the hilly areas of West India. They do not cause any damages to local people but they fight against the strategies of feudal land lords who are in power and those who exploit the poor landless tribes. Their helpless state forced them to commit rebellious activities. Mahasweta Devi writes in this context:

> Dulna and Dopdi worked at harvests, rotation between Birbhum, Murshidabad and Bankura. In 1971, in the famous operation Bankura, when three villages were cordoned off and machine gunned, they too lay on the ground, faking dead. In fact, they were the main culprits. Murdering Surja Sahu and his son, occupying upper caste wells and tube wells during the drought, not surrendering those three young men to the police. (2010: 19-20).

Even though both the genders of the tribal community fight, it is the female gender that suffers greatly. This is the story of a woman Dopdi who represents the Naxalites' group in their area. Dopdi was popularly called as Draupadi in their area. Whatever the group may be, the women belonging to that group face humiliation, marginalization and most importantly, sexual abuses. Draupadi, being the leader of the group, is first in the list of the most wanted by the government officers. Unfortunately, she was caught by the group of seven police men. She was raped and sexual tortured by those police men. The cruelty of rape was stated as:

> Rape is worse than death
> Rape is always spoken through the lips of dead woman

> For a live woman rape means dishonour
> Silence is the only choice for a victim
> Rarely do families give victims the space to speak about their condition. (2005: 312)

Mahasweta Devi, being a social activist, and a fighter of tribal growth, brought out the real essence of pain and sufferings of tribal women. She was a stern worker of development of marginalized communities. To bring out the real contribution of Mahasweta Devi on tribal people, Radha Chakravorty writes:

> Mahasweta's current reputation as a writer rests largely on her own self-projection as a champion of the tribal cause and decrier of class prejudice. (2008: 94).

Though Draupadi was an accused criminal in the point of view of the police men, she was a fighter of her own rights and for that strength and firmness she was raped ruthlessly by those brutal powers. Mahasweta Devi introduces Draupadi as:

> "NAME: DOPDI MEJHEN, age 27, husband Dulna Majhi [deceased], domicile Cherakhan, Bankrahjarh, information whether dead or alive and/or assistance in arrest, one hundred rupees…" (2010: 19).

Draupadi was sexually assaulted by seven police men continuously. When she woke up next day, she found herself in a very pathetic condition. Her pains and sufferings are expressed through her red teary eyes. Her arms and legs were tied in four different posts. She lay down naked and she found something sticky under her waist and she recognized later that it was her own blood. She could not even cry aloud as her lips were already torn by them. She was brutally assaulted by those animals and her condition was written by Mahasweta Devi:

> Shaming her, a tear trickles out of the corner of her eye. In the muddy moonlight she lowers her lightless eye, sees her breasts and understands that, indeed, she is made up right. Her breasts are bitten raw, the nipples torn. How many? Four-five-six-seven – then Draupadi has passed out. (2010: 35).

The instances where the untouchables are denied from taking water from the wells are exactly described by Mahasweta Devi. The real-life sufferings of those people are brought in front of retina by her words. When Draupadi was caught by the police men, she asks for water after the brutal attack. But she was denied water by the police men. She closes her eyes and thinks of the incident that happened earlier. She stands as a perfect representative to stand against the brutal marginalization. Starting from the drinking water, they were marginalized from everything. Mahasweta Devi has brought the feudal and imperialist mindset of post-colonial Indian governance. The marginalization by the dominant Hindu society was written by Mahasweta Devi in a beautiful manner. They followed a technique that the previous generation's debts were collected in installments by the labour that the present generation does for the landlords. By saying this and showing illegal bonds, they were denied proper wages. Mahasweta Devi narrates it in the following words:

> Surja Sahu's house was surrounded at night. Surja was tied up with cow rope. His whitish eyeballs turned and turned, he was incontinent again and again. Dulna had said, I will have the first blow, brothers. My great-grandfather took a bit of paddy from him, and I still give him free labour to repay that debt. Dopdi had said, his mouth watered when he looked at me. I will pull out his eyes. (2010: 30)

Operation Jharkhani was in action against the rebel groups. Senanayak leaded the group as he was a special seasoned military officer. He used many strategies to get closer to the rebel groups. One of the strategies he used was to become acquainted with the rebel groups and know their future attack plans. Senanayak was a tricky man who always wanted to make his thoughts into success for which he dedicates himself. He was equally brutal too. He amazed the strength of Draupadi and planned to arrest her. He made special plans and finally took her into his control. Senanayak's theory of executing plans has been depicted in these words:

> In order to destroy the enemy, become one. Thus, he understood them by becoming one of them. He hopes to write on all this in the future. He has also decided that in his written work he will demolish the gentlemen and highlight the message of the harvest workers. (2010: 22).

Mahasweta Devi compares Dopdi to the Draupadi of the *Mahabharata*. When Mythological Draupadi was humiliated by her own family members for being born and being married to five men, she raises up each time with the same strength and determination. Likewise, Mahasweta's Draupadi rises up every time with the same determination and strength. When their group faces a fall at a particular place, she raised her hands and encouraged other comrades to move further. This strength was written by Mahasweta in these words:

> Now Dopdi spreads her arms, raises her face to the sky, turns towards the forest, ululates with the force of her entire being. Once, twice, three times. At the third burst the birds in the trees at the outskirts of

> the forest awake and flap their wings. The echo of the call travels far. (2010: 34).

Dopdi had all the strengths that the mythological Draupadi had but when the Gauravas tried to take off the veils of mythological Draupadi, Lord Krishna protected her by giving her veils. But the fighter Dopdi, even though she was pure and strong, was raped by seven brutes and no any God like Lord Krishna saved her from the shame. The next morning when she found herself in a pathetic condition, she tried crying aloud but she could not even do that. The furiously wiped her tears and looked at them furiously. One of the seven police men threw a bit of dress on her. But she threw away the cloth and stood up naked. She made a wild laughter on his face and walked towards Senanayak. All the police men in the tent looked at her with fear. Her actions in front of Senanayak were something unpredictable to everyone. She proved her strength once of a last time. But it was really furious and forceful in the words of Mahasweta Devi:

> Draupadi's shakes with an indomitable laughter that Senanayak simply cannot understand. Her ravaged lips bleed as she begins laughing. Draupadi wipes the blood on her palm and says in a voice that is terrifying, sky splitting and sharp her ululation, what is the use of clothes? You can strip me, but how can you cloth me again? Are you man? What more can you do? Come on, Kounter me – come on, counter me? –. (2010: 37).

Dopdi was a greatest victim of rape but she did not suppress herself into a secluded place. She proved her strength to the animals that made her suffer. She wiped out all the pains and fears through her strong determination. She was an actual fighter. She proved herself great at the end of the story. Draupadi was considered as the symbol of purity even though she married five men at a time. This Dopdi was considered pure as well even though she was brutally raped by seven animals. Dopdi is a symbol of unlimited courage and determination. Her character in the *Mahabharata* proved what a courageous and intelligent woman could do. Starting from an unnatural birth Draupadi stood courageously even after marrying five brothers all at a time and eradicating the evils. She was portrayed as a perfect warrior. Lakshmi Bandlamundi perfectly states:

> Draupadi, as a character, commands a whole range of contradictory meanings. She goes all the way from a non-existent being of nothingness to a full-blown character. She is both nowhere and everywhere and inhabits multiple times. (2010: 153).

Even though she was powerful and courageous, she could not come out of the patriarchal views. She consciously or unconsciously followed the patriarchal ideas even from her birth. Her birth was not an ordinary one. She was born out of fire and this signifies that she was extremely pure but her purity was tested after she got married to five men. All those men fallen in love with her charm and intelligence. She was supposed to live with five men and followed patriarchy. But Mahasweta's Dopdi did not give her ears to patriarchy. Even after she was raped by seven men, she did not give up on her. She stood courageously in front of them. That proves the power of a woman. Kavita Sharma beautifully stated the power of women in these words:

> Their (women) words and actions make them the driving force behind men. They constantly intervene, manipulate, subjugate and subvert to make a place for themselves and to exercise power. The men think they control them and are superior to them but these are intelligent, brave and beautiful women who cannot be easily brow beaten or subdued. (2007: 12)

Thus, Dopdi, being a subaltern woman, undergoes many sufferings and assaults in the society. Bearing all those unbearable pains she still stands as a perfect image of courage. The story of a subaltern woman is compared to an aristocratic queen Draupadi. Mahasweta Devi made it successful by saying that whether it may be a queen or a subaltern woman, woman generally faces many humiliations and assaults but they overcome everything with their inner courage and determination. Even today, there are millions of 'Draupadis' fighting every single second for their freedom and life.

Works Cited

Badrinath, Chaturvedi. *The Women of the Mahabharata*. Hyderabad: Orient BlackSwan, 2010. Print.

Bandlamundi, Lakshmi. *Dialogics of Self, the Mahabharata, and the Culture: The History of Understanding of History*. London: Anthem Press, 2010. Print.

Chakravorty, Radha. *Mahasweta Devi: A Luminous Anger in Feminism and Contemporary Women Writers: Rethinking Subjectivity*. New Delhi: Routledge, 2008. Print.

Devi, Mahasweta. *Breast Stories*. Trans. Gayatri Chakravorty Spivak. Calcutta: Seagull Books, 2010. Print.

Hameed, Syeda. S. "Sexual Abuse in Revenge: Women as Targets of Communal Hatred." *The Violence of Normal Times: Essays on Women's Lived Reality.* Ed. Kalpana Kannabiran. New Delhi: Women Unlimited, 2005. Print.

Nisha and Phogat, Geetha. "Women of Substance and Heroism: A Study from *The Mahabharata*". *Research Journal of English Language and Literature*. 5.1 (2017): 256-260. Print.

Sharma, Kavita. *Queens of the Mahabharata*. New Delhi: Rupa & Co., 2007. Print.

Chapter - 15

'The Policy of Exclusion': In Search of 'Marginal Voices' in Rushdie's *Midnight's Children*

Anup Barman and Sabuj Sarkar

> *The marginal subject continues in any case to maintain relations or contacts with some segment of society, because exclusions (in terms of nonparticipation) from a certain subsystem is not the same as saying that the same person occupies an analogous position in all the social subsystems he/she belongs to.*
>
> **– *(Mauro Giardiello 2016: 118)***

Marginality study is an offshoot to the postcolonial studies. Enriched, multi-foliated, differed as well as deferred, marginality studies encompass a huge range of social and cultural history. Highly philosophical in thought, marginality studies are based on the structure of so called 'colonial rule' and hegemony. "Confrontation", "Transgression", "Opposi-tion", "Resistance" and "Retrieval" are the key pillars of the intellectual base of marginality in the society. Marginalization is a way of categorisation in which a group of socially discriminated people are always in a struggle to get access to the mainstream of the society and are always in a hope against the hope for the full participation in the main course of the life which gets hardly fulfilled. This paper on Rushdie's *Midnight's Children* primarily focuses on the marginal sections of the society and questions how and why 'marginality' is a process of social exclusion. Several minor and major characters are encountered in course of the journey of the text in which they are not given space for their voices. Such characters are kept in the margin and they are cornered. This paper attempts to reveal the social and cultural position of those voicelessly voiced human beings.

Marginality can be described as a dynamic social process in which an individual or a group of individuals becomes victim of the norms and traditions of the dominant sections of the society and undergoes various complexities and social suppressions. The cornered sections continue to live in the periphery of the society and hardly get access to be in the centre. They are often endowed with inferior attributes. When the marginalized are relegated to the lower status or the outer sphere of the society, they sometimes show effort at resisting the dominant hegemony of the society. It may lead them either to get excluded or to be included in society. But marginalization has its own broad spectrum. The legacy of marginality is extended in historical, religious and cultural contexts too. In social sciences, the concept of marginality refers to the racial and ethnic minorities, migrants, the physically challenged members, the deviants of the mainstream of the society and so on. Such categories of people are deprived of adequate social or political privileges. Marginality refers to the limitations of an individual's or certain group's access to power. In literature marginality can be shown in terms of women, gender, family, caste, colour and race. The machinery of exploitation, suffering and suppression through various ways is never ending. On the contrary, counter response is also evident through the ways of language, silence, resistance and power. Generally, it is the centre or centrality that creates the conditions of marginality. The aim of this paper is to deal with some facets and perspectives of marginality with reference to the novel *Midnight's Children* by Salman Rushdie.

It is not possible to fully define marginality in a single specific term. There are different dimensions and experiences of marginality in literature. To quote Mauro Giardiello:

> Marginality belongs to central/peripheral polarity, which affects spatial and social thresholds and borders and marginal areas. This distance is no longer configured in relation to a single centre but is gradually assuming an increasingly polycentric aspect where the processes of marginalization no longer follow morphological or spatial line....The concept of marginality allows shedding light on the role of power and domination as played within both central zones and classical areas of central/peripheral dichotomy. The role of unequal distribution of power becomes one of the fundamental characteristics of the process that produces the peripheralization that impacts on central and outlying territories not only at the macro and spatial level, but also at the individual level.... (12).

G. Germani refers to "marginality as the lack of participation of individuals and groups in those spheres in which, according to determined criteria, they might be expected to participate" (49). Robert Park states: "It is the mind of the marginal man that the moral turmoil which new cultural contacts occasion manifests itself in the most obvious forms. It is in the mind of the marginal man – where the changes and fusions of culture are going on – that we can best study the process of civilization and of progress" (1967: 206). Marginality includes a broad range of positions. The following lines from the book *Marginality and Modernity* by Mauro Giardiello throw another sort of light on marginality: "...marginality is the product of an abnormal condition where individuals and groups find themselves assuming the norms and roles of the reference groups while still being unable to belong to it for lack of prerequisites, remaining on the margins of their original group as well as of the group they have chosen to refer to" (50). Peter McCarthy shows a different notion of marginality through these lines: "marginality is today no longer limited to minority groups, but is rather massive and pervasive;...Marginality is becoming universal. A marginal group has now become a silent majority" (37). The book also informs us that "conflation and erasure are central to the politics of marginalism ... fantasy gives form to our desires and at the same time mediates between our gaze and its object: it is an agent of conflation and collusion" (130, 132). To quote Leah F. Vosko: "It is necessary to rework the norsmative principles for gender equity underpinning the universal caregiver model such that they foster global universal caregiving. The difficult task is to deepen the antipoverty, anti-androcentrism...to expand the anti-exploitation principle to respond to the harsh (and discriminatory) treatment of woman...to develop the anti-marginalization principle..." (243).

Salman Rushdie creates such a space within his novel *Midnight's Children* as explores various binaries such as centre/periphery, reality/imagination, religious/secular, history/imagination, truth/fiction etc. moreover, the novel also explores many other issues such as subversion, hybridity, societal hatred, religious violence, partition, problematisation of identity, history etc. Some women are made subject of dominant ideologies or patriarchal rule and are compelled to enjoy a degraded position in society. They seem to be exploited both physically and socially. They are instrumental in giving birth to child. Within the narrative of *Midnight's Children* women are treated as powerless, and insignificant subjects. They yield to male desire and domination. They are not given primacy. Catherine Cundy states, "women in Rushdie's novel are invoked to prove a point about social injustices and inequalities, and then effectively demeaned... or marginalized by the writing itself" ("Rushdie's Women" *Wasafiri Magazine*1993: 13-16). Some characters of the novel are brought from the sphere of marginality to that of centrality by the novelist. To quote Catherine Cundy, "*Midnight's Children* ... serves as a testament to the importance of memory in the recreation of history and the constitution of the individual's identity" (32). Some characters are deprived of their space for social status. Some are victim of political and historical incidents, cultural and religious traditions.

In the novel *Midnight's Children*, we find that women have the traditional custom to be in *purdah*. In course of time it is also seen that women come out of *purdah*. But, women do not consider this as an act of liberation on their parts because they are victim of male domination. To quote Nicole Weickgenannt Thiara: "Imperialist discourse portrayed *purdah* as yet another instance of female subjugation, symbolising the inferior status ..." (68). We see that Naseen is a victim of conservative patriarchal norms. When she falls ill, her father Ghani does not allow her body to be seen by the Doctor Adam Aziz. Naseem is in *purdah*. Aziz has to examine only the ailing portion through a perforated sheet. Naseem and Aziz fall in love and it is against the desire of Aadam Aziz's mother that the two are married. After their marriage Aziz finds that Naseem is so traditional wife. Aziz tries to destroy her orthodox and conservative thoughts which have taken a firm root in her mind. Education of women is important for their entry into the class of respectability. Naseem is placed in a position of inferiority in terms of her education. She tries to instil narrow-minded traditional beliefs and customs into her daughters by bringing a Maulavi to her house, but her husband Aadam Aziz's interference turns the man out from the house eventually. Naseem develops into Reverend Mother but motherhood is rarely discussed here. It is seen that she cannot satisfy her husband sexually. Woman's role as traditional wife and sexual partner is highlighted. Let us now quote the following lines of the novel:

> ... she lived within an invisible fortress of her own making, an ironclad citadel of traditions and certainties. [...] It was perhaps the obligation of facial nudity, coupled with Aziz's constant request for her to move beneath him, that had driven her to the barricades; and the domestic rules ... (Perhaps, too, it wasn't a system of self-defence at all, but a means of defence against herself.) (47-48).

Naseem cannot forget her traditional upbringing and customs. She is very unhappy with her domestic life. She is dominated by her husband. We find evidence of it when Aadam Aziz refuses to offer Naseem reasonable arguments for giving Nadir Khan shelter in their house and utters in patriarchal manner:

> 'Be silent woman! The man needs our shelter; he will stay'. Whereupon an implacable perfume, a hard cloud of determination settles upon my grandmother, who says, 'very well. You ask me, whatsitsname, for silence, so not one word, whatsitsname, will pass my lips from now on' ... woman, spare us your crazy oaths!' (66)

It causes Naseem's silence. Naseem's silence signifies a kind of obedience towards her husband Aadam Aziz's command. She has always to compromise her protests because her husband always appears to dominate her. Rushdie's men are indifferent to women's interests, feelings and individuality. Naseem's husband is indifferent to her desires and opinions. Viewed from this angle, Naseem's position is marginal.

The colour of skin may also lead someone to a degraded position. It is found in the following comment of Zohra who is a distant cousin of Ahmed Sinai: "How awful to be black... proof of inferiority!..." (90). In Book Two we find that Amina also criticizes and tries to degrade Ahmed Sinai's secretaries:

> 'Those Anglos,' she said to Mary, revealing a touch of snobbery, 'with their funny names, Fernanda and Alonso and all, and surnames, my God! Sulaca and Colaco and I don't know what. What should I care about them? Cheap type of females. I call them all his Coca-Cola girls. (181-182)

Amina Sinai, who is one of the three daughters of Aadam Aziz, gives birth to Saleem, the central character of the novel, at the exact hour of independence of India. Wee Wilie Winkie's wife Vanita also gives birth to a child. It is found that the child is not by her real husband but by an Englishman William Methwold. Now things are complicated by a nurse Mary Pereira:

> ...when she was alone – two babies in her hands – two lives in her power – she did it for Joseph, her own private revolutionary act, thinking He will certainly love me for this, as she changed name-tags on the two huge infants, giving the poor baby a life of privilege and condemning the rich-born child to accordions and poverty ... (157)

The following lines from the book *Salman Rushdie and Visual Culture: Celebrating Impurity, Disrupting* Border by Ana Christena Mendes also focus on the complication:

> Saleem's multiple parentage and the inherent multiplicity within himself narrows his own multiplicity: fathered by the departing British colonialist William Methwold, he is born to a Hindu mother, raised in a Muslim household by a Christian ayah. (141).

William Methwold is a British estate owner. He represents the superior race and attempts to keep the inheritance of his race intact. In the Introduction to the book *Midnight's Children: A Reader's Companion* Tapan Kumar Ghosh states, "The British transfer of power is parodied through the symbolic takeover of the intact Englishness of the Methwold's Estate. Rushdie ruthlessly attacks British colonialism through his caricature of characters like Methwold and attempts to link many of the ills which plague independent India to the mischief done by the British during their rule. What was invisible or forcibly silenced in the British history (like the story of the nationalist Muslims in 'Hit-the-Spittoon' and 'Under the Carpet') is brought to focus..." (25). The conflict regarding the ideas of superiority in the matter of religion is presented through the employees – Musa who is a Muslim and Mary Pereira who is a Christian.

The novel shows that women have a degraded position in the society. Women are quite different from men in thoughts, activities, and status. Breakdown of their virtues often leads them to peripheral status. Sometimes it is found that Wives choose other sexual partners than their real husbands. Vanita, Pia, Lila are unfaithful wives. Vanita is lured into sexual relation with Methwold. Later, she is in protracted labour, gives birth to a son and bleeds to death. Women play the role of daughters, wives, mothers and perform other household activities. Female characters are only there to help and serve the male characters who occupy the central position to produce and shape the actions and incidents of the novel.

In rural areas or tribal areas, people have faith in the existence of witches. It is taken to be the result of the superstition of backward people. The novel *Midnight's Children* gives rise to an idea of the witches by marking all women as witches. Generally, children are the most helpless and vulnerable to the witches. There is also hallucinatory atmosphere in this novel. It is also seen that a few of the children of midnight do not express magical power because they have fear in witches. Some women such as the Rani of Cooch Nahin, Alia, Indira Gandhi, to name a few, are marked as witch characters in the novel. Amina's sister Alia hoped to marry Ahmed Sinai. But it is Amina who marries Ahmed Sinai ultimately. Alia practises 'culinary witchcraft'. She harms the family of Amina by her wicked power. But it is evident that witch theme is a marginal issue in the main narrative of the novel.

The novel shows a history of the Indians and their struggle for independence from the domination and imperialism of the British. The colonized Indians were marginalized by the British. The condition of pre-independence is shown to us through the stories of Aadam Aziz, his family and friends, Boatman Tai and many other characters and incidents. Boatman Tai does not belong to the central characters of the novel. He is of lower class of individuals in the society. He is a drunkard. The smell of his body, often, offends his passengers.It is found that he refuses to wash in retaliation to Aadam Aziz's coming to Kashmir with Western culture. He goes away from the scene of the novel with the departure of Aadam Aziz from Kashmir. His arrival in the scene of the novel is known in 1947 when a battle between India and Pakistan takes place over Kashmir. We find his sympathy for the Kashmiris who claim separate Kashmir. To protect his Kashmir, he goes to fight the armies. The result is that he is shot dead. His role is marginal in the central story of the novel.

Various issues of the history of India such as pre-independence, domination, freedom etc. are highlighted through the midnight's children. To quote Tapan Kumar Ghosh, "All the important historical events in the sub-continent, from Jallianwala Bagh massacre (1919) to the Emergency (1975) are ingeniously linked with the crucial turns in the story of Saleem and his family so that the autobiography of an individual reads like the history a country and the Odyssey of a family becomes the Odyssey of a nation from 1915 to 1977, the period of Indian history Rushdie charts in the novel" (23). The midnight's children are suppressed after Indira Gandhi orders the arrest of the midnight children with miraculous powers. Saleem is first to be arrested. He is tortured by the police. Consequently, he gives information and address of the remaining 580 children as out of 1001 midnight children, 420 were dead earlier because of disease, famines, strikes and other hostile incidents. Ultimately, all the children are taken to tubectomy-sections and made impotent. In the Introduction to the book *Midnight's Children: A Reader's Companion* Tapan Kumar Ghosh states:

> "The hopes of the nation generated at the moment of independence were drained with the castration of the midnight's children by Indira Gandhi, ... and her sinister minions. Saleem retires to the privacy of a pickle factory and decides to preserve ('chutnify') his version of India's history for future generation before his demise. Saleem's progress from unlimited optimism to disenchantment, from illusion of centrality to marginalization and impotence, which parallels the journey of independent India from an optimistic and vibrant nation to a despairing and comatose state, is a telling comment on the postcolonial history of the country. (30).

So, it may be said that marginality is caused by disparity, disadvantage, degraded position, unequal status or deprivation, suppression, silence, sufferings, exclusion, inferiority of an individual or group of individuals in the spheres of society, culture, politics, history etc. The perception of marginal experiences is also produced by other factors such as patriarchy, imperialism, ethnocentrism etc. In most cases, the centre is responsible for creating the margin. To quote Mauro Giardiello:

> Generally speaking, these peripheral realities represent the milieu that produces poverty, dependence, and cultural subordination and, more and more frequently, areas of marginality and degradation where ... the most vulnerable ... easily and severely subjected to processes of social exclusion. [...] new instances of marginality are not easy to identify and fix within stable and circumscribed configurations, like degraded neighbourhoods or new postmodern territorial ghettos, but that they present shifting borders, follow superimposed and intersecting line...(11).

Salman Rushdie's novel shows the female characters as not possessing equal status. Some elements of patriarchal structure and misogynistic strategies underlie this novel. Harold Bloom shows a different layer of notions, "In *Midnight's Children*, women are seen to be powerful practitioners of yet another mode of connection, the passive-aggressive. In spite of their seeming lack of control in the public spheres, they loom large in Saleem's family life, feeding all their repressed sorrow, guilt, jealousy, and bitterness. [...] women's status within a patriarchal structure and the weapons of the weak that they yield mirror the weapons that the post-colonial subject can wield in the uneven struggle for self-determination" (164). Salman Rushdie seems to empower the powerless and give voice to an entire section of the society – women, men, slum-dwellers as well as the leaders of the nation. Obviously, Rushdie aims at rich inclusiveness in regard to the structure of the novel which shows us some facets of marginality.

Works Cited

Bloom, Harold. *Bloom's Modern Critical Views – Salman Rushdie.* United States of America: Chelsea House Publishers, 2003, Print.

Brennan, Timothy. *Salman Rushdie and the Third World: Myths of the Nation.* The United States of America: Palgrave Macmillan, 1989, Print.

Crewe, Jonathan. "Defining Marginality". *Tulsa Studies in Women's Literature,* Vol. 10 No. 1, (Spring, 1991), PP. 121-130, www.jstor.org/stable/463956.

Cundy, Catherine. *Salman Rushdie.* Manchester & New York: Manchester University Press, 1996. Print.

F. Vosko, Leah. *Managing the Margins: Gender, Citizenship, and the International Regulation of Precarious Employment.* The United States: Oxford University Press, 2010, Print.

Fraser, Kathleen. "The Tradition of Marginality". *Frontiers: A Journal of Women Studies:* Vol. 10, No. 3, Women and Words (1989), PP. 22-27, www.jstor.org/stable/3346436.

Germani, G. *Marginality.* New York: Transaction Publishers, 1980, Print.

Ghosh, Tapan K. *Midnight's Children: A Reader's Companion.* New Delhi: Asia Book Club, 2004, Print.

Goonetilleke, D.C.R.A. *Macmillan Modern Novelists.* London: Macmillan Press Ltd, 1998, Print.

Giardiello, Mauro. *Marginality and Modernity.* New York: Transaction Publishers, 2016, e-book.

J. Blasi, Anthony. "Marginality as a Societal Position of Religion". *Sociology of Religion.* Vol. 63, No. 3 (Autumn, 2002), PP. 267-289. www.jstor.org/stable/3712470.

Malhotra, Inder. *Indira Gandhi. A Personal and Political Biography.* London: Coronet Books/Hodder & Stoughton, 1989. Print.

Mehretu, Assef, et al. "Concepts in Social and Spatial Marginality". *Geographiska Annaler. Series B. Human Geography,* Vol. 82, No. 2, Development of Settlements (2000). PP. 89-101, www.jstor.org/stable/491067.

Miri, Mrinal. "On Mainstream and Marginality". *India International Centre:* Vol. 27, No. 2, MARGINALISED (SUMMER 2000), PP. 3-10, www.jstor.org/stable/23005483.

Mc, Peter. *Writing Diaspora in the West: Intimacy, Identity and the New Marginalism.* The UK: Palgrave Macmillan, 2009, Print.

Mendes, Ana Christina. *Salman Rushdie and Visual Culture – Celebrating Impurity, Disrupting Borders.* New York: Routledge, 2012, Print.

Park, Robert. *On Social Control and Collective Behaviour.* Chicago and London: University of Chicago Press, 1967, Print.

Pieris, Ralph. "Bilingualism and Cultural Marginality". *The British Journal of Sociology:* Vol. 2, No. 4 (Dec., 1951), PP. 328-339, www.jstor.org/stable/588086

Riesman, David. "Some Observation concerning Marginality". *Phylon (*1940-1956). Vol. 12, No. 2 (2nd Qtr., 1951), PP. 113-127, www.jstor.org/stable/271565

Roberts, John. "Art and Marginality". *Circa,* No. 30, (Sep.-Oct., 1986), PP. 44-46, www.jstor.org/stable/255715

Rushdie, Salman. *Midnight's Children.* London: Vintage, 1995. Print.

Teverson, Andrew. *Salman Rushdie Contemporary World Writers.* New York: Manchester University Press, 2007, Print.

Thiara, Nicole Weickgenannt. *Salman Rushdie and Indian Historiography: Writing the Nation into Being.* The UK: Palgrave Macmillan, 2009, Print.

Weisberger, Adam. "Marginality and Its Directions". *Sociological Forum:* Vol. 7, No. 3 (Sep., 1992), PP. 425-446, www.org/stable/684659.

Chapter - 16

The Journey of a Woman in Kavita Kané's *Lanka's Princess* and Manini J. Anandani's *Mandodari: Queen of Lanka*

Shikha Khandpur

In her ground-breaking work, *The Second Sex*, Simone de Beauvoir, one of the renowned pioneers of the Feminist literary theory, mentioned that, "One is not born, but rather becomes a woman" (Beauvoir 301). This statement at once touches the question of nature versus nurture, and makes it possible to dissect the gender roles that have become the norm in the prevalent structure of society. Nivedita Menon, in her work *Seeing Like a Feminist*, speaks of Feminism and explains, "Feminism is thus not about individual men and women, but about understanding the ways in which 'men' and 'women' are produced and inserted into patriarchies that differ according to time and place" (Menon 8). This chapter takes up two works, Kavita Kané's *Lanka's Princess* and Manini J. Anandani's *Mandodari: Queen of Lanka,* both of which are a retelling of *Ramayana*, a famous epic of Hindu mythology. These retellings of this popular epic are written from the perspective of two different women, with wildly different characters, yet it is remarkable to notice the similarities in the factors that contribute to making them who they were and the role they played in this epic tale. Over the course of the years that this tale has been passed on from generation to generation, the voices of these women were lost behind the epic battle that took place between the armies of Rama and Ravana. But this chapter is an attempt to trace the stories of these female protagonists, Meenakshi, the Princess of Lanka, and Mandodari, the Queen of Lanka. Their stories, though influenced by the same events, showcase entirely different ways in which a woman's character is forged in the clutches of patriarchy. While these women are mythical characters from an age old saga, yet the society they live in is true to the definition of a patriarchy, which in many ways reflects upon the position of women in India today, though many factors like the class and caste of a woman play an important role in deciding the struggles she may face in this social setup, but the fabric of the misogynistic system is consistent as presented in these novels, and the one that is prevalent in this country. This chapter then aims to trace these similarities and highlight the subtle ways in which the distribution of power is maintained with men having the upper hand, and women, finding themselves subjugated, and in a marginalized position in the society, and brings into consideration the need to reflect upon these problem areas and work upon moving to a more accepting, diverse and balanced society.

It is believed that the formative years of a child are the most important years in shaping the personality of an individual, and when we glance at the references to Meenakshi's and Mandodari's childhood and their upbringing, we see the discrimination in the way they were being raised as opposed to how their respective brothers were being raised. While Meenakshi was not encouraged to pursue academics with the same enthusiasm as her brothers were, Mandodari was discouraged from partaking in activities like hunting while her brothers were expected to cultivate such hobbies. Children are receptive and can sense this discrimination and so starts the process of forming personalities that are set in traditional gender roles. *Mai* or the caretaker provided to Mandodari tells her that "Princesses don't go hunting, Princesses are born to marry a handsome Prince" (Anandani 1), while Meenakshi presents her doubts regarding her education to her maternal grandmother as seen in the following lines:

> But why am I not allowed to study the Vedas like my brothers, Nani? I kmow I am not as fast in my calculations as Vibhishan or clever as Ravan…Am I not Rishi Vishravas' child too? Then why am I not studying the shastras and the Upanishads like my brothers? (Kané 24).

Both these references from the texts are hinting at the early categorization of children as based on the gender roles that are ascribed to men and women. Men are encouraged to pursue activities that make them self-sufficient and independent, while women are raised to be family oriented and gentle in their conduct. Such fixed roles take away the chance for people to choose their own paths and identities, and aid in maintaining the power play between the two sexes. This difference in upbringing pre-decides the division of labor between men and women, where women do substantially more housework and childcare than men, and men have to be the breadwinners and finance providers for their families. This unfair division of work takes away the chance from women to gain work experience and for men to be an active part of their family life. This problem is well explained in the following lines:

> Since so many good jobs are incompatible with substantial childcare responsibilities, employers will quite reasonably end up hiring workers who are not primary childcare providers. Women are, statistically, far more likely than men to be primary childcare providers. In addition, women, in general, undertake by far the greater proportion of household labor...Due to the incompatibility of better paid, full-time work with childcare, women who are primary childcare providers often end up in part-time work, or lower-paid full-time work. (Saul 8).

It is said, "Nearly 60 percent of women hold jobs in traditional women's work such as clerical, sales, and service occupations, which typically pay half of two-thirds of the wages in blue-collar work" (Williams 81). In this way, this vicious cycle, continues and keeps up the power hierarchy distributed amongst the sexes, where women hold a submissive position, and struggle to provide a quality life for themselves. As explained in the following lines:

> This, in turn, results in a system of cultural identifications in which masculinity is associated with income-earning, and femininity is defined in terms of sexual and domestic service for men, and the nurturing of children. So men and women enter marriage with different income earning potential, and this disparity widens during marriage, as the man acquires valuable job experience. Since the woman faces greater difficulty supporting herself outside the marriage, she is more dependent on him maintaining the marriage, which allows the man to exercise greater control within it. (Kymlicka 382).

Besides this lack of pushing women towards being ambitious and goal-oriented, the accepted idea of beauty, and the extreme emphasis of finding a woman's worth in her looks, takes women further away from finding substance in their identity, and works on creating an atmosphere that constantly takes away from their sense of self-worth and self-esteem. This is especially visible in the case of Meenakshi, whose looks are constantly mocked by her family, as a result of which she develops a sense of insecurity about her physical appearance, as can be seen in these lines:

> Meenakshi grimaced at her reflection in the mirror. What she saw never pleased her. It did not today too. There was a change in her physical appearance, but not a pleasant one. She was now twelve years old –

> yet she was still dark, skinny, gangly chit of a girl with a burgeoning bosom, too large for her tiny waist and slight, short figure. (Kané 20).

Not only is women's identity reduced to how they look and how they carry themselves, but this is a cog in the bigger machinery that ensures the subordinate position of women in the gender hierarchy. As correctly pointed out in these lines:

> Women's typical body language, a language of relative tension and constriction, is understood to be a language of subordination when it is enacted by men in male status hierarchies. In groups of men, those with higher status typically assume looser and more relaxed posture: the boss lounges comfortably behind a desk while the applicant sits tense and rigid on the edge of his seat...What is announced in the comportment of superiors is confidence and ease...women tend to set to and stand with legs, feet, and knees close or touching...One thing is clear: woman's body language speaks eloquently, though silently, of her subordinate status in a hierarchy of gender. (Bartky 74).

In his famous work, *Discipline and Punish: The Birth of Prison* (1975), Foucault discusses the nature of power and points out that it is dispersed throughout the structure of society. He draws on Jeremy Bentham's idea of a panoptic surveillance state, which allows an omniscient presence of power and discipline that makes the people live under fear and themselves keep a check on their actions, and in such a way, be the oppressors while also being the oppressed. Similarly, the stress on women's appearance and conduct binds them in a cycle of always watching, judging, criticizing, and self-policing.

Another thing that the selected texts showcase is the restraints put on women's sexuality in a patriarchy. Even though there are communities like the Khasi tribes of North-East India, that are matrilineal in nature, the majority of the Indian communities are patrilineal in nature, "where property and the family 'name' flow from fathers to sons" (Menon 6). The reason behind this policing of women's sexuality is explained in the following lines:

> The fact is, no man can ever know whether a child is his. A woman knows a child is hers, but a man can never know whether it is his, not even with a DNA test. A DNA test can only tell you if the child is *not* yours, but if your DNA matches, it only indicates 'a high statistical probability' that it is your child. As they say, 'Motherhood is a biological fact, fatherhood is a sociological fiction.' It is this knowledge that creates

permanent anxiety for patriarchy, an anxiety that requires women's sexuality to be strictly policed. (Menon 7)

This predominant fear is clearly visible, as even though Ravana himself continued to marry new wives in the name of political advancement by making new allies with different kingdoms, and even had a palatial building called *antapura* that housed the many concubines that were there for his pleasure, yet when his wife, Mandodari simply pleads the case of a sage who wished to extend his stay at their palace for a few days until he finished his *tapasya*, Ravana's immediate response to Mandodari was to accuse her of having intimate relations with the said sage. It instantly captures the insecurity that comes to men living under a patriarchal setup. The hypocrisy of his comment highlights how different the responses are expected to be from two people sharing the same relationship, as he throws a fit and kills the sage he suspected to be in an adulterous relationship with his wife, while, when he married another woman, Mandodari found herself thinking, "I still didn't know if I was supposed to respond like a queen – calm and collected – or if I could scream like an angry wife who had been betrayed" (Anandani 29).

While in the case of Meenakshi, her sexuality is dealt with in great detail. Not only does she show unrestrained passion for her husband Vidyujiva, but also does not shy away from pointing out Ravana's philandering ways when he accuses her of misconduct upon catching Vidyujiva in her chambers before they were married. She reminds him of the women he raped, and the curse he brought upon himself in the process when Vedavati burned herself upon being defiled by his touch, and she prophesied that she will come back in her next life and be the cause of his downfall. Not only that, but Meenakshi played a major role in triggering that prophecy into action, when she meets Rama and Lakshmana in the Dandaka forest- the place where she had retired after her husband's death, where her attempt to seduce them brings Lakshmana to disfigure her face by chopping off her nose and her ears.

This incident is a major example of the treatment of women's sexuality in a patriarchy. When she feels desire for these men, she finds herself questioning her own impulse, as shown in the following lines:

> She stopped. She could not run away from herself, from her desires. She had not had a man since Vidyujiva's death, and slept with loneliness as her only companion. She shut her eyes in shame and grief...Was it not a simple, untamed urge coming out of spontaneous desire, essential for satisfaction. Is that not what her Nani had taught her: that there was

no shame in desiring a man, that a self-assured woman be comfortable with her flowing urges and desires? (Kané 194).

In contradiction to Mandodari, who suffers in silence, Meenakshi is a character who calls it out when something is wrong, as she did when she met Sita, and pointed out the hypocrisy of the self-proclaimed righteous brothers, as seen in the following lines:

> If they found me so crass and crude and unwelcome, could they have not just politely refused me like the chivalrous warriors they claim themselves to be? You claim the immediate reason for my disfigurement is my attempt to attack you. But is it, Sita? I think, however, the implied reason is my attempt at adultery. Yet, how proper was Ram's jest? If he is so upright as you claim, and had refusal in his mind all along, why, then, did he send me – a woman who has openly come to him – to his younger brother knowing he was married too and very much in love with his wife? Could he not have refused me directly? Both the brothers thought it was a game and tossed me to and fro like a playing ball between them. (Kané 239).

These lines highlight the misogynistic mindset that restrains women's sexuality, as we see, both Ravana and Vidyujiva had multiple sexual partners and their sexual appetite did not raise any eyebrows, nor got them any ridicule from society. But, Surpanakha's unapologetic attitude towards her sexuality led to the tragic outcome of her face getting disfigured at the hands of Lakshmana. In response to Surpanakha's accusations, Sita simply thinks to herself:

> How could she explain to Surpanakha that in the world she lived, there was a deep suspicion of women's power and desirability flaunted so openly and when unchecked by male control. Surpanakha's overt sexuality had taken the men by surprise, amused them greatly and they had played along till the amusement had gone awry. Surpanakha had been the predator and they the prey, but in a swift stroke of the sword, from an aggressor, Surpanakha had become the victim. (Kané 240).

As it is further emphasized in these lines, "Infidelity was born on the day that natural flows of sexual desire were bound into the legal and formal permanence of marriage; and in the process of ensuring male control over progeny and property, women were chained with the fetters of identity." (Verma 135).

So far, it is evident through the stories of these two women that so much of a woman's life is depending on how society constructs it, and as it is clear from the stories, it is a rather lonely life that women are made to live under the garb of patriarchy. As we see, while Mandodari is estranged from her family after she gets married, and is reduced to the titles and the roles she has to play, Meenakshi fails to feel loved and appreciated in her family from the very start. Upon the wedding of her son Meghanath, Mandodari thinks to herself, "My life was neatly catalogued; first a daughter, then a wife and mother, and now a mother-in-law" (Anandani 167), while Meenakshi chooses to live in denial, by ignoring her husband's affairs and focusing on the acceptance she found in his love. He was her safe haven in a world that felt cold and lonely. She describes these feelings thus:

> Women, she knew, were reduced to the elemental, their most vulnerable when they were facing love and family...She had been unwanted in her family, and it was Vidyujiva who had saved her from them. He had given her the love that none of them could offer, that warmth, that peace, that sense of being wanted, the belongingness. (Kané 170)

In a way, both these women lost themselves in an attempt to stay loyal to their sense of duty towards family. Meenakshi's tale takes us on a journey of her transformation from being Meenakshi – one with beautiful eyes, to Surpanakha – one with long, sharp nails or one as hard as her nails. This shift in her name also marks a shift in her personality, from being a young, innocent child, to becoming a vindictive, scheming individual. This cruel name was given to her by her brother Ravana when in a fight between siblings, she attacked him and hurt him badly by scratching his skin with her nails. Though cruel, but Meenakshi took this name proudly and gave it her own meaning. Her first thoughts upon receiving this title are written in the following lines:

> The word echoed in her ears. Surpanakha. Meenakshi looked down at her bloodied nails, some of her brother's skin still hanging loose on them. *If this could protect me, then well, I am Surpanakha*, she thought with perverse pleasure. (Kané 8).

The need for vengeance upon the murder of her husband at the hands of her brother, fuelled the fire she needed to make a plan so vicious that it would guarantee the downfall of Ravana. She was so consumed with that rage that the entire city of Lanka, once called the golden city of Lanka, burnt down in that war between Rama and Ravana that was orchestrated by Meenakshi to avenge the death of her husband. Even though no one suspected it, she was the one pulling the strings behind the curtain, as she used her skills to manipulate people and events in order to get the results she wanted. On the contrary, Mandodari lost her husband, and despite her desire to go back to her paternal home, she once again, had to live up to the role of being the queen of Lanka, and this time, she had to marry the man whose betrayal cost them the war, and her husband's death. Vibhishana was crowned the king of Lanka, and she his queen. For the first time, she was the one marrying for political advancement as Ravana used to say. The irony of the situation was not lost upon her as she thought:

> My marriage with Vibhishana was a political necessity. Thinking about Dashaanan's many wives that I had envied and he had claimed to be 'political necessities' made me laugh now. For the first time, I was a queen before I was a wife. (Anandani 265).

Looking at these stories now, it is visible that both the women were in an unequal relationship, where they had to make peace with their fate and accept their husbands as they were, even if it meant looking the other way when they found something they couldn't tolerate. As Mandodari's state is shown in these lines:

> It was four months since Dashaanan had last visited my chamber. Every night I yearned for my husband. I was lonely. Apart from the daily chores at court, I had nothing to do the whole day. Some nights as I would lie alone in my bed listening to the insane noises coming from the antapura, I felt envious. At times I heard screams of pleasure, laughter from wines they consumed and that made me feel even more lonesome. (Anandani 73).

Perhaps the ending to these stories could be different if they had the choice to step out of such situations that did not allow them the same level of respect in the relationship. But that was not an option available to them. In the time when these stories were set up, divorce was not a practice, but in the prevalent times, when it is possible, many women still fail to remove themselves from such toxic relationships. Speaking of the current family system practiced in the country, Menon explains the reason why women find themselves helpless in situations where they need to end a marriage:

> The three key interlinked features of this 'Indian' family are – patriarchy (power distributed along gender and age hierarchies, but with adult men trumping older women); patriliny (property and name passing from father to son); and virilocality (wife moving to the husband's home.) In this configuration, patrilineal virilocality is the key, isolating women from all previous support systems and leaving them entirely at the mercy of their husbands' families. (Menon 32).

A rising need for seeing things through the feminist lens are further elaborated in these lines:

> The word feminism came to stand for a belief in sexual equality combined with a commitment to eradicate sexist domination and to transform society. In order to centralize women's experiences of sexuality, work, and the family, feminists are inevitably forced to challenge the traditional frameworks of knowledge. (Kalpana 19).

Government schemes like *Beti Bachao, Beti Padhao* are an attempt to spread awareness and eradicate malpractices like female feticide, child marriages, and the dowry system, which are a major concern to the Indian society, and are causing hindrance to the overall development of the country. Through the reading of these stories and the understanding of the various methods employed in the above mentioned system of keeping women isolated and incapacitated to make their own life decisions or to lookout for their own welfare, the pressing need to cover these gender gaps is highlighted through this paper and acts as a step in doing the same.

This research paper has focused on discussing the treatment of women in a patriarchy, and the intrinsic web of customs, traditions and mannerisms that are employed to subjugate women in such a misogynistic setup of society. The findings of this research paper shows how it is that women continue to be a marginalized section of the society, and that, through generating consciousness about the silent weapons of patriarchy that include a rigid outlook on gender roles, it is possible to tip the scales against this grave injustice done to one section of the society, and bring about a more balanced and just environment that allows and provides everyone an equal opportunity to flourish in the society, irrespective of their biological sex. This research paper is one small step towards encouraging this conversation around gender equality, and towards moving on to a more progressive outlook regarding women and their place in society.

Works Cited

Anandani, Manini J. *Mandodari: Queen of Lanka.* Haryana: Penguin Random House India, 2018. Print.

Beauvoir, Simone de. *The Second Sex.* New York: Vintage Books, 1973. Print.

Bartky, S. "Foucault, Femininity, and the Modernization of Patriarchal Power", in *Femininity and Domination.* New York: Routledge, 1990. Print.

Foucault, Michel. "Discipline and Punish". *Literary Theory: An Anthology.* 2nd ed. Eds. Julie Rivkin and Michael Ryan. Oxford: Blackwell Publishing Ltd., 2004. Print.

Kymlicka, W. *Contemporary Political Philosophy,* 2nd ed. New York: Oxford University Press, 2002. Print.

Menon, Nivedita. *Seeing Like a Feminist.* Haryana: Penguin Random House India Pvt. Ltd., 2012. Print.

Verma, Archana. "Stree Vimarsh Ke Mahotsav". Trans. Nivedita Menon. Kathadesh, 2010. Print.

Williams, J. *Unbending Gender: Why Family and Work Conflict and What to Do About It.* Oxford: Oxford University Press, 2000. Print.

Kalpana, R.J. *Feminism and Family.* New Delhi: Prestige Books, 2005. Print.

Kané, Kavita. *Lanka's Princess.* New Delhi: Rupa Publications, 2017. Print.

Saul, Jennifer M. *Feminism: Issues and Arguments.* New York: Oxford University Press, 2003. Print.

Chapter - 17

Shades of Female Marginality in Toni Morrison's *Sula* and Alice Walker's *The Color Purple*

Dr Sumitra Singh

Much drawn are the ethos and sensibilities of a woman in a patriarchal society where violence may be muted, thawed, stalled or further aggregated and later on and even then sublimed by silence and moderation in speech. Much is because of abjection of their gender which though is supposed to be the supreme, as it nurtures the human kind but when portrayed in a common lens, gender-based violence speaks of discrimination faced by women on grounds of physical, sexual, psychological and economic suffering. The suffering becomes suffocation and ultimately, the woman lives a tumultuous life. Toni Morrison's works have brought the black literature in spotlight whereas Alice Walker's works are influenced by the atrocities on black women in America; much is also drawn from the personal experiences of Walker.

The pages of history tell expressly about female domination in different parts of the world. Many of them were deprived of their human rights as well. Both the novels, *Sula* and *The Color Purple* reflect major themes of feminism and oppression in the African-American context, with some differences. However, the major part remains the same. Abuse in its worst form was seen.

Alice Walker's *The Color Purple* portrays the subjugation of African American women, being black and being women together. The novel actually is a strong narrative of Celie who, as a poor, uneducated and ugly black girl, raped by her own father, did not have the temerity to be with her own two children. Celie gets married to a man who further abuses her both physically and mentally. The trauma that strikes Celie is tremendous, heart-wreathing and traumatic. Efforts by Celie lead her further to mentally prepare herself for a better, at least not a suffocated life any more. The narrative talks about how she tries to come out of her suffering. Celie at first appears to be powerless to be against the oppression and brutality of both black and white men. Slowly, with a long passage of time, and with the help of her friends Sofia and Shug Avery, she realizes that she is also born to act according to her will. She had to overcome her fear. Albert's sisters, Kate and Carrie tell Celie, "You got to fight them, Celie, I can't do it for you" (Walker 21). Celie knew that much fear had been inflicted upon her and that she had a deep agony in her heart and soul. It's evident that men try to inflict fear upon women and keep them undermined!

She can't be subjugated by anyone. With this thought in mind, after so many years of racial oppression, sexual abuse and brutal sufferings at the hands of black women, she starts speaking against such evils in the human society and strives to liberate other such women from the clutches of both black and white men. Celie, over a period of time, gains internal strength and become revitalized.

In *The Color Purple*, Albert asked Harpo to beat his wife and Sofia to make her do what he tells her to do (Walker 35). Harpo once asked his father why he hit Celie and to that, he replied, "Because she is my wife" (Walker 22). Therefore, we see such emotional and physical abuse also in the novel. Men, who boast of belonging to a particular class and domination, always show that they controlled their women and therefore, had power and status and the other way round too. Many a time, they controlled their children so as to have full control over their families. The Chief of Olinka village had forced the children to carve identification onto their faces in desperation to save their culture; much to undergo scarification (Walker 239). Therefore, Tashi, a character was left with no choice and felt ashamed of her scars; she could hardly lift her face and face others! Similarly, Celie was told by her step father to be married to Albert so that she could take care of her children and also submit to his sexual demands after the death of Annie Julia, his late wife (Walker 12). All these instances truly show how the men, as a ruling, dominant class gains control over their women. Walker says, "It is such. The husband has life and death power over the wife. If he accuses one of his wives with witchcraft or infidelity, she can be killed" (Walker 163). Men are allowed to go anywhere, behave anyhow as they wish but women can't, they are not free!

There is some difference in the sexual orientation of the lovers in Alice Walker's *The Color Purple*. Shug holds Celie, totally reclaiming the female sexuality, talking virginity and female genitalia. Enjoyment through sexual pleasure or sensual pleasure by reinventing female sexual desires sets the major narrative in the novel. Shug believed that and also made Celie believe that female sexual pleasure acts as a liberatory mechanism.

The story of *The Color Purple* is written in an epistolary manner where the protagonist, Celie feels the need to tell her story using the black vernacular. The novel showcases letters filled with elements of desires, emotional sufferings etc; the letters like letter from Celie to Nettie, Celie to god and Nettie to Celie form the spine of the novel. Through the letters, Celie is able to tell about the abuse that she had suffered and ultimately able to speak about it. Nettie's letters talk about difficulties of communication between men and women, black and white, both in America and Africa.

Celie's belief in god gradually changes from fear to hatred, "What God do for me"? Iast…he give me a lynched daddy, a crazy mama, a lowdown dog of a step pa and a sister I probably won't ever see again. Anyhow, I say, the God I been praying and writing to is a man. And act just like all the other mens I know. Trifling, forgetful and lowdown" (Walker 173). She writes in her first letter to god, "Last spring after little Lucious come I heard them fussing. He was pulling on her arm. She say, It too soon, Fonso, I ain't well. Finally he leaves her alone. A week go by, he pulling on her arm again. She says, "Naw, I ain't gonna. Can't you see I'm already half dead, an all of these children" (Walker 3).

The story proceeds when Celie's alleged father tries to strike another sexual encounter with his wife, who had shortly delivered a baby; she shows discomfort. He then rapes his oldest daughter and pressurizes her to do what her mother did not want to do (Walker 20) Alphonso imposes the bond of silence on Celie stating that she should keep silent on each instance, otherwise, he would kill her mother. She could, however, tell everything to God! Celie becomes pregnant with his so-called father's child, which her mother never knew, because of Celie's silence. Eventually Celie is sold in a slave auction.

In this novel, much sexual abuse and violence towards women is seen to be executed by black men and not the whites. Celie has been completely objectified…controlled by her father and also by her husband later. Shug Avery describes Albert as a person who mistreats others through verbal and physical abuse, "You black, you pore, you ugly, you a woman. Goddamn…you nothing at all" (Walker 187). Similarly, abuse can be seen when Harpo insists in marrying Sofia, he says gain in the same fashion,

"Young women no good these days, got they legs open to every Tom, Dick, and Harry" (Walker 31). Women in the novel are continuously degraded and subdued. Once Celie also told Harpo that in order to make Sophia work or react or act, he needed to beat her up into submission. But then hurriedly, Celie realises her mistake and apologizes, "I'm so shame of myself, I say. And the Lord he done whip me little bit to. The Lord don't like ugly, she say. And he ain't stuck on pretty. This open the way for our talk…." (Walker 39).

Celie and Shug slowly develop good relations and now Celie, after a long time of subjugation and oppression realizes that she would be able to speak her heat out. But then, Shug demands of another fling to which Celie remains uncomfortable. Shug appears to be highly independent, aesthetic, expressive but erotic and spiritual in the novel; one who actively tries to shape Celie's character to live life with boldness and style in the face of adversity and absurdity. Much of her independence came from her profession of singing. Shug had three children from Albert, her intended husband and lover but she left the children with her parents and moved out to pursue her career. Celie was sick of becoming pregnant and bearing children. When Celie loses her ability to menstruate, she literally becomes happy as she had become free of becoming pregnant from the man who she hates. Celie had faith in God but the object of faith is replace from god to a white man to the love for nature by Shug, "I think it pisses God off if you walk by the *The Color Purple* in a field somewhere and don't notice it" (Walker 177). Although Celie suffers a lot, yet she channelizes her rage into creativity and eventually becomes a designer of folk pants. Shug makes it a point to provide her with full artistic freedom. Celie's pants follow the "ethical and aesthetical shift from worshipping the white male God to appreciating the presence of spirit and color" (Walker 227). Celie's creative geniuses of pants are not white but purple and red and have various prints on them. Her art work could define thoughts beyond what she had suffered – from child bride to capitalist entrepreneur.

Walker portrays her women as mentally stronger than men and reflects various shades of men who try to adapt to the female culture of nurturing philosophy, and acceptance. Sexuality and feminism has been therefore dealt with both as a power tool and as a liberatory device.

Toni Morrison's works have brought the black literature in spotlight whereas Alice Walker's works are influenced by the atrocities on black women in America; much is also drawn from the personal experiences of Walker.

In *Sula*, also, we find similar narratives. Eva's marriage was very short lived. Her husband was totally insensitive. He used to drink, abuse, cheat on his office and leaves a negligible sum of amount for his three children, when he left her (Morrison 32). He had a negligent attitude, carelessness, treated women like an object which may be thrown anywhere. At the same time, we can see a different picture with other characters in Sula. The character Sula had the ability to take control over a situation by means of violation in order to protect herself from more oppression.

Sula tries to create and control her identity. That's the way she could also control her life. She developed relationships with many men. She does not care about what others would think about her and also did not believe in the traditional, conventional role of the women in her society. She did whatever she wanted; she was highly independent too! But we have other characters also. Nel is in the clutches of the cultural myths of the society. A woman in a male dominant society can never have to face the fate of it; to listen to the men and live their lives according to their wishes. This novel revolves around two characters Nel and Sula, their friendship and kinship and relationship. There are other themes like violence and deaths, sadness and tragic ends. Many people argue that the novel has a lesbian theme. But the fact is that, Morrison uses a female as an image. The essence of the story lies in self realization, self-understanding, understanding of each other and other emotions that can be really expressed. The initial sexual encounter between Nel and Sula unites them in a bond and it is the same sexual encounter that drives them apart (*Sula* 64). It was Sula who declines to be with Nel, in fact, she decides not have sexual conduct between them. This betrayal sets them apart. Sula also feels apart from her immediate community and surroundings. She felt alienated; stopped all communication, gets exhausted, and ultimately dies. There are other characters also, but Sula and Nel continue to be the main characters. It is difficult to understand who was good and evil between Nel and Sula. Both were much committed to each other. Both of them evolve as characters in the novel, although they may initially not be centric to the novel. But the deat of Sula in the story appears to be a high element in the story. Because Sula dies because of alienation, being incommunicado. She actually loses herself to herself. However, Nel moves on ahead in her life and many a time denies the loss of her childhood friend. The character of Eva appears to be a dominant and undisputed character (Morrison 65). She appears to be prophetic when she comments," It was the last as well as the first time. Nel was ever to leave Medallion" (Morrison 29). The novel focuses on the life events of all the characters from 1919 to 1965 whereby all the themes are structurally placed.

Many argue that the novel has discontinuity, missing subjects and other elements in form and content.

Many characters in this novel appear for a shorter time, some disappear, or die, like Sula. This actually becomes a mourning affair for others in the novel. That people miss their kins is an integral part of the novel and also reflects African American Culture and its history. There are gaps in time in the novels. Nel and Sula spent five years as girl friends. Nel gets married to Jude and when Sula has a sexual encounter with Jude ten years later. Both Nel and Sula get physically separated thereafter. Apart from this the novel reflects major world events like World wars and the period of Depression. But the lives of Sula and Nel, their personal struggles are more important in Bottom, their town. History says that African American communities had been subjected to an organized racism, with brutality and oppression, destruction of communities etc. The town, Bottom, functions as symbol in the novel, and the prologue of the novel sets the perfect setting of the theme of destruction in the novel. The concept of self and the other has been developed in the novel. The women were perceived as the other and men as self.

Bottom, was a black neighborhood in America and the existing black neighborhood including this is demolished for construction of a big golf course. The women have been objectified and the men treated as subjects. In African American literature, the women have been treated as the double other. In such a society and situation, Sula creates a self outside of society. In fact, both Nel and Sula created the concept of 'another self' but with an innate bond. This 'self' could not exist without the other and therefore with the loss of friendship with Nel, Sula loses herself and dies. Women in this novel represent different aspects of class, colour, matrilineal genealogies. Eva, Hannah, Sula are representative of the working class and Rochelle, Helene and Nel represent "the bourgeois ascendance from disavowal of subaltern black origins rendered shameful and inaccessible by the bourgeois morality of domesticity and respectability" (Morrison 47). Nel has been portrayed as daughter of Helene Wright, who was herself was the daughter of a prostitute, brought up by her grandmother "under the dolesome eyes of a multicolored virgin Mary" (Morrison 17). Helene tried her best to imbibe in Nel the values of orderliness and humility and to be constantly on guard and of subjugation. Nel had once witnessed public humiliation with her mother and decided to be on guards ever since.so that no man could ever look at her in that way or behave with her in a demeaning manner. "That no midnight eyes or marbled flesh would ever accost her and turn her into jelly" (Morrison 29). Nel definitely followed her mother's track as a leading pathway in life. That day was an eye opener and the trip "was the last as well as the first time she was ever to leave Medallion" (Morrison 29). Nelintialy did not befriend Sula as she thought that Sula's mother was kina sooty (Morrison 29). The story also its instances where Helene talks about men with whom she had multiple affairs (Morrison 69) and with that a growing Sula learnt that female sexuality has a great meaning, sexual intercourse needed to be frequent and it was pleasant (Morrison 44). Evidently, theses relationships would separate her from Nel, later; the ones who considered themselves as two halves when they met at the age of twelve. It appears as if there is a spiritual connection between Sula and Nel, who are totally dependent on each other for the things that they lack in themselves and find expression in the 'other halves of each other'. Their selves melting into each other, both Sula and Nel, as if in dreams, felt solace in each others' company as if there was nothing to hide, to reveal…intoxicated with each other's presence (Morrison 51). Indeed, there was a sexual attraction, developing into a relationship between the two girls; however, it gave them strength together (Morrison 52).

"In concert, without ever meeting each other's eyes, they stroked the blades up and down, up and down. Nel found a thick twig and, with her thumbnail, pulled away its bark until it was stripped to a smooth, creamy innocence" (Morrison 58). One thing is taken for granted and that is Nel and Sula were inseparable from each other; that they were one and the same thing (Morrison 119). At the age of 17, Nel marries Jude, an African American who desperately wishes to fulfill whatever he can. He is denied a job on the New River road and he promptly decides to tell about this to Neland not Sula. He believed as if women would love talking about misery, real miser considered as their singly own (Morrison 83). He makes efforts to distance her from Sula.

There are other narratives in the novel talking about Hannah's increased appetite for men, while Eva's hatred for her husband grew! There are dialogues between the people, despite, all love and hatred prevailing. Many of them appear to be ethical deliberations. Eva eventually learns to control her situation, but keeps herself in synchrony with the African American neighbourhood.

Morrison uses death as an aesthetic image in the novel as could be seen through the characters of Shadrack, a soldiers experience of the hallows of death in the battlefield. This is also seen when Chicken Little disappears in water. The drowning is described as "peaceful. There was nothing but the baking sun and something newly missing" (Morrison 61). It is quite mentally disturbing to the readers when they experience how Sula says on the death bed that she enjoyed in the aesthetics of the burning Hannah, wrapped in flames (Morrison 78). Morrison ultimately talks about the stream of consciousness through the character of Nel. Morrison describes Nel's thighs as a "truly empty and dead too, and it was Sula who had taken the life from them and Jude who smashed her heart and the both of them who left her with no thighs and no heart just her brain raveling away" (Morrison 111). There are two different things booth represented through sexuality – she becomes sexually rejuvenated with the news of Sula's return and again loses her personal sexuality with the loss of Sula.

Thus, feminism is portrayed in a distinct form of sexuality in *Sula*. The major aspect of the novel continues to be the relationship of Nel and Sula, reflecting features of imagination, emotional turmoil and displacement through the character of Sula. Her "idle imagination" is blamed for her whims, "Had she paints, or clay, or knew the discipline of the dance, or the strings; had she anything to engage her tremendous curiosity, she might have had a meaningful life" (Morrison 121). Sula disbelieved her mother's opinion on loving the men with whom she slept with, and considered that "a lover was not a comrade and could never be – for a woman" (Morrison 121). With the relationship that Sula had with Ajax, she believed that at least, she have some genuine conversations and that she would come out aesthetically in the relationship, as Ajax has aesthetic temperaments. (Morrison 127-128). Although, Nel spends another twenty-five years following Sula's death; mourning the loss of her marriage and exercising the role of a victimized woman, she says, "Leaves stirred; mud shifted; there was the smell of overripe green things. A soft ball of fur broke and scattered like dandelion spores in the breeze." All that time, I thought I was missing Judge, "We was girls together", she said as though explaining something. "O Lord, Sula", she cried, "girl, girl, girl, girl, girl." (Morrison 174).

Both Morrison and Walker present different shades of the same thing – A female's world in the African American parlance. The women through various incidents become depressed, subjugated and live in man's world where they face brutality and oppression. Then where is the question of male and female companionships, camaraderie and friendship, love? Both the authors have beautifully penned down the sufferings of women and the ways and means through which their lives proceed. Both the novels demonstrate some friendship between black women and also reflect various aspects of emotional health and seeking spirit of happiness. The oppressed community seeks its participation in influencing social structure through cultural and aesthetic mirrors of the society. The characters appear to argue against alienationand isolation and try to interject themselves into the dominant class.

Works Cited

Abel, Elizabeth. "Emerging Identities: The Dynamics of Female Friendship in Contemporary Fiction by Women." *Signs* 6.3 (1981): 413-435. Print.

Bell, Bernard W. *The Afro-American Novel and Its Tradition*. USA: The University of Massachusetts Press, 1987. Print.

Bloom, Harold. *The Novels of Toni Morrison*. New York: Peter Lang, 1990. Print.

Byerman, Keith. "Walker's Blues." *Modern Critical Views: Alice Walker*. Ed. Harold Bloom. New York: Chelsea House, 1989. 59-66.

Cooke, Michael G. *Toni Morrison*. New York: Chelsea House, 1984. Print.

Morrison, Toni. *Sula*. United States: Knopf, 1973. Print.

Walker, Alice. *Meridian*. New York: Pocket Books, 1986. Print.

Walker, Alice. *The Color Purple*. New York: Pocket Books, 1985. Print.

Chapter - 18

Humanism, Feminism and the Established Socio-Economic Order in the Works of Shashi Deshpande

Dr Parveen Bala and Dr Vijaylakshmi

Shashi Deshpande is one of the famous humanist and contemporary Indian novelists in English. Basically she writes about human relationship and feminism. The main themes in her fiction are human relationships and feminism. Shashi Deshpande, as a writer, always valued human relationships more than anything else and endeavours to portray the conflict of an educated middle-class woman in relation to the women of modern society for socio-economic dependence.

Shashi Deshpande belongs to the generation of the post-Rushdie Indian English novelists who try their hand in dealing with human psyche. During this period novels took various shapes and forms such as domestic novels, regional novels, campus novels and feminist novels. Shashi Deshpande is basically a feminist novelist. She has attempted to analyze the meaning of being a woman in modern India. The dominant themes in her fiction are human relations, feminism and the problems related with the life of Indian woman in the context of modern Indian society. She asserts that a writer is generally involved with human relationships; the relationship between human beings and the relationship of a person with its society are the two primary concerns. She also says that the relationship between persons is what is enormously significant to her.

However, the fact remains that Deshpande's views and thought are guided by Indian philosophy. Her father Sriranga, called the 'Bernard Shaw of Kannad', was a great Sanskrit scholar as well as Kannad dramatist of repute.

Naturally, she must have passed her childhood in a family that upheld traditional values. Sita and Savitri must have been the ideal women for her mother. Guided by such thoughts, the early years of her married life were devoted to the upbringing of her two sons and to the care of her husband. The family background contributed immensely to the shaping of her personality as a writer who valued human relationships coupled with human values more than anything else. She asserts that women should understand this point but men too must take care of their happiness. She asserts:

> It's necessary for women to live within relationships. But if the rules were rigidly laid that as a wife or mother you do this and no further, then one becomes unhappy. This is what I have tried to convey in my writing. (*Literature Alive* p.13).

Deshpande's father influenced the attitude of this girl deeply who appreciated human values. He contributed a lot in shaping her personality and she, as a receptive girl, adopted consciously what he gave her. Though born in a very orthodox family, she developed a rational approach to the problems of life and began to condemn orthodox beliefs and superstitions more prominently after she had availed an opportunity to go abroad and stayed there for four years. It was here that she and her father developed the feelings with western ideology. Her father was influenced by Gandhian thoughts which indirectly formed part of her childhood. At several occasions she owned that she was inspired and influenced greatly by her father. Thus she had mixed reaction towards women's questions in relation to society.

Deshpande's visit to and stay in England, the medium of instruction and the availability of English books at home made her a lover of English language. She read Jane Austen, Charles Dickens, George Eliot and Thomas Hardy who influenced her deeply. Besides this, her home as a 'harmonious mixture of language' with a Marathi mother and a Kannad father who taught Sanskrit, wrote in Kannad and read English, there was, thus, a curious combination of oriental and occidental thoughts and conceptions of feminism in her mind. She has attached equal importance to both of them in her novels. As such she stresses the point that everyone has to live within relationship, "it's needed".

Shashi Deshpande's short stories are collected in five volumes: *The Legacy and Other Stories* (1978), *It Was Dark and Other Stories* (1986), *It Was the Nightingale and Other Stories* (1986), *The Miracle and Other Stories* (1986) and *The Intrusion and Other Stories* (1993). They had been regrouped into two collections: *Collected Short Stories I* (2003) and *Collected Short Stories II* (2004). Her first novel *The Dark Holds No Terrors* was published in 1980. It was followed by *If I die Today* in 1982, *Roots and Shadows* in 1983, *Come Up and Be Dead* in 1983, *That Long Silence* in 1988, *The Binding Vine* in 1992 and, *A Matter of Time* (1996), *Small Remedies* (2000) and *Moving On* (2004). *Come Up and Be Dead* and *If I die Today* were detective serials that were expanded and published as novels. The detective serials, subsequently, expanded and published as novels are- *If I Die Today* (1982) and *Come Up and Be Dead* (1983). Her famous novels are *Roots and Shadows* (1983), *The Dark Holds No Terrors* (1980), *That Long Silence* (1988), *The Binding Vine* (1992), *A Matter of Time* (1996), *Small Remedies* (2000) and *Moving On* (2004). Besides novels and short stories, she also published several children's books in English and wrote the screen play for the Hindi feature film "Drishti". The Narayanpur Incident was written based on "Quit India Movement". Her short story "The Legacy" was prescribed for the graduate students in Columbia University. K.R. Srinivasa Iyengar compared *The Legacy and Other Stories* to Raji Narasimhan's *The Marriage of Bela* (1978) and Juliette Banerjea's The Boyfriend (1978) and commented as, it talks about the tears in things, the little upsets in life, the price one has to pay for one's acute self-awareness, and the loneliness that becomes more pronounced as one gets older and older. All her creative writing reveals that she is an intelligent, sensitive and sympathetic writer who shows sympathy for women and the oppressed. Thus she becomes the protagonist of oppressed women.

Deshpande is a humanist. She seeks to highlight the conflict of tradition and modernity in general and particularly in relation to the position of modern, educated, middle-class Indian women. She produces woman as the central figure in each of her novels. She deliberately focuses her attention on woman to portray her grievance. She craves for self-expression, individuality and independence but she is forced to submit in silence by the long established patriarchal social structure. Deshpande feels more for the female characters and understands the harsh reality of their life.

However, Deshpande frankly accepts the importance of a male person because she has been inspired, encouraged and helped by men in all spheres of her life. But she wants to remove the confusion from the minds of people that a woman cannot take up any job as seriously as man is supposed to be. She strongly refutes:

> ...that women's writing, like their lives, somehow lacks weight and substance. That there was something embarrassing about such writings and had to feel apologetic about it. For long, I had to fight against the feelings that my writing is second-class writing for the sole reason that it is about women. (Shashi p.34).

Deshpande broods over man-woman relationship and gives a judicious analysis of their position. In the domestic field, she finds that a woman is a sufferer. In the field of writing, she feels that a woman writer's writing about the problems of a woman is not supposed to be a serious writer. But she champions the cause of women. She is perhaps the only Indian author who prominently expresses the agony and anguish of a woman. In doing so she brings in some of her bitter experiences that she faced in the society. But she does not like to be called a feminist writer. She says:

> A woman who writes a woman's experiences often brings in some aspects of those experiences that angered her, roused her strong feelings. I don't see why this has to be labeled feminist fiction. (*The Literary Criterion* p.35).

Deshpande takes both the sexes on equal terms since both are complementary to each other. She feels that she has not been denied freedom to display her talent in different roles-as a wife, a mother and a writer. However she does not write with social purpose. On the other hand she asserts that if a writer writes in the true spirit of a writer, social purpose will naturally come to him. She realizes that literature comes to a writer spontaneously. Though she is not a committed writer yet she believes in the greatness of an artist concerned with human predicament. The only thing a writer has to keep in mind is that he should keep a judicious balance between the principles of construction and the principles of compassion.

Deshpande has an aversion to being called a feminist writer because she thinks that the word 'writer' is an umbrella term and it covers a large variety of issues to be treated. She is not hesitant in being called a woman writer. In her opinion a woman writer should not take herself to be inferior to a male writer.

Come Up and Be Dead and *If I Die Today*, two of her detective novels were the outcome of her analysis of *A Woman's Eye: New Stories by the Best Women Crime Writers*. She developed interest in detective novels so much so that she wrote down her two novels dealing with a series of criminal acts and murders in a girls' school. Her novels evince her interest in the stories of blood and violence but she failed to capture the attention of her readers. However, there is much material to delight the readers – the element of suspense, variety of characters, their whims and idiosyncrasies – but she is unable to hold the attention of the reading public who feel disappointed.

Deshpande is an upholder of human values. At any cost she argues equality, not that women should get upper hard. Nor can she tolerate that a woman should groan under male tyranny. In that case she would recommend revolt but ultimately the rebellion should subside in mutual understanding, peace and harmony.

Admittedly, Shashi Deshpande writes to create general awareness among women against the social evils and not against male person. She is the representative of the aggrieved women and shows great sympathy for them.

She confesses:

> ...what is to be a woman in our society? My writing comes out of my consciousness of the conflict between by idea of myself as a human being and the idea that society has of me as a woman. All this makes my writing very clearly women's writing. (Deshpande p.33).

Deshpande has produced middle-class educated young women as the protagonists who struggle to define the concept of feminism anew. She voices forth their grievance continuously in her novels thereby creating a space for herself to be their protagonist. It is, however, worth-noticing that her women are strong and bold. They face the difficulties though ultimately surrender. Talking about her own stand as a protagonist of the oppressed women, she has declared in an interview:

> I am a feminist. In my own life, I mean. But not consciously as a novelist. I must also say that my feminism has come to me very slowly, very gradually, and mainly out of my own thinking and experiences and feelings. I started writing first and only then discovered by feminism. (Holstorm p.26).

Deshpande has sought to create protagonists who, like her, are the architects of their fate. She becomes the embodiment of courage to the women who have lived under the protection of either parents or husband or their children. They have begun to shed their timidity and shun abject surrender to the protective cover of men. Encouraged by such writers as Deshpande, they are earning money independently, and are struggling against the age-old slavery. Indu, in her novel *Roots and Shadows* seems to recall Henrik Ibsen's words:

> ... I must take steps to educate myself. You are not the man to help me there. That's something I must do on my own. (Ibsen p.26).

Deshpande's statement regarding feminism proves that she is a feminist though not consciously. It seems she did not basically begin with the ideology of feminism. She only wrote about the misery of the female world without being conscious of writing about them. As a sensitive writer, her humanism came to the fore. Reviewers began to call it feminism. In an article she has stated that she writes about women merely because she wants to share the pain of humanity. She says:

> My writing has been categorized as 'writing about women' or 'feminist' writing. In this process, much in it has been missed. I have been denied the place and dignity of a writer who is dealing with issues that are human issues, or interest of all humanity. (Deshpande p.37).

There have been several western writers namely, Simon de Beauvoir, Germaine Greer, Betty Friedan, Kate Millet and Virginia Woolf etc., who wrote more pertinently about woman's question than Deshpande has. But apparently Deshpande's own thinking and experience might have motivated her to write about women and their problems. She owns:

> Perhaps being a woman. I find myself sympathizing with women. If others see something feminist in my writing; I must say that it is not consciously done. It is because the world of women is like that and I am mirroring the world. I find a lot of men unsympathetic to my writing and a lot of women extremely sympathetic. This is because the world is viewed in different ways by men and women. (Deshpande in *The Sunday Observer*).

Deshpande deals with man-woman relationship judiciously. She is objective and impartial in weighing the importance of both the sexes. She realizes that men and women are complementary to each other; they are equal and honoured life partners. Neither of them is to be ignored. Nor is it proper to prefer one at the cost of the other. She asserts that both of them are required to play their allotted roles. She appreciates the positive role of male persons as she affirms that it is her husband that has changed her and gives the credit of getting connected to people, to live life blissfully and to view the world in an improved way to her husband.

Apparently, Shashi Deshpande does not regret for being a woman. Actually her feminism, in relation to the importance of society, is not meant to reduce the position of man. She observes great strength in woman and only motivation would create in her the awareness to utilize her strength in the best possible way. She does not uphold the idea of women's strength being wasted in tolerance, submission and suffering. She takes pride in being a woman who is lucky enough to get full support of her husband in displaying her talent as a creative writer who could create a new social order in which both men and women are treated as persons and equal partners. She admits that her father and her husband helped her a lot in her growing into a writer. She says:

> I have been able to write…., what I want, the way I want, and at the place I want. I have never had to compromise on anything in my writing. I have been lucky that both in my childhood home and in my married one, I have had the full freedom to think, to live and work my way. (Deshpande p.37).

Deshpande is a humanist. She writes without resorting to any personal commentary or moralizing. Nor is she a propagandist. She realizes that good Literature should aim at doing well to humanity. If any writer writes to serve his own ends or writes for a limited circle, he can never produce good literature having universal appeal. She is sympathetic towards woman in all her roles as a wife, a mother and a writer. She thinks of her family, her society and her country. But above all she broods over the problem of humanity.

Deshpande's third novel, *That Long Silence* published by 'The Virago Feminist Press', London, made her popular all over the world. Surprisingly enough, she is not the woman writer who is associated with any Feminist Movement, nor is she conscious of the reader's interest in the feminist writing. She calls herself an ordinary woman who writes while at leisure. She holds the view that if one becomes publicly conscious, one's writing is automatically affected and also states that she is contented to be anonymous as this gives her the liberty to write.

Deshpande holds the view that a writer need not make conscious efforts to get publicity otherwise it would distract him from his work. Explicitly, he would become more interested in himself as a person and would forget his basic duty as a writer. He should only write, his books would naturally make him known to the world. If he has anything within to contribute to literature, he should present the reality of the middle-class Indian women. She has firsthand experience of the predicament of India women whom she has sought to portray in her writings with greater sensitivity than other women writers born in India and educated in foreign countries. Undoubtedly, the depiction of the world of Indian women is more prominent, more authentic, more credible and more realistic than that in the work of other woman writers like Anita Desai, Nayantara Sahgal and Ruth Prawer Jhabvala etc.

Urmila (Urmi) in her novel *The Binding Vine* is a very bold and courageous crusader who is far ahead of her predecessors. She becomes highly sensitive to the suffering and despair of others. She makes friends with helpless Shakutai, sympathizes with Madhu, Mira and Vaana. Deshpande creates in her the best of the protagonist of the oppressed woman. *The Binding Vine* gives the message, obviously Deshpande's message to the oppressed humanity:

> Come, my brother, come, my sister
> Let us join our hands,
> A new road. A new way
> A new age begins... (*The Sunday Observer n.pag.*)

Shashi Deshpande derived creative impulse from so many sources. She read Virginia Woolf, Simone de Beauvoir, Betty Friedan and Kate Millet but it was after she had started her career. Hence, it would not be justifiable to state that she was influenced by them because she had already produced some feminist literature. She is not influenced by any particular conception of feminism. Admittedly, she has deep concern for women, their problems, and their quest for identity, their dehumanization and exploitation. She treats her themes in the context of Indian situations. She focuses her attention on Indian woman before and after marriage, she realizes that the real problems of a woman begin after her marriage. She is positive in her treatment of the subject because she does not have an anti-male stand.

Works Cited

Deshpande, Shashi. Interview by Vanamala Viswanatha. "A Women's World (…) All the Way!" *Literature Alive*, Vol. I, 3 Dec. 1987.

—. "Of Concerns, Of Anxieties." *Women in Indo-Anglican Fiction: Tradition and Modernity*. ed. Naresh K. Jain. New Delhi: Manohar Publishers, 1998. Print.

—. *The Binding Vine*. Delhi: Penguin India, 1992. Print.

—. "The Dilemma of the Writer." *The Literary Criterion,* Vol. 20, 1985. Print.

Carvalho, Stanley. Deshpande Shashi in an interview to Stanley Carvalho. "Everyone has a Right to Choose a Language." *The Sunday Observer,* No. 11, Feb. 1990. Print.

Holmstrom, Lakshmi. "Shashi Deshpande's Interview to Lakshmi Holmstrom." *Wasafiri,* No. 17, Spring 1993. Print.

Ibsen, Henrik qtd. in Sree Prasanna Sree. "In Conversation with Shashi Deshpande. Woman in the Novels of Shashi Deshpande: A Study". S. Prasanna Sree (ed.) New Delhi: Sarup & Sons, 2003. Print.

Chapter - 19

'Size-ism' in Literature: Marginalising Fat Women as Non-Brandish

Disha Sharma

> *I accept you, and you get the same respect from me whether you are black, white, gay, straight, Asian, bisexual, Australian, tall, fat, whatever it is. We are all people, and I look at the people of the world the same way, as my brothers and sisters.*
>
> **– Nash Grier**

Until 1960s the discriminations in the society that were largely put into mainstream generalised to be on gender (women), caste (Dalits), race (Black), and social class divide (workers/ proletariats). But, a wave similar to feminism rose in late 1960s when a large number of people in New York gathered to voice a new parameter of discrimination i.e. anti-fat bias. This was consequential of the warnings from doctors and pro-health freaks that soon majority of the masses will fall under the spell of 'obesity' leading to health hazards. The prevalence of dominant health discourses has been observed earlier in many Western countries and now has taken its toll in India too which is perhaps good to an extent unless they categorize a few lot of people into a bin, marginalizing their esteem at the stake of their appearance. Instead these discourses tend to associate fatness with ill health, perpetuating stigma and negative attributions about bigger bodies. Public health campaigns used by governments to encourage people to lose weight have frequently employed messages and images that portray body fat, and fat people themselves as not 'fit' and 'unhealthy'. It has often seemed that rather than "waging a war on fat", such campaigns are directly attacking fat people. In response to these portrayals and intense indifference towards people who were deemed to be too large, activists have called up on 'fat acceptance' and curb 'fat discrimination'. And to spread the wave activists-cum-writers turned their propagandas into fiction writing highlighting the issues of acceptance and assimilation of these 'oversized' people in the society.

Literature echoes the society and in a way helps breaking certain stigmas prevalent in it. Different genres help in manifesting the truth through various forms. Novels are one such pieces of our leisure reading that we get to interact with daily. As the society comes up with modern issues, so the novels are incorporating those issues to lend literature its contemporary role. The purpose of this chapter is to ponder light over the most neglected issue of the times that is spreading rapidly. This chapter will talk over the acceptance of fat women in the society: how fat is categorically marginalized not to be accepted as normal in case of females more acutely. This study involves the operating mindsets of children, at one stage in the novel *Blubber* by Judy Blume and the adults at later stage in the novel, *Venus of Chalk* by Stinson. Both the novels hinges back on females, be it a child girl or an adult woman not to be taken as important, for their body sizes do not fit in the regular shapes of women in society. To get the facts straight, a more fresh lens is intended to be applied for the accomplishment of findings needed and that is 'Fat Studies'.

The eminent theorists of Fat Studies are Esther Rothblum and Sondra Solovay. According to them, Fat Studies are defined as "an interdisciplinary field of scholarship marked by an aggressive, consistent, rigorous critique of the negative assumptions, stereotypes, and stigma placed on fat and the fat body" (2). In their anthology *The Fat Studies Reader*, they conceptualize about how fatness and over-size are being used to oppress identities. In the beginning of the book, Rothblum and Solovay affirms, that a critical methodology 'Fat Studies' requires approaching the construction of fat and fatness exactly the same sort of progressive, systematic academic rigor with which we approach negative attitudes and stereotypes about women, queer people, and racial groups (2).

Rothblum and Solovay, relating the hype of fatness prevalent in the society as a mark of oppression asserts, "the assumption that fat people are unhealthy is so ingrained in western society that it is hard to get people to face the facts" (3). Recent studies including Fat Studies emphasises on the idea that people who are fat are not always unhealthy. And thus for theorists like, Solovay and Rothblum, stresses on the need to accept the statement as an initial step to practice Fat Studies. At a later stage, Fat Studies involves drawing out the programming of thought process towards fat and the plus-sized body eventually leading to fatphobia. The negative culture in the society of not assimilating the fat is consequential of inhabiting 'Diet culture' which certainly helps in getting oneself fit into the self-constructed frame of society. Marilyn Wann, in her Foreword to *The Fat Studies Reader*, explains:

> If you believe that thin is inherently beautiful and fat is obviously ugly, then you are not doing fat studies work…you are instead in the realm of advertising popular media… in other words, propaganda (ix).

Wann tries to link the representation of fat body only to the personal identity of a being. She highlights how simply showing a fat body in media does not equal affirming that identity. This is especially true when the fat body being "represented" is used as a means of perpetuating negative thoughts and assumptions towards fatness. For this, flood of advertisements are being broadcasted on Televisions, radios, print media etc. which are derogatory in terms of their presenting a fat body as flabby, bulging out, sluggish, dull and directly points towards one's lower confidence level (a negative trait of being fat). Interestingly, Fat Studies showcases how the society gradually pushes out bodies that do not fit normative sizes. Moreover, the most contributing part of the society, Literature, had also been neglecting the representation of fat female protagonists. The same has been talked of by Susan Stinson in her one of the essays in *The Fat Studies Reader* titled "Fat Girls Need Fiction". She points out towards the absence of proper fat representation in the genre of fiction. Stinson challenges common notions that fat girls need fiction "because [they] are fat" (231) and argues that the contemporary novels are doing more than simply comforting fat girls. She states,

> When I say that fat girls need fiction, I mean that we need to read and encourage the writing of a wide range of fiction about subjects both close to our various hearts and past the far-reaching imaginations. Beyond the desire to see our own lives and experiences reflected in fiction, we need those habits of mind and heart that deepen empathy with others. (233).

Stinson acknowledges the need for fat identities to claim more hands in literature even further. The purpose of calling for representation of these fat characters in literature is not only to identify them as beings but also want these identities to foster empathy and understanding in others. Stinson attempts to project a change in the readers of these novels as the underpinning of such complex characters will encourage them to challenge their previously held perspectives towards fat and the body. The major issue barring the literature here, is the less sold copies of such fictions and thereby rejection of publishers for such manuscripts. This made Stinson to publish with only those presses that align with the targets surrounding Fat Studies and fat activism.

The novels taken up for the purpose of showcasing demeaning role of the society regarding the commonly attributed fat characters in fiction clearly stipulates the stigmas they attempt to break down, and hence offers an original contribution to literary Fat Studies.

The novel *Venus of Chalk*, focuses on the lead character Carline and her failure to control her own body seeking to get success in getting a "normal" so to fit in society. The novel thus questions how ones identity gets parallel with these unneeded desires for a normative body. It is a critique on one's mental health issues that get developed over time for being not accepted in the society, rather than on outside contributions to her negative behaviours. The novel presents moments where the stigma surrounding fat bodies often get thwarted by the author's use of common tropes. The novel depicts no matter how positively created fat characters happen to be there, they are always limited by flakes of self-doubt, self-harm, and other stigmatized actions.

Susan Stinson's main protagonist is Carline, a fat woman staying with a loving fat partner-cum-friend Lilian (Lil), and a pet cat named Minnaloushe. Carline and Lilian eke out all alone, where Carline works for a magazine, Lilian enjoys cooking healthy and delicious food especially tofu and she does performs slam poetry too. At the beginning, the novel is all about their relationship, and their bonding. Carline affirms in the earlier pages, "We shaped each other's tastes. Lil fed me raw parsley, and I taught her my mother's recipe for cornbread" (*VC,* 18). They have divided the house chores and often work together as a team, preparing home cooked meals, working on DIY projects, and taking care of Minnaloushe. The novel embarks on relationship that does not bother over size and their relation is evident that fat women can feel complete and still live life to the fullest. Through their normal healthy routines, the taboos and assumptions surrounding fat bodies is challenged. However, the turning point in their relationship came when Lilian was away at poetry competition; some teenage boys harassed Carline for her fat body, making her question her own identity. The incident stirred Carline through inside and created a spell of doubt about her appearances. Carline spends a long time drifting in this identity crisis even when she had to take a road trip that leads her to temporarily live with her mourning aunt Frankie in Texas, and later return home to Lilian, there she realizes that she needed time away to move on from her feelings of internalized fat hatred. This parallels Audre Lorde's statement in her essay, "The Master's Tools Will Never Dismantle the Master's House" where Lorde sheds light over this dynamics:

> Those of us who stand outside the circle of this society's definition of acceptable women; those of us who have been forged in the crucibles of difference; those of us who are poor, who are lesbians, who are black, who are older, know that survival is not an academic skill. It is learning how to stand alone, unpopular and sometimes reviled, and how to make common cause with those other identified as outside the structures (99).

The society's capability of attaching negative connotations with things that make people different is beautifully explained by Lorde in the above statement. These differences are nowhere to be seen as desirable and acceptable simultaneously and so such differences get stigmatized thereby encouraging people who fit into the "normal" category to look at these bodies and identities with pity, seeing them as weak, and undesired. This idea is generalised by promoting negative stereotypes in relation to fatness; such as assumptions towards health, self-control and sickness. The only survival for these identities, according to Lorde is to take these victimized pieces of identity and reclaiming them as strengths, which is not mostly seen fat fictions.

Along with Carline, there are two other fat women too in the novel, *Venus of Chalk*, but Stinson features the trait of victimization on novel's most developed character, Carline. She adheres to the victim trope. Though the novel unlike *Blubber*, presents only one such incident of ridiculing the fat character, it does focuses on the many conflicts caused by that only episode of verbal harassment from teenage boys outside her apartment. It was only when Carline leaves the apartment to take her trash down to the dumpster, some teenage boys approach her on their bicycles. A gush of hateful words started pinching her; "Somebody yelled 'Sooee,' as if calling a pig. Somebody else started repeating the word, 'fat'" (*VC*, 20). Here, Stinson herself equates fat to denote negativity. In their utmost funny crack, the teenage boys compares Carline's body to that of a pig, an animal that is seen with greed, bad hygiene, and overconsumption. Carline is not only stripped off from her identity as a magazine writer to an animal but also is deprived of any human sentiments. To mock one's appearance is the pleasure of other's moment. The teenagers simply by calling her an animal, publicly body-shamed her, hence objectified her identity. They see Carline as an object to be shamed rather than a normative body able to freely exist in society. Though the novelist attempted to break down victimized assumptions, but this single incident remains so influential that Carline is seen struggling to get over those remarks throughout the rest of the novel.

The character of Carline is presented as a complex one, where on one hand she was living her life to the fullest before that single incident, she becomes apparently in contrast to what she used to be earlier after that scene. She is haunted constantly by the projections of her own insecurities. The words of those boys pierced down to her heart and she was left with self hatred only, her self-respect and feelings of self-worth quickly deteriorate. She started hating her body to the extent that she almost harm herself as means of finding stability.

> It hurt. Moving the flame in a tight circle, I watched the spot turn red. I was suspended and impersonal. I didn't live in the sparse hairs, the dry layers of skin that had risen to the surface to be sloughed off. It was a feeling I remembered from high school, when I was the age of those cigarette boys…Physical pain had been a focus, almost a relief. (*VC*, 21).

Carline's burning herself is significant in a way that it intensifies a pattern of self hatred-that how external forces have an impact on a individual's mind that it detaches himself not from the environment only but also from his/her own body. Carline describes this incident as "impersonal" since it was done to cope up with that traumatic event. Pain, here, for Carline is an act of getting relief. She causes her body to suffer as a penance for the trauma her mind bear. This pain that she causes herself acts as a release from her body. Instead of sharing her problem with Lilian, she resolves to isolation and inflicting pain. Carline detaches her soul from the body by harming herself as she was no more inside that fat body. Stinson projected this internalization of fat hatred by making the protagonist a victim. Carline could have been on the other side of victimization if she does not internalise the matter that was external.

Being a theorist of fat studies, Stinson could have projected Carline as a strong character who would have shown resilience towards harassment, rather she manipulated the whole event to emphasize how she victimizes herself against those uneducated teenagers whose identities are expanded on no further than this one singular scene of harassment. This form of outward hatred towards fat bodies is still prevalent, but the way Stinson chooses to unfold this reaction places Carline in a victimized position. Had Carline been contended with the way she was or had she chosen to call Lilian the moment or started caring about herself and kept doing things that bring her joy, such as doing some DIY or cooking, the entire premise of the book could not exist. The conscious part of Carline permitted her to rethink the moment of her self-harming and she realises that it had never occurred to her to stand up to these teenagers. She adds:

> The fact that I was bigger than every one of them had been useless. I never considered defending myself. Burning my own arm had seemed inevitable. I struggled to hold the thought that perhaps it was not. (32).

To an extent, the bullies of society can be controlled but an individual's self esteem about his/her flaws are build within, as Carline allows the big size of her body to become her weakness, where it was not needful. Stinson simultaneously presented Lilian, who is also fat though the projection of how much fat is not explicit, but she is also fat and confident. Any such incident would have not affected her. Carline loses her worth with one such incident of external harassment, leading her to multiple instances of internalized hatred. She avoids the actual root of the issue, and chooses to risk her life and security. By criticising herself, she resorts to find the source of this conflict within herself instead of recognizing the social structure and ideologies of size.

The problem with all these fat fiction novels though they may feature a fat female protagonist, their entire identity develops surrounding their wish to fit into the structure of a normative body. The expectations of the society make them not only shrink physically but in the process their emotions squeezes too. There is necessity to see these characters affirming to their current identity, which is to be explored in *Big Fat Manifesto* by Susan Vaught. Vaught creates a character named Jamie, who is fat and ordinary high school senior. She does work on her body, to get control of it, but not furtively from some external constraints. She is morbidly obese as per doctors and friends, but she remains confident in spite of the fat-phobia she endures. In fact, she chooses to write creating awareness about the injustices fat people suffer through.

Another aspect of not assimilating fat in the society is to profuse diet culture, that assists in procuring desired body. In the novel, *Venus of Chalk*, the characters, Carline and Lilian themselves criticize this dieting culture and Stinson explains Lilian's healthy eating routine as, normal liking not as a need to shrink herself. Stinson candidly relates dieting to self harm, and it is apparent when Carline visits her aunt Frankie and express her desire of procuring a likable body. Her control over the taste buds is delineated as sheer exploitation of the self. Kate Harding in her book, *Lessons from the Fat-O-Sphere: Quit Dieting and Declare a Truce with Your Body,* Kate

Harding rigidly believes that women are more concerned with body appearances as compared to men and lethally be their own worst enemies, indoctrinated by society and media. sKate along with Marianne Kirby in this book voices out the idea that lean body does not certainly verify well being and moreover, exercise is healthy to remain fit, irrespective of its aiding in weight loss. The way an individual manages his relationships is exactly the reflection of how worthy he thinks of himself. Like most usually till fat acceptance movement came to stir the societal norms, novelists such as Sidney Sheldon, had used fat women characters in his novels. But they are at first, the peripheral characters and shown as more prone to drinking, kind of ugly over flowing bodies, that no one is interested to sit across too. This context of fatness makes the marginalised attaches his body to negative connotations, the identities that fit within the mode of fatness then get seen as undesirable. The usage of these fat characters in fiction were mainly to treat them as a device used for humour or the best friend that occupies these negative stereotypes as a means of making their counterparts seem more attractive. The role of Carline in the novel is not to highlight the beauty of other two characters, who are also fat like her. But it was indeed to portray as a matter of humour for the society. The reader becomes most immersed in Carline, whose inner thoughts towards her own body are on a downward spiral mirrored by her recent life decisions. Her relationships and decisions she makes in regards to these dynamics continue to develop how Carline's self image affects her ability to continue to be a healthy friend/partner.

The novel *Blubber*, by Judy Blume, is a stark critique on the childhood bullies that gets ingrained in an oppressed mind for the lifetime. The main protagonist and narrator of the novel is Jill Brenner, a V grade student of Highland School. *Blubber* is not about the protagonist Jill whose life is held at details but a fat child whose actual name is Linda Frescher, a classmate of Jill. The novel begins with Jill elaborating on the class scene where some students are getting bore with the report making tasks by the class teacher, some are busy playing Tic-Tac-Toe silently and some has got their turns to read aloud their reports on animals. Jill explains how class had no interest in the formality where suddenly Linda's report on whale turns the whole class alive. Linda asserts the qualities of whale and her thick body:

> "Blubber is a thick layer of fat that lies under the skin and over the muscles of whales," Linda said. "And uh…it protects them and keeps them warm even in cold water. Blubber is very important." (2).

> As Linda was reading her report, Jill sheds more focus on Linda's body appearance. She remarks: Linda's head is shaped like a potato and sits right on her shoulders, as if she hasn't got any neck. She's also the pudgiest girl in our class, but not in our grade. Ruth-Ellen Stark and Elizabeth Ryan are about ten times fatter than Linda, but even they can't compare to Bruce. If we had a school fat contest he would definitely win. He's a regular butterball. (2).

Here, Blume attempts to point towards one of the serious matters of livelihood, where parents are not able to prevent their wards from these stigmas of the society. Such stigmas then pass on to generations automatically. This modern society has cultivated some issues that are not confined to the adult generations of the era, rather it has spread its evil wings to circumscribe little children in its wrath. A class fifth student's description of the batch mate in terms of his appearance is alarming in its sense of evoking shallow behaviours of the coming generations. However, most significantly is the part where Jill talks about a boy named Bruce, who is fattest of all but he still remains out of the bullying situation perhaps nobody dares to poke him because of his size or it hardly matters if a boy is fat. What remains disgusting is that how can a girl not take care of her appearances and thus becomes a matter of humour for the rest of the class, primarily being scoffed at by girl children only. Moments after Linda finishes her report on whale and the class is over, the class representative Wendy, who is shown as a powerful figure of the class, spreads the word to everyone, that from now on Linda's name will be 'Blubber'. The first time when Linda becomes a child victim, she was called on in the novel as "Here comes Blubber!" (5) Linda was entrusted a name that has relevance for animals. 'Blubber' the title itself denotes flabby, swollen, fat like substance that does not have a life. Linda just like Carline is demeaned to a level of an animal, with no sense and intellect, keeps roaming around without purpose.

Linda never retorts back whenever she used to encounter such harassments. The class obeys what Wendy commands them, nobody dares to challenge her ill intentions and Linda never got Jill at her side too. Blume was cautious of the fact that children can be insensitive at times because their purpose behind prodding someone could be taken as childlike. But the novel is much more than only scoffing. It has become a ritual for Linda's classmates to strip her off her worth whenever, wherever they confront her. One such incident is when Linda was about to come back home from school bus, she was thwarted by Wendy's group to board on the bus and when she does, everyone started meddling with her stuff:

> Then Irwin grabbed her jacket off her lap. "She won't need a coat this winter," he said. "She's got her blubber to keep her warm." He tossed the jacket up front and we played Keep-Away with it. (5).

In one of their Halloween fancy dress competition, Jill decides to wear something extraordinary to get the prize, she decides to dress like a flenser (a person who cuts out blubber from whales). There all these girls Wendy, Jill and Caroline started torturing Linda in the bathroom. Until this scene, Wendy and her friends used to bully Linda psychologically and emotionally by making her say, 'I am Blubber, the smelly whale of class 206'. But here, they attempted to torment her physically:

> "Strip her, flenser!" Wendy called. "Now! Then we'll throw her cape out the window and she'll have to walk down the hall in her blubbery birthday suit..."No!" Linda said. "Don't you dare strip me"... "Let go of me!"... Linda started to cry. (20).

Judy Blume sensitively approaches the limits of children in terms of understanding diversity of beings. She places Linda at every hurdle be it in school bus, an unsupervised classroom at lunchtime or girl's bathroom. Linda is teased, tripped, humiliated and physically controlled while her skirt was lifted. Blume silently questions the parent's role at home that does influence the society as whole. Blume realistically challenges the atmosphere of the schools, their breeding on moral grounds and capability of turning the stigmas into normal behaviours. Rather than providing comfortable environs to the kids, modern schools are a leading factor for deteriorating a child's mental health. Just like Carline, Linda, a child of eleven years ventures on a diet plan, in a hope that losing weight will vanish all such criticism for her. At lunchtime, when Linda opened her Tiffin box, everyone spied her grub and Jill asked if she is on diet:

> "Yes," Linda said. "I'm going to lose ten pounds and then you won't be able to call me that name anymore." (36).

Blume harshly comments over the inhuman nature of modern society, that no single student including Jill in the class felt a little remorse over what they have been doing to Linda. The novel charts out different pictures of stereotypes and discriminations in the society and challenges the Marginalization of fat – at a child stage or an adult. During the ending of the novel, the victim changes, keeping the victimization constant. On Tracy's word of knowledge, Jill realizes that she is scared of Wendy, and just as when she voices her opinion against Wendy, the whole plot changes—from Linda V/S class it becomes Jill V/S class. Later Linda also enjoys bullying

Jill with Wendy. The novel in a way encourages girls to torment rather than being tormented. Blume hints towards the survival of the fittest. The novel does not end up happily as Blume stick to make it realistic since happy endings are not truly attainable in the real world. Even at the end, the book does not clue any regret or change of heart. The novel ends as a usual endurance of humiliation suffered in lower classes that quietly completes its session within four walls of a classroom.

This is the conditioning of the society that enables people to believe that fat is undesired and distasteful, which is not necessarily a natural reaction. The negative connotations about fat assimilation are not inherently created by God rather they are socially constructed. This is well explained by Lilian when she tries to calm down Carline, Lilian says, "If it's not fat it's something else. Don't you know that much about the world Carline?" (*VC*, 44). Lilian attempts to bring Carline back to her senses by explaining to her that anti-fatness is socially constructed. Lilian wants Carline to see the ways in which she gives in to the negative thoughts others have about her body. The authors' taken up for the purpose of study have proven inefficient to create self-affirming fat characters. Carline and Linda did not fight up for their rights and did not have strong self worth which contributed to their internalized fat hatred, lending them an inclination towards diet plans. The socially constructed mold of the society for normative bodies stirs a spark in them to hate their bodies and yearn for the one where they would appear as normal.

Though the novels discussed were written in the late 1970s, we still need more fictional examples of fat identities that feel fulfilled, are paying attention to and taking care of their mental health and have strong support systems. Such characters will better represent the possibilities for positive fat identities. A novel that adheres to what has previously been done in fat fiction is a novel that perpetuates common stereotypes of what it means to be fat today. Fat identities are aware of weight oppression, of negative views towards the size of their bodies, they know what it is like to be bullied, they know that their bodies are under surveillance. This Fat fiction has become an umbrella term where novels discussing the issues of identity crisis, mental health, diet culture, abusive hatred are to be seen propagating. But the genre does encapsulate novels like, *Dietland* by Sarai Walker who writes of the fat women as strong characters in the world quite enraged by the misogyny present in their times and resolves to brutally punish the rapists in their own guerrilla gang way. This novel tries to break down the stereotypical norms of the society and pushes the society a step forward. Such fat fiction authors' claims do justice to the society for they endeavour to draw out the taboos for general well being. A novel that subconsciously reinforces these ideas is not a novel for the fat community, but a novel for their oppressors. A new level of visibility that pushes against our preconceived notions of what it means to be fat in society would be a powerful tool, and more fiction should look into the prospect dealing this realm.

Unlike Carline in *Venus of Chalk*, Linda does not succumb to her everyday encounters with these traumatic events. Linda cries, weeps, and begs to her class mate to stop ridiculing her, in fact, she once went on to threaten Jill for the repercussions of tormenting her. Here, Stinson and Blume successfully charted the characterisation of their victims where they relate more to reality of common masses. Carline being an adult, independent woman lets herself gets afflicted by only one such incident of harassment while Linda keeps her patience and does not let her inner peace be broken down by the frequent bullying of her class mates. These novels highlight how growing up in this non-fat acceptable society, makes one psychologically unfit and more unwelcoming of one's flaws that at a child's age the hardships of the life are almost negligible if compared to the struggles of an adult.

Works Cited

Blume, Judy. *Blubber.* Downloaded from www.ibatefl.com.

Lorde, Audre. "The Master's Tools will Never Dismantle the Master's House." *This Bridge Called My Back: Writings by Radical Women of Color*. Cherrie Moraga and Gloria Anzaldua. New York: Kitchen Table: Women of Color Press, 1983, pp. 94-101.

Rothblum, Esther D., et al. *The Fat Studies Reader*. New York University Press, 2009. Print.

Stinson, Susan. "Fat Girls Need Fiction." *The Fat Studies Reader*, 2009. Print.

—. *Venus of Chalk.* New York: Firebrand Books, 2004. Print.

Chapter - 20

The Mirror Images of Marginalization in M.R. Anand's *Untouchable* and Arundhati Roy's *The God of Small Things*: A Comparative Analysis

S. Divya Bharathi

> *Dalit literature is not a literature of vengeance. Dalit Sahitya is not a literature which spread hatred. Dalit Sahitya – first promotes man's greatness and man's freedom and for that reason it is an historic necessity.*
>
> **– (Bagul 56-57)**

Dalits and untouchables are the synonyms for each other. Dalits are considered marginalised due to their ostracized status from the mainstream society. Two novels Mulk Raj Anand's *Untouchable* and Arundhati Roy's *The God of Small Things* have been taken for study in this paper. Sohini and Bakha from the novel *Untouchable* and Velutha and Ammu from *The God of Small Things* remain the victim of the caste sensitive society.

Excellent literature is a manifestation of human feelings, predicaments, sufferings and happiness. Actually, literature is called life and the representation of life can be seen in the society. The surviving writers present the true image of the society through their works. The people of different castes and communities can be found in every society. Some parts of society can be seen organized whereas some parts are totally disarranged and without any order. Those who have lost their socio-economic opportunities for their livelihood are victims of economical, cultural, social, and political exclusion. The poor and the socially backward people from low castes are considered marginalized.

Our Indian community is divided into different classes such as the upper class, middle class, lower-middle class and low class which have further many castes and subcategories which follow many practices and applications, each of which is unique.

Subaltern theme is important in current contextual literature. The word "bottom line" is a German word which means the "lower quality" or "second importance". Antonio Gramsci, Ranjit Guha, Gayatri Chakravorty Spivak and Julian Wolfs think about the marginalised people. Marginalization has neglected, oppressed and exploited groups based on cultural, political, social and religious grounds. Marginalization deals with form of repression, gender discrimination, slavery of the working class, neglected women, deserted sections of society, and curved classes. Both women and downtrodden are considered community groups. Both male and female writers have raised the dilemma of women and backward classes in conservative and traditional societies.

For example, Nuruddin Farah and Buchi Emecheta have recorded experiences of African immigrants. Many writers like Shashi Deshpande, Bharati Mukherjee, Kamala Markandaya, Arundhati Roy and Geeta Hariharan etc. have paid some attention to women in classical and high-profile Indian society. Rohinton Mistry has been portrayed by the Indian untouchables for survival in a hostile and caste-based society in "a good balance." Taslima Nasreen's *Lajja* condemns repression of breeding through patriarchal ideology. Vijay Prasad observes:

> The institutional and ideological independence of these castes, despite the atrocities visited upon them by dominant castes, allows for a certain amount of political flexibility. That the Jatavs, for instance, have at their disposal a reasonable amount of collective capital to finance a political movement is of some significance. (Prasad xiv).

The most important issues of the untouchables and the freedom of pre-Independence and the marginalized areas of post-Independent India are portrayed by novelists. The caste plays an important role in Indian society. The untouchables are called the dirt of society. Such caste discrimination is the most humiliating setback for Indian society. It is the experience and interest of society that creates the truth about the social evil of the untouchables.

Arundhati Roy's novel *The God of Small Things* was published in 1997 and it has its setting in Ayemenem in Kerala. It has been written from a third person omniscient view. The novel projects Marxism. The novel has bagged Booker Prize. The plot has its setting in 1969 and 1993. In this novel, it has been depicted that the Indian society decides whom to love, why to love and to what degree. The novel depicts the story of twins Astha and Rahel who live with their mother Ammu. Ammu's mother is Mammachi and brother's name is Chacko.

This novel also tells the story of Mammachi and Pappachi and their unhappy life. Pappachi was not a good husband and he would beat Mammachi. Their children Ammu and Chacko's life also does not remain satisfactory. Chacko goes to England for studies where he married Margaret but she leaves him for Joe. Chacko feels broken and he comes back to Ayemenem and handles his family business of pickle.

Ammu was also an aspiring girl and she married Baba. But Baba also would beat her and he used to drink alcohol. Ammu's husband forces Ammu to sleep with her boss and when she denies, he beats her black and blue. Ammu gets back to her family home.

In this novel, Ammu gets attracted towards Velutha and she develops physical intimacy with him. They sleep together for a week. One day Velutha's father Velleyaappen notices their lovemaking and he reaches to Mammachi and tells her that her daughter is in a relationship with his son and they should get them married now. Mammachi and Baby Kochamma were strictly against this marriage because they did not want that Ammu may get married with a low caste man. They lock Ammu in a room. Mammachi thinks:

> She (Ammu) had defiled generations of breeding and brought the family to its knees. For generation to come, forever now people, would point at them at wedding and be funerals. At Baptism and birthday parties. (Roy 258).

Baby Kochamma plays a trick. She goes to the police station and lodge an FIR that Velutha has tried to rape Ammu and he has kidnapped Astha and Rahel. Inspector Thomas Mathew sends six policemen to arrest Veltutha and beat him badly but soon the police inspector comes to know that Kochamma has played a trick. After so much beating, Velutha dies in the jail. Ammu tries to save him but she failed.

The novel *Untouchable* (1935) describes how untouchables lived in an unhealthy and humane environment. Many events of the novel highlight the marginalized lives. The untouchables were not allowed to touch the well and were not allowed to get water from it. They needed someone to pour water into their pots and they depended on the people of upper castes so that they may pour water into their pitchers. Such humiliation is common to them as they are untouchables.

In the novel *Untouchable*, Bakha returns after completing the cleaning work of toilets. He is extremely tired and thirsty but he does not find water to drink at his home. Sohini goes to well to bring water for her brother. Sohini has to wait for a long time because she finds a long queue and great rush on the well. Moreover, she notices that all the low-caste women were waiting for some upper-caste person so that he may pour water into their pitchers. Nobody comes and all had no option but to wait. Finally, Pundit Kali Nath comes and he pulls water for Sohini on the condition that she would come to clean his toilet the next day. Sohini was an innocent girl and she silently nods in affirmation to Pundit Kali Nath. Sohini could feel the thirst of her brother Bahka but she was helpless. His brother was tired and thirsty also and Sohini was unable to give him water. This situation shows her helplessness.

The untouchability is a social evil and it has been described in the novel in a lucid manner. In the novel *Untouchable*, Bakha belongs to a sweeper class and he has to bear the pangs of his caste. Firstly, his duty is very odd which cannot be performed by any person of the high caste. Secondly, he is not allowed to mingle or touch even the upper caste people. Bakha has to announce his arrival with the message that he is an untouchable and the upper caste people must stay away from him. Even after his warning, if he comes to touch anybody, he is beaten mercilessly by the upper caste people.

The position of the low-caste women has also been described badly. In this novel, Sohini is the victim of the caste decimation as well as the gender disparity. She becomes the subject of jealousy among the other women of the low caste. She has an attractive figure and people like Pundit Kali Nath get attracted towards her. When Sohini goes to Pundit Kali Nath's home to clean his toilet, he catches him from the back and tries to molest her. Sohini cries loudly and Bakha, who was working nearby and the other people also, come to see what has happened there. Pundit Kali Nath shows his crook nature and he puts the whole blame on the innocent Sohini.

When Bakha comes to know the whole story from his sister, he asks Sohini whether he had done something more to her but she denies. Bakha is on the verge of attacking the pundit but Sohini prevents him. On that day while returning to their home, Bakha also feels that his sister's beauty has become a curse to her because the upper caste people's evil eyes are falling on her and it is becoming difficult for them to save her honour.

In the novel *The God of Small Things*, the rules of the caste are broken by Ammu and Velutha. In this novel, Velutha is a Paravan or an untouchable. He works in Ammu's pickle factory. As he is an untouchable, he is paid less for the same work. He is not liked by other people due to his low caste.

The upper caste Hindus believe that the birth in a low caste is a punishment given by god for their evil deeds. Velutha thinks:

> It was not entirely his fault that he lived in a society where a man's death could be more profitable than his life had ever been. (Roy 267) .

Velutha's love affair with Ammu breaks all the social taboos of the caste system and thus, Velutha invites the wrath of Ammu's family and the Kerala police. Untouchability has so strong roots in Kerala that Velutha is not considered even a human being by the upper caste people. Even the woman having affair is also deserves punishment and Ammu is also considered the part of the sin. Ammu is a Syrian Christian divorcee having two children and Velutha is a carpenter by profession. The story is woven in the complex web of relationships and

The Syrian Christina community has been depicted in the novel. The Christians of Kerala have been divided into five churches: Roman Catholic, Nestorian, Marthoma, Orthodox Syrian and Anglican. Thus, the novel describes the differences on the basis of religion.

In the present context also, the caste system is still prevalent in India especially in the rural areas. Arundhati Roy's *The God of Small Things* has many themes like caste discrimination, feminism, and social discrimination. There are few female characters in the novel and these women's lives are full with many ifs and buts and ups and downs. This novel turns into a tragedy when Ammu comes in touch with Velutha:

> Paravan were expected to crawl backwards with a brown, sweeping away their foot prints so that Brahmins or Syrian Christian would not 178 defile themselves by accidentally stepping into a paravas foot prints. (Roy 75).

Velutha is a talented carpenter who has special skills and he is best friend of Estha and Rahel. He is seen in the novel for the first time when the family is going to theatre to watch a movie and Velutha is seen with the other communists marching on the street. Ammu sees Velutha there for the first time, "Velutha marching with a red flag. In a white shirt and Mandu with angry veins in his neck" (Roy 71-72). Ammu starts liking the feelings of revolt in Velutha and that's why she falls in love with him which leads to the illicit relationships between them.

Ammu dies in Bharat lodge in Allepey. She had gone there for the post of an office secretary for someone. When the sweeper comes in the morning, he finds Ammu dead there. Thus, her life comes to an end just at the age of twenty-four. She had also become 'virtually untouchable' in the eyes of others after having her relationship with Velutha. Baby Kocchamma comments, "A married daughter had no position in her parents' home. As a divorced daughter, she had no position anywhere at all" (Roy 45).

In this way, the above description presents a clear picture of women that they are inferior to men. She is a woman having a good character and she is bold enough to divorce her husband and moreover, she is strong enough to bear one suffering after another. Ammu's life turns into a tragedy after her marriage with Velutha. Even after death, she is considered a low caste woman and even her last rites are not performed according to Christian rituals because the church denies burying her.

Work Cited

Anand, Mulk Raj. *Untouchable.* India: Arnold Publishers, 1970. Print.

Bagul, Baburao. "Dalit Shitya: Man's Greatness, Man's Freedom." *Asmitadarsh*, Vol. I, 1973. Print.

Prasad, Vijay. *Untouchable Freedom: A Social History of a Dalit Community*. New Delhi: Oxford University Press, 2000. Print.

Roy, Arundhati. *The God of Small Things*. New Delhi: India Ink Publishers, 1998. Print.

Chapter - 21

Geeta as a Caged-Bird of Haveli: A Study of a Marginalised Woman

Dr Budhnath Parihast

Even in the twenty-first century, the duties and works of women are assigned by men. They are not allowed to take any decision of their own. In the childhood, a girl remains in the total control of her father. Her husband rules over her in her youth and the son nourishes a woman in her old age and she remains under man-domination throughout her age. The decisions of education, marriage and jobs are taken either by the elders or the men of the family. Thus, a woman's place remains marginal.

Many female writers have projected the positions of women through their works. In this context, Rama Mehta has also written a very beautiful novel *Inside the Haveli* that was published in 1977 and this novel has won the Sahitya Akademi Award in 1979. The novel presents the conflict between the modern ideologies and traditional mindset.

Rama Mehta was born in Nainital and she gets educated from St. Stephens College under the University of Delhi. The novel, to a lesser extent, presents some incidences of her life but in a different way. Rama Mehta was in IFS and she also marries to an IFS officer, Jagat Mehta and starts living at Udaipur, Rajasthan where novel has been set up. She had to resign from her job under the pressure of her husband. Thus, Rama Mehta herself had been the victim of the male domination even after being an educated and well-settled girl.

She tries to change some repressive practices prevalent in the society. She was one of the first women who was appointed for the Foreign Services. She was a novelist, sociologist, feminist and a lecturer. She has written children fictions and some academic books also.

The novel *Inside the Haveli* tells the tales and traditions which were prevalent in ancient time and some people are also following the same rules in the present time.

Geeta is the female protagonist of this novel who was brought up in Mumbai. She had lived her life in the liberated and unrestricted environment of Mumbai. She got her education in a co-education college and she had enjoyed the metropolitan life. When she was nineteen years old, she was married to Ajay who was a professor of science. Ajay belongs to the ministers of Ranas of Udaipur. They had the biggest haveli in Udaipur which was known as Jeevan Niwas.

The traditional world of Udaipur was like a cultural shock to a vivacious and aspirant girl like Geeta. When she reaches to Udaipur Railway Station after her marriage, she feels herself surrounded by many women and their children. Many maids of the haveli also had come there to see her. She feels astonished further when one of the maids named Pari comes forward and tells Geeta to observe purdah which is compulsory for every woman. She gets admonishing even by a maid servant Pari who takes pride in narrating such kind of state of women and she tries to tell her the importance of the custom:

> One of them came forward, pulled her sari over her face and exclaimed in horror, 'Where do you come from that you show your face to the world?' Geeta, bewildered, frightened managed to get in to the car without talking to the women who followed her, singing as loud as they could ... [When] Geeta had lifted her face and pulled the sari back to see. 'No, no, you cannot do that,' Pari had snapped, pulling back the sari over her face. 'In Udaipur we keep purdah. Strange eyes must not see your beautiful face.' (17).

The story begins in the flashback technique and later in a chorological order. Through the character of Geeta, the novelists interprets that a change is to come. Geeta comes to know that a boy is given preference by the people in the haveli.

Geeta finds the environment of the haveli totally different. She notices that there were separate apartments in the haveli for servants and the family members. There is a strange thing to note that there is no boundation of purdah on the maid-servants and only the women of the haveli are expected to follow it. Jasbir Jain writes in her article "Erasing the Margins: Questioning Purdah" writes:

> The practice of purdah in many Asian countries is not merely a form of dress or custom, but is indicative of a whole social system. Purdah

> reinforces the idea of female subordination in built in patriarchal societies; it also defines family and political structures and constitutes the basis of gender ideology. (Jain 243).

Geeta is not allowed to go to the chambers of men. The haveli is a symbol of a traditional mansion or a large beautiful building that is a symbol of a big and strong system which is unable to change. She cannot see her husband during the day and even the arrival of the men during the day time has been marked with an announcement. The novel presents a world of women that follows the traditional rules of the patriarchal system.

The haveli is following the traditional rules for many years like its existence. No any woman ever tries to break these rules. When she goes in the haveli, she feels a total metamorphosis in her life. Geeta also tries to adjust herself there:

> The main theme of the novel starts with Geets's alienation from the life of the haveli and leads to her gradual acceptance of its mores and rules. She learns and comes to respect some of the traditions. She starts feeling pride in these traditions. She came to love the veil that her face, this allowed her to think while the others talked. To her delight she had discovered that through her thin muslin sari, she could see everyone and yet not be seen by them. (23).

The other women who come to see Geeta's face tell that she is not like other women and she will never be able to adjust in the environment of haveli. Perhaps they said such words because they thought that the people of the haveli have committed a mistake by bringing a bride who hails from a big city Mumbai but Geeta's mother-in-law states with pride that they can change even an educated girl also. Thus, the novel presents a conflict between the traditional mentality and the modern dreams.

Marriage remains a fantasy world for a girl and Geeta also, like other teenage girls of her age, thinks to enjoy her life after marriage but Geeta does not find even a day of romance in her life. She finds every day full of waiting and patience. She is now in the hope that her husband, as he had promised her, will take her to Delhi and thus, she will get rid of this suffocated life of haveli but that day also never comes. Though the traditions of the haveli were much difficult to follow, yet Geeta is determined not to surrender:

> What if I cannot trace my ancestry beyond my grandfather? That is no reason why I should surrender; she was filled with rebellion and her face stiffened. She was determined not to be crushed by the haveli. (100).

Time passes by and Geeta gives birth to a girl Vijay and Geeta sends her to school. She starts taking some revolutionary steps in haveli. She decides to send a servant girl Sita also to school. It was a strange and awkward step taken by her because if servants will get education who will serve them? But Geeta gets the support of her father-in-law Bhagwat Singh. She starts teaching other women and children of the haveli. This incidence becomes a topic of discussion everywhere. Geeta faces many protests but she remains firm on her decisions and keeps continuing her duty.

She breaks the rule of the haveli openly when her daughter Vijay is tried to engage at the tender age of thirteen. She raises her voice against it because she thinks that her daughter's life will be much difficult after marriage. She remains successful in this effort also.

Gradually, Geeta becomes the mistress of the haveli after the death of her in-laws. Her in-laws are the symbol of patriarchal dominance. The life of the servants was miserable. The maid-servants do not get time to rest and they so their duties without break. The strange thing in the novel is that the women of the haveli make all the rules themselves for women which are against them.

This novel depicts the strong and the weak points of a joint family also. There are many people who are living together. The novel's title "Inside the Haveli" also depicts that all the actions are done only inside this big building i.e. a cage for women. This haveli is their world and they are not allowed to get out of it. Haveli suggests a big mansion to control the women from the outside activities. The proposition of the novel is to present the true assessment of the condition of the women in the traditional society. Geeta feels entrapped in the haveli after her marriage. She has now no way of escape.

Geeta's mother suggests Geeta to cover her face all the time and speak less after her marriage. It is an inkling to Geeta that she is going to a different world where she has to follow many unknown rules of a new place. Geeta's parents think that Geeta's in-laws will not force her to the age-old and rotten traditions which are obsolete in the present context but they prove wrong and Geeta has to make sacrifice due to decision taken by her parents without seeking her permission.

So far as Geeta's character is considered, she is considered an outsider in beginning of the novel but when the novel ends, she becomes the mistress of the haveli. Geeta yearns for the independence and piece in her life. Geeta realises later that Jeevan Niwas can be a befitting place for her and what she needed at this moment is just to have some patience.

Geeta remains undecided and unbroken till the end of the novel. She is a strong character who faces all the challenges and hurdles coming on the way. Her husband Ajay is fully cooperated to her. Chotte Lal Khartri says, "In this enterprise Ajay always stands by her as a docile fellow" (Khatri 106). He gives her books to read and sometimes even breaks the minor rules of the haveli to give love and company to his wife.

The novel has some sorts of rules that run the life moving inside the haveli. The novel is about the asserting the autonomy of women. Geeta's disgruntled self looks for a free environment and that's why she wants to go out of the haveli but Geeta gets fewer chances to go out of the haveli.

The novel is a mirror image of women living in a traditional family. In the novel, purdah is a symbol of control and repression. The haveli presents a strong traditional custom that had deep roots and remains undamaged despite of many efforts. The bazaar is a symbol of liberation and freedom for women.

As a conclusion, it can be stated that Geeta faces all the problems after her marriage but she keeps fortitude and bears everything silently. She remains victories in the end of the novel when she becomes the mistress of the haveli and her rules are followed by all:

> Geeta is successful by changing the rules of that custom-ridden haveli though she has to break the rules of the haveli and has to disobey and displease her in-laws but this is how she is successful in her motives. (Singh 4).

Works Cited

Chotte Lal Khatri."Rama Mehta's *Inside the Haveli*: A Synthesis of Tradition and Modernity." *Studies in Women Writers in English*. Ed. Ray, Mohit K. & Kundu, Kama. Atlantic Publishers & Distributors, 2005. Print.

Jain, Jasbir. "Erasing the Margins: Questioning Purdah." *Women's Writing*. Jaipur and New Delhi: Rawat Publications, 1996. Print.

Mehta, Rama. *Inside the Haveli*. New Delhi: Penguin Books, 1996. Print.

Singh, Bijender. "Feminist Consciousness in Rama Mehta's Novel *Inside the Haveli*". *Variorum Multi-Disciplinary e-Research Journal* Vol. 04, Issue-II, (November 2013): 1-5.

Chapter - 22

Self Identity, Ambition and Womanhood in Mahesh Dattani's *Dance Like a Man*

S. F. Filomine White Sheela

A woman in a man's world would may be considered being progressive. But a man in woman's world is pathetic.

– (**Dattani, *Dance Like a Man* 150**)

Mahesh Dattani is a very renowned Indian playwright who is best known for the social issues in his plays. He was the first English playwright, actor and director having won the Sahitya Akademi Award in 1998 for *Final Solutions and Other Plays*. His plays are the strong voice on the social issues and problems. He has written his novels on the problems of women also. His novels deal with those issues which are related with the problems of many men.

His play *Dance Like a Man* (2000) was published in two Acts. This play narrates the story of the three generations, their struggle, hardships, relationship, frustration, sacrifice, marginality of women, patriarchal dominance and domestic conflicts.

In the play *Dance Like a Man*, Jairaj Parekh and his wife, Ratna Parekh wanted to take dancing as a career. For them, dance had become the part and parcel of their life. They were passionate for dancing and they wanted to be successful in the field of dancing. Jairaj thought that dance is the perfect medium through which he can express his hidden emotions. Their father Amritlal Parekh had a different mentality and he did not like that his only son may take dance as his career because according to him, dancing is not taken as a profession for the members of the respectful families.

Jairaj Parekh does not pay much attention to the views and warnings of his father. He emerges as a rebel in this play. He becomes more interested in it after getting the support of his wife, Ratna Parekh who was also practicing the traditional form of dancing. Jairaj's father was not happy when Jairaj was growing his hair like a woman because the long hair suits the dancers. He did not want to see his son as a Bharatnatyam dancer. He thought that dancing is the profession of the prostitutes and this would give him nothing but frustration and hopelessness. Amritlal says that dance is:

> "The craft of a prostitute to show off her wares – what business did a man have learning such a craft? Of what use could it be to him? No use. So surely no man would want to learn such a craft" (425).

Amritlal does not like to tolerate the dancing bells in his home and his son dancing like a woman during his rehearsal. He hates the effeminate guru also who had long hair like women. Likewise, he did not like that Ratna may go to learn dance from a woman who lived in a brothel. He forbids Ratna to go to the old *devdasi* who used to teach her the old forms and techniques of Bharatnatyam.

His father's worries for Jairaj were also justified to some extent because dancing cannot give enough money to him to support his family. There was not a bright future behind dancing. He had fear in his mind that dancing would not help him gain enough money and then his wife Ratna would also consider him unworthy and good for nothing. Asha Kuthari Chaudhuri writes in this context:

> The underlying fear is obviously that dance would make him 'womanly' – an effeminate man – the suggestion of homosexuality hovers near, although never explicitly mentioned. (Chaudhuri 68).

Jairaj's wife Ratna would think that she would have bright career in dancing. She encouraged her husband also to go ahead with dancing but she knew it well that Jairaj was not perfect and intelligent enough to go to the acme of his career in dancing. Not only this, she supported her daughter Lata also so that she might also become a traditional dancer. Lata was not unaware of it and she used her own brain over that decision. That's why she did not come into the sway of her mother and thus, could not become an object at the hands of her mother. Ratna would like to fulfill her dreams through her daughter as a traditional dancer. She would see her own self in her daughter and she would see her childhood through Lata.

The dominance of patriarchal society is clearly visible in the play. According to men, the traditional dance is an act of women only and there is no any place for men. The dancers are expected to have long hair like women, having womanly gait and the same effeminate style of speaking.

The play brings tensions in the family. Rachel Bari and M. Ibrehim Khalilullah write, "What is interesting about Dattani is the fact that in every human drama of his .... everything is placed in the family mould" (Bari and Khalilullah 61).

In this novel, Jairaj takes dancing merely as an enjoyment and he did not know the hurdles coming on the way. He did not know much about the background of this dance. He had never thought that the traditional dancing is considered merely the prerogative of women and there is no any place for men. Jairaj's step was just to take a path that was untrodden by men and he had less hope that he would get support by anybody in taking dance as his career.

Ratna thinks that it is only dancing that can give her a platform of popularity, status and money. That's the reason that she married Jairaj because she knew it well that he would never prevent her from dancing. She sacrifices Jairaj's skills and abilities so that she may achieve her goal as a dancer. She plays with Jairaj's emotions also. Ratna seems to be dominant over her husband and she challenges his maleness also and Jairaj does not oppose it. She says:

> "You! You are nothing but a spineless boy who couldn't leave his father's house for more than forty-eight hours. You stopped being a man for me the day you came to his house." (442).

Ratna finds that her husband is not independent enough to take the decisions of his life and he is not standing on his legs and is depended financially for his parents. That's why when they needed a mridangam player for their daughter, Jairaj takes this task as a test of his manhood and he tells Ratna, "Will finding a musician make me a man?" (442).

Jairaj is a submissive husband who never becomes the cause of her wife's tension. Instead his wife keeps pricking the thorn through her bitter words. He remains silent and even does not put the blame on his wife when their son Shankar dies due to her carelessness. Neeru Tanton writes, "What one loves about them is the way he brings in the dynamics of personal and moral choices while focusing on human relations" (Tandon 91).

The play has many dominant themes like revolt, sacrifice, ambition and domination. There are few main characters and each of them is running after one or the other objective. One character does not respect the feelings of other and there is lack of mutual understanding among the characters. Both the father and son have a different mentality in the play having their different world. The father is practical and he is an experienced person while the son is just trying to test the fruit of life and he dreams to live in his own world. He took dancing because it would give him satisfaction while his father was not allowing him to take dancing as a career because everybody needs money to run the family and this career will not provide his son enough money and he may fail in running his family smoothly.

Both the persons are right from their own perspectives but they never try to sit together and find the solution. The father just gives order and the son knows disobeying his father. Jairaj remains adamant on his decision of career as a dancer. He considers his father a deceiver and when he gets extremely angry with his father, he leaves his father's house. But he is forced to listen to his father and he returns later.

In this play, Lata is the only character who seems to be connected with the realistic grounds of life. This quality of Lata makes her different from other people of her family. She knows it well that traditional dance can become merely as a hobby but it cannot be a career for her. She knew it well that her parents are traditional dancers and she enjoyed their dancing also but she knew well about her career also. Lata takes dance just as a part of life but not like a passion like her parents. She does not let dance come on the way of love.

This play is a conflict between the older and younger generations. Amritlal has been projected as an autocratic father who is adhered with the masculinity and he wants to see that kind of stance in his son also. This play has its setting in Chennai and dancing is liked by many people there. Jairaj's father thinks that Bharatanatyam has become a socially neglected art and it can be practiced only by the low-graded women like *Devadasis* and it must not have any link with the well-established and respected people. The following conversation between father and son reveals that Amritlal will never allow his son to take Bharatanatyam as a career:

> Jairaj: You promised you would allow me to continue with my hobbies.
> Amirtlal: That was when you were a boy and dance was just a hobby. Grow up Jairaj.
> Jairaj: I don't want to grow up! You can't stop me from doing what I want.
> Aritlal: As long as you are under my care. (422).

Thus, Jairaj remains under the constant pressure of his father in his home. Sometimes, he becomes impulsive also and that's why he decides to remain aloof from his father. He says, "As from now we are no longer under your care. And will never be again. Never" (424). He fails to run his family without the support of his father and soon realizes his mistake. He returns to his father's house within two days but this time his father puts certain restrictions on him. He tells Jairam to have his hair trimmed like a man and Ratna is also not allowed to learn dance. Amritlal's conversation with his son is a clear indication that he will never allow to have long hair to his son because it would make his son womanly:

> Amritlal: I have never seen a man long hair.
> Jairaj: All sadhus have long hair.
> Amritlal: I don't mean [...]
> Jairaj: What are you trying to say?
> Amritlal: All I am saying that normal men don't keep their hair so long. (417).

Amritlal shows his dominance in the family not only to his son but his daughter-in-law Ratna also. He tells Ratna which was to be said to his son only. Amritlal should have told the words which are related to his son instead he warns Ranta that if Jairam keeps long hair, he would shave his head and will kick him out of his house without giving any attention to the point that Jairam is his only son. Thus, Jairam's life becomes a tragedy by his father.

Jairam wants to fulfill his desires through his son Shankar. He wants to take the revenge of the oppression through his son. He says that his son would dance on the head of his grandfather. Jairam says, "I'll teach him how to dance- the dance of Shiva. The dance of a man. And when he is ready, I'll bring him to his grandfather and make him dance on his head-tandava nritya" (441) but this dream of Jairam also remains unfulfilled because his son dies a premature death.

Amritlal allows Ratna to dance on the condition that her husband would not dance. Ratna becomes happy to get the permission of dancing by her father-in-law. But Ratna does not remain much happy over the decision and she becomes passionless because in this way, her husband Jairam's career gets spoilt. She feels happy when her daughter Lata becomes a shining star of Bharatnatyam.

Amritlal strikes a deal with Ratna that he can allow her to learn dance if her persuades her husband not to dance like a woman. He wants to see his son a 'manly man'. Ratna has been shown as a selfish woman who puts her husband's dancing career at stake. She becomes so passionate for dancing that she joins hands with her father-in-law against her husband's hopes and aspirations. She gets married with him for the selfish motives because being a dancer; Jairam would not prevent her from dancing. When Jairam comes to know about his wife's secret plans, he becomes so sad that he becomes alcoholic. Thus, Jairam becomes the victim of the whims and dreams of his wife and she and his father were responsible for his undoing.

Ratna is so selfish that she keeps dancing career at the priority and the family comes at the secondary place. She leaves his son under the care of the nanny and the latter gave his son the overdose of sleeping medicine so that he may not cry and sleep peacefully. But unfortunately, Shankar dies due to overdose. Towards the end of the play, Jairam holds her responsible for his son's death and his unsuccessful career.

Thus, Mahesh Dattani's play *Dance Like a Man* is about the selfish motives of Ratna and Amritlal who do not think about the feelings of other persons in their family. Amrilal shows the patriarchal dominion over his son and daughter-in-law and Ratna also keeps Jairam under the pressure and tensions because all the things of house are under the control of his father. In this way, the play makes Jairaj as a marginalised character. Mahesh Dattani remains successful in giving the message to his readers that dancing for men is still a forbidden area under the eyes of the traditional people like Jairaj but overall, Dattani remains successful in conveying his message to his reader. K. Ramya writes about Dattani's plays:

> Mahesh Dattani draws attention to the complexities of relationships under patriarchal hegemony in his play *Dance Like a Man* (1989). He unveiled the ill effects of patriarchy in Indian society through his portrayal of the sufferings of women characters as well as men characters. In this play Dattani examines the relationship among the members of the family with truth and genuineness. (Ramya 543).

Works Cited

Chaudhuri, Asha Kuthari. *Contemporary Indian Writers in English: Mahesh Dattani: An Introduction*. New Delhi: Foundation Books, 2005. Print.

Dattani, Mahesh. *Collected Plays: Dance Like a Man.* New Delhi: Penguin Books, 2000. Print.

Khalilullah, Ibrahim and Rachel Bari. "The Literary Criterion: Special Number on Modern Indian English Drama". *Reading Dattani: A View Point*. Vol. 42. No 3 & 4, 2007. Print.

Ramya, K. "Patriarchal Subjugation in Mahesh Dattani's *Dance Like a Man*." Vol. 19:4 April 2019. 542-46.

Tandon, Neeru. Ed. *Perspectives and Challenges in Indian English Drama*. New Delhi: Atlantic Publishers & Distributors, 2006. Print.

Chapter - 23

Addressing the Euphemism of "Better Life" in Pratibha Ray's *The Primal Land*

Sumedha Bhandari

Gustava Estava while discussing the terms of development and progress argues that these are better understood as "forms of 'colonizing anti-colonial in which poor countries of the world are simultaneously seen as socially and politically 'backward,' and in which the positive meaning of the world 'development" profoundly rooted after [at least] two countries of its social construction – is a reminder of what are…" (21).

Pratibha Ray's novel *The Primal Land* is a translation of Oriya novel *Aadibhoomi*, a saga of embattled Bonda tribe that inhabits the mountains and forests of Malkangiri region of Koraput, Orissa. The novel is a fictional portrayal of the Bondas whose population of around 9378 has been fast dwindling to 6676 (as per 2001 census); thus, relegating them nearer to the threat of extinction. Though, the British government framed the tribals by the Criminal Tribes Act of 1871, Pratibha Ray is more interested in presenting their story without the lens of judgment or condemnation. This fictionalized reconstruction of little known Bonda tribe, sets a meta-narrative that helps in resurfacing their traditions and taboos which have stood the test of time for thousands of years. The primal tribe is marked with the chief characteristics of pride, honour and unmannered aggression. They are extremely self-independent and at the same time conservative in the pursuance of their traditional ideologies. "This is the self proclaiming land of the Bondas, where few outsiders have ventured and life has changed but little since the Stone Age" (Preface vi). The fictionalized account of the Bondas is chiseled by the art of folklore and mythology, so, intricately woven into the fabric of the novel. The ethnic and cultural traits of the Bondas are superbly explored to present forth a novel that seems more so a cultural biography rather than a fictional account.

In *The Primal Land*, Pratibha Ray unravels the image of Bonda as "naked like the mountain and the river, the sky and the earth, like the beasts of the forest" (3). For the people of the plains, he is brute and barbaric; because for them the nature is also wild and uncivilized. Since the Bondas do not conform to the rules of civilization, they are considered wild too. For the Bonda the cycle of life and death coincides with the cycle of growth and decay as in nature. As a "primitive, aboriginal society" (2), the Bondas have been in constant interaction with nature with their "back turned to civilization" (2). They chose to call themselves "Remo" (Man), so that the people of the plains do not mistake them for an animal. In this context Mohapatra and Mohanty state, "neither they want to leave their original place, nor like to settle with the outsiders ... Here, the question of dominance by plains people ... was at the back of their mind" (38).

Geographically the Bonda community establishes its identity as original settlers of villages collectively known as 'Bonda Ghati'. It comes under Mudulipada and Anthral village under Khairaput block of Malkangiri district, Odisha. The community of 'Bondadesh' comprise of thirty two villages, with each having its own nayak, or a headman. For the tribe the nature is their biggest teacher. They roam about in its care, taking from it what it gives willingly and returning what is needed to maintain the equilibrium. Since, they have no conception of "civilized world, the "remos" are aggressive and animalistic in most of their traits. Ignorant of the western concept of anthropocentricism, the 'remos' are well-perceived as uncivilized, and backward. As Cary Wolfe citing Jacques Derrida, puts it, "... the full transcendence to the human requires the sacrifice of the animal and the animalistic, which in turn makes possible a symbolic economy in which we can engage in a 'non criminal putting to death', as Derrida phrases it, not only of animals but of humans as well by marking them as animal" (39).

In India, the subalternisation of the indigenous tribes is ecologically and historically linked with the colonization of their traditional forest in the name of development and civilization. In *The Primal Land*, Pratibha Ray recognizes this severing of links between the tribals and their land due to their historical encounters with other cultures, ideologies and hegemonic structures. In this context, Mahasweta Devi observes: "They had no sense of property. There was communal landholding, because, just like Native Americans, they also believed that land and forest and river belonged to everyone. Their society was of course broken under mainstream onslaught...("Author in Conversation" *IM* ii) For the Bondas, the land is not a piece of paper to be owned, but a living spirit, a family to be celebrated.

"Wherever the eye can travel is sky, but not divided into fragments, "thine" and "mine". In the sky there are no fences separating village from village, caste from caste" (2). They owe it a responsibility towards the land, as the mother Earth "offered her soft lap, the valleys and settlements where the Bondas rested his head" (3).

Just like Gabriel García Márquez's *One Hundred Years of Solitude* (1967), an epic tale of seven generations of the Buendía family, the story of Bondas narrated by the oldest living member of the tribe Soma Muduli spans over hundred years showcasing the life, birth, marriage and death of the Bondas. In spite of Bondas having a reputation of being ruthless murderers, Bonda tribesman Soma Muduli has never killed a man in his life of hundred or more years. Since the rules of civilization seem conforming and stifling to the Bondas, they take refuge in a hostile mountainous terrain that has on the one hand made their life hard but has on the other hand given them the freedom to lead a life of their choice, secure and undisturbed. The danger associated with the wild terrain accompanied by the fear of wild animals has given them a safeguard from the onslaught of modernity and progress. The over-enthusiastic entrepreneurs and the missionaries of religion have though tried to penetrate their circle, but the unpredictability and hostility of the terrain and Bondas alike has worked in their defense. At the Pansatti (Assembly of five elders) the Bondas observe an oath, "No remo will give up his country, except to go to jail. No remo will work for any foreigner" (90).

The real threat to their way of life arises with the fast developing world making entry into their tribal world. The Bonda is suspicious of civilization; he despises everyone who is clothed. They are tired of the pressures of civilization and mistrust all plainsmen. The only outsiders are the Dombs who act as mediators between them and the plains people. Since, only Dombs can understand the language of the Bonda, they exploit all the interactions of Bonda with the civilization to their own advantage. They assure them: "You Bondas are good people – you are our brothers. We will protect you: have no fear" (81). Mindful of the killing tendencies of the Bonda, they are fearful of them and live together in different 'kudus' (hills). Though, they act as genuine interpreters for the Bonda, through their treachery they extract maximum benefits for themselves and nurture the seed of suspicion towards civilization in the mind of the Bonda. They question the integrity of any outsider, "Are they really coming to help us or to destroy us?" (81). The suspicion is also caused by their intense need to maintain their freedom; and hence, their association with nature. It is against the Bonda tradition to leave one's homeland, "It is not important to live longer what matters is to live like a man what use is it if you have to sell yourself to survive" (88).They believe that the spirits of their ancestors reside in the forests to guide the future generations. In fact, when one of the characters Lachma leaves the Upper Bonda region after the death of her husband, she is instantly questioned, "Life and Death follow us everywhere, but is that the reason to give up the mother Earth?" (61) as they believe that if they leave the land, they will be rudderless and their tribe will cease to exist.

However, the march of civilization continues with its flag march and penetrates the circle of Bondas with the weapon of religion. Karl Marx rightly asserted, "Religion is the sigh of the oppressed creature, the heart of a heartless world, and the soul of soulless conditions. It is the opium of the people". Here, religion is used to dominate, subjugate and domesticate a tribe which does not follow the dictates of civilization. The narrative of the story unweaves instances, where the jailed Bondas are freed after buying the photo of a God from the Jailer. The problem arises when every freed Bonda is given a different photo. Perplexed at the different faces of bought Gods, the Bondas compare them with Mahapuru, their stone-god living under the Banyan tree. Comparing the strength of the Gods, they leave the photo of bought Gods near the banyan tree and decide to pray to the one who maintains its ground till morning. Notwithstanding the forces of wind, the photos are lost in the eternity of time. Hence, the Mahapuru turns victorious and Bondas solidify their faith in the pagan Gods. The Bondas eat cow meat and do not want any Hindu temples in their region and are happy with their own gods and ways of worship. They believe that "The gods create human beings, but human beings do not create gods" (199). Their reverence of pagan gods not only allows them to preserve the ecosystem, it also provides them the wisdom to consider themselves a part of the ecosystem and not the one directing it. Having a communion with nature provides them the tools to sustain in the wilderness, while also, lending them the freedom to enjoy their existence. Since, they have not entered the folds of any conformed religion; they are able to devise rules for themselves that are both eco-centered and eco-sustainable.

When the agenda of mistrust towards faith finds not many takers, the neo-colonizers instill fear with the power of money. The Bondas, who had, earlier, survived on the economics of the barter system, have no conception of money. They are happy exchanging rice for salt and consider money useless as it is inedible. If they need more than their means to carry out the rituals of the tribe, the sahukars keep their sons and daughters as goti and give them the requisite things necessary for the ritual. They do not mind this arrangement as they believe that the remos belong only to the sun, sky and the mountains. However, with the mobilization of few Bondas into the tea-gardens of Assam by the Christian missionaries and their constant interaction with the plains people, the Bondas are slowly introduced to the concept of money. Their ignorance in the field of economics makes them an easy target for both the sahukars and the Domb people. The sahukars exploit the goti system to their advantage and the Domb people convey a higher price for a purchased product to the Bondas. The sarkar in the garb of their development carpets and re-carpets roads, opens schools with no buildings, appoints teachers with no requirement of attendance, and build housing complexes named Indira Awas that never stand the test of time. These yardsticks of development are never assessed by the standards of the Bonda nor are they ever implemented keeping in mind the requirements of the Bondas. In fact, they are specifically aimed to cater to the western models of development and to fill the pockets of the government officials.

The new leader of the Bonda Development Project, Bijoy Bal, orders the felling of valuable teak trees "to make chairs, sofas, dining tables and desks" (263) for his office. He also imports exotic flowers from nurseries in Cuttack and Bhubaneswar, sets in power lines to install an electric bulb in his residence, shuts the tailoring workshop and starts the carpet weaving centre that does not use indigenous material but imports raw material from far-away cities. The aim of the Bonda Development Project is to civilize Bondas, educate them and include them into the mainstream populace. However, all it is reduced to: "If the Bonda had learnt the value of money it had to be admitted that the project was a success" (202). A divide is imitated in the Bondas based on the wealth amassed by each. When the time comes to allot the Indira Awas houses to the Bondas the government representatives ask he Bondas, "Who among you is poor?...Who is the poorest?" (248). The plan is to allot the houses only to the poorest Bondas, so that at the time of inspection, the higher officials are impressed by the scale of development. Conversely, the Bondas respond, "There is no poor among us Bondas. What is 'poor'? To which caste does he belong? We don't need your gulang houses! Go way and leave us in peace, you Khangars!" (248). To succeed their plan, the sarkar babus, finally start to offer money for settling in the new houses; this offer few accept as bogged down by the loans of shahukars, they don't have much to survive on. Hence, the "Bondas are divided into the rich and the poor. Those who lived under thatches and those who lived under tin roofs" (249).

Pratibha Ray's *The Primal Land* evaluates the cause of the tribals in a world that is fast changing its dynamics to suit the "better life" perspective of western notions of development. The Bondas who believe that the "...

remo [who] falls from the yong's womb into the Earth Mother's lap clutching hunger and death in his fist" in the end of the text asks the question, "But who was responsible? The stones and the bricks of Indira Awas?" (297); consider nature as a giver, the protector and the preserver. But when their bond with nature is questioned in order to provide him the clothing of civilization, he is left helpless and disappointed. Adibari, the first woman to leave traditional Bonda clothing to wear a sari and keep long hair is ultimately left by the proprietors of "better life" to survive on the mercy of a sexual pervert who exploits her on the pretext of giving her a roof. She is made to abandon her new-born in the woods, something never ever heard of in the Bonda community. She lives with the hope that upon her death, "… spirit will return to the mountain… I cannot go back into the sacred land to pollute it with my presence" (199). On the other hand, Sombari Toki, the second woman to wear a sari, returns back to her tradition disgruntled by the false promises of development: "Which babu from the city would have come to marry me? Can any city babu be trusted? That was the mistake Adibar Toki made. My place is here, with my people. You can do nothing for us" (205). The third Bonduni to accept sari, Mangli "remained unmarried, clinging to both her sari and the mountain where she had been born" (209).

Another important issue that emerges is the loosing of one's identity when in acceptance of the commandments of progress. For the characters of Pratibha Ray, they are left dangled yearning to go back but transported to a mythical place that lies between the civilized and the uncivilized. When Soma Sirsa calls for help from his fellow Bonds, he is told: "He is not one of us now, because he is educated. But the city babus do not want him as he is a Bonda. He belongs to no one…" (210). The identity of the Bondas is strongly woven in their interaction with nature. They wear a small piece of cloth, survive on natural produce and are content with their life. Their edenic existence allows them to be a part of the ecological existence. The flora, fauna and the air are their strongest ally and they worship them with utmost devotion. These traditions have helped them survive for numerous decades. However, in the name of civilizing them, the proprietors of progress take away their beliefs, faiths, traditions, customs and attire. Since the Bondas are illiterate they cannot understand the real meaning of progress and blindly follow the gulang babus in the hope of "better life". Ironically, they are unaware of the meaning of the words "better life" and chase a dream that finally turns out to be nightmare for their tribe.

To suffice, the text questions the pace of development and re-defines the meaning of progress for the indigenous. It is a statement against the hazardous effects of western model of development on the indigenous ecology along with sending a lucid message that for the survival of tribal race the models of development and the euphemisms of "better life" need to be positively structured.

Works Cited

Devi, Mahasweta. "The Author in Conversation." *Imaginary Maps*. Trans. Gayatri Chakravorty Spivak. Calcutta: Thema, 2001. i–xvi.

Gupta, Vandana. *Mahasweta Devi: A Critical Reading*. New Delhi: Creative Publications, 2009.

Guha, Ranajit, ed. *Subaltern Studies IV–Writing on South Asian History and Society*. New Delhi: Oxford University Press, 1985.

Huggan, Graham and Hellen Tiffin. *Postcolonial Ecocriticism: Literature, Animals, Environment*. USA: Routledge. 2010.

Marx, Karl. *Karl Marx: Selected Writings*, 2nd edition. David McLellan (ed.). Oxford: Oxford University Press, 2000.

Ray, Pratibha. *The Primal Land*. New Delhi: Orient Blackswan Pvt. Ltd., 2001.

Chapter - 24

Appropriation of Mythic Women through the Lens of Counter-Narration in Divakaruni's *The Palace of Illusions* and Parameswarans *Sita's Promise: A Dance Drama*

Anupama Rai

Chitra Banerjee Divakaruni was born in India. After her marriage, she migrated to the U.S.A, and built her career in the literary and non-literary domain. Her creative oeuvre comprises a diverse body of writing, both in terms of genre and themes of writing, ranging from *The Mistress of spices*, *Queen of Dreams*and *Sister of My Heart*, to the well-known collection of short-stories *Arranged Marriage* and *The Unknown Errors of Our Lives* etc. Expectantly, for her works, she acclaimed numeral awards and honors including the PEN Oakland Josephine Miles Prize and the Bay Area Book Reviewers Award for fiction. Similarly, Uma Parameswaran was also born in India, and later on, moved to U.S.A. and finally to Canada. Likewise Divakaruni, her creative output is extensive one which includes works from various genre of writing like *Trishanku* (poems), *Sons Must Die and Other Plays*, *What was Always Hers*, *The Sweet Smell of Mother's Milk-Wet Bodice*, *Sisters at the Well* (poems) and *Riding High with Krishna.*

Moving to the topic of discussion, out of the existing definitions of myth, there is one definition given by Marian Webster dictionary of English language, which defines myth in the simple words. According to it, the word myth is derived from a Greek word "Muthos", which stands for the story-telling tradition, and for the set of beliefs of a particular sect that is also in an exaggerated form and formulation. Similarly, its scientific study is known as mythology, and its strong oral tradition somehow directly correlates it with the history of human existence whereas, some scholars have directly co-relate it with story, and try to establish a direct link between the myth and story. Further, others have tried to condense it to a single unit of literary discussion and debate, by attributing purgatory and diagnostic purpose to the anatomy of myth, as it is elaborately discussed by Aristotle in his *Poetics*. In the lieu of it, *Sita: An Illustration of the Ramayana* is worth quoting, as it proclaims, "The story pours out in different ways, in different tongues, different words, different nuances and different emotions. Sometimes, it is poetry, sometimes prose and sometimes just a gesture" (Pattanaik xi). Moving to the other definitions of myth, some litterateur have found a strong co-relation between the culture of a community and myth, and sum up"

> Myth fulfills in primitive culture an indispensable function, it expresses, enhances, and codifies belief; it safeguards and enforces morality; it vouches for the efficiency of ritual and contains practical rules for the guidance of man. The myth is thus a vital ingredient of human civilization; it is not an idle tale, but a hard-working active force; it is not an intellectual explanation or an artistic imagery, but a pragmatic charter of primitive faith and moral wisdom. (Malinowski 100-101).

Undoubtedly, a glance at the formative influence of the mythic tradition is enough in itself to arrive at the conclusion that it stimulates scholars to culminate a new trend of writing in the garb of 'contemporize the past' or 'radicalization of the past' in literature, which has flooded the literary domain with multiple discourses. In a similar fashion, Hans Robert Jauss has succinctly tried to capture the nerve with the assistance of his theorem 'horizon of expectation' which propounds, "A literary work is not an object which stands by itself and which offers the same face to each reader in each period. It is not a monument which reveals its timeless essence in a monologue" (Cuddon 339). Similarly, it motivates littérateurs to contest the past in the light of Present. Following the trends of writing, there are certain writers, who not only add a novel meaning to the mythic characters but also, re-interpret mythic women characters to consolidate their points and positions, both in the domain of narration and notion. Again, it largely depends on the taste and type of readers, as there are two ways of reception of an artifact; one is "culinary (totally consumable) reading, and on the other, there are works which have casted seminal impact on the psyche of the readers" (Cuddon 339).

So far as the matter of women's representation in our canonical literature is concerned, the words of Adrienne Rich can turn out to be seminal to further clarify our vision in this context. For her "Re-vision,act of looking back seeing with fresh eyes, of entering an old text from a new critical direction is for women more than a chapter in cultural history. It is an act of survival" (Rich18). In Indian context, Nabneeta Dev Sen has expressed the same thing and promulgates:

> While reading the epics I have always felt that the place of women was very piteous in the world of male war poetry where bodily strength and valor was all. It was all the same whether she was considered a *Lakhshmi* the obedient one; or an *Alakhsmi*, the disobedient one who brings misfortune and misery. Whether Sita or Draupadi, Taraka, or Surpanakha, it was as if the women were born only to suffer misery. As if they had to pay with their suffering the price to prove the glorious valor of the heroes. Thus, it was that some stories came to be written (perhaps some more would be) about the women of the epics. The classical stories have not been changed, only some imaginary events have been associated. But, by the very nature of the stories, they have been dissociated at the end. Otherwise, the characteristics of the epic stories could have been altered. These stories merely offer the tint of alternate possibility in the mind of the readers (*Sita Theke Shuru* 9).

The paper attempts to unlace the mooted theme and meaning in the select work of Chitra Banerjee Divakaruni and Uma Parameswaran, whose writings attempt to unpack the literary objectives behind their literary endeavor. The potential issues of debate are, The politics of representation of mythic characters in our folk tradition in general, and women characters in particular, how their power and position are relegated to periphery, and if it is done, then what would be the impending reasons behind such presentation. The paper raises some pertinent questions like-Why are the writers interrogating traditional images of mythic women of our society? And if it is imperative, then what can be the possible repercussions of such literary debate? Why are they (mythic women) so much important to us, even after centuries of their commencement? How / How far are these women characters influential to direct our lives? Thus, the paper tries to find out some answers to the questions which are still need to be answered by scholars.

There are some key points of similarity and dissimilarity between the select texts of the paper. So far as the matter of genre is concerned, Divakaruni's *The Palace of Illusions* belongs to the genre of novel, while Uma Parameswaran's *Sita's Promise* is a dance-drama, both of which map the ideological shift of meaning of the text from the conventional to the unconventional one. The main reason behind the selection of the theme and writers is obvious and strong one, as it is directly related to my topic of research as well as of interest. Though, there are some points of differences which can be easily traced at the level of narration and methodology. For instance, both of them are representing the mythic women, but in different setting. Both try to re-narrate the earlier version of the text in a new form by applying their analytical and logical strands; Parameswaran's Sita represents the memories of past and present, while Divakaruni's Draupadi represents past in the light of the present.

In addition to this, the point can be easily elaborated through the words of Urmi, as she asserts,

> Neither feminism nor mythology is a modern construct. Strong feminist characters have long been the hallmark of Indian mythology. In fact, a famous ancient verse brings together quite a fiery bunch...the five maidens from the Indian epics:
>
> Ahalya Draupadi Kunti Tara
> Mandodari tatha/ Panchakany
> Smaranityam mahapataka nashaka (n.p.).

The lines connote multiple things about the women characters who are capable of escorting others, directing the course of lives of many, pacing the emancipation and elimination of their sins, and acting as the guardian of the weak. They are famous among us by names such as Ahilya, Draupadi, Kunti, Tara, and Mandodari. So far as the purpose of the writing is concerned, the texts are powerful enough to proclaim the potentiality of the women characters which is deliberately incorporated by Divakaruni and Parameswaran in the persona of Draupadi and Sita. For example, Divakaruni's Draupadi at the very starting of narrative declares:

> I couldn't breathe, I would go to my nurse and ask for a story. And though she knew many wondrous and edifying tales, the one I made her tell me over and over was the story of my birth. I think I liked it so much because it made me feel special, and in those days there was little else in my life that did. Perhaps Dhai Ma realized. (P I01).

For instance, there is a bulk of Indian women, who still observe fast, and celebrate festivities like 'Vat Savitri Pooja' 'Tulsi Vivah' etc. under the impression of the mythic women. One such event was covered by my colleague, Nausheen, who is a research scholar from the department of history at Banaras Hindu University, and her research work centers on 'the inextricable relationship between the festivals and Hindu myths' especially from Awadh region of Uttar Pradesh. During the recording of the event, we had observed that these women had a staunch faith in the saga of Savitri who was still there among them, according to them, in intangible form. She hoisted the flag of dedication, determination, love, sacrifice and productivity among them. The image of ideal woman stems from Indian mythic tradition, since woman stands for "An image of womanhood that has a profound effect on the Indian psyche is that of Sita, the heroine of India's most beloved epic, the Ramayana. Sita's chastity, obedience, and unflinching loyalty to her husband represent the ideal path for an Indian wife (Rangaswamy 145). Moreover, there is a proper method of the festivity celebration with slight differences in the manner of observation, which can be easily perceived among the different parts of India and the differences often times ascribe to the differences of time and place of observation.

The other side of such practice can be sum down to following proposition that patriarchy has consolidated its position in the society through the myths of Savitri and Sita. It has often tried to manipulate the sexual independence and liberty of Draupadi through the creation of many sub-narratives which are directly related to the backdrop of her choices and of her sexual freedom. Yet scholars have produced multiple-versions of theirs keeping the strong-hold of Draupadi and Sita in the society. Though they are apparently pole apart, still there is some sort of co-relation between these two. For example, manner of their birth is the first point which establishes a direct bond between them. Both of them are not biological children of their parents, as the first one is directly heralded into the world of ours from the womb of the fire, while the second is born out of the womb the earth that shows their independent individuality.

Moving to the next point of similarity between Sita and Draupadi, which can be certainly marked down in the very manner of their birth, as "two epic heroines parallel each other in their birth from the sacrificial altar, *yajnavedi* (Draupadi) and the altar ground, *devayajana* (Sita). Again, the Puranas celebrate each as the destructive "Shakti' of her era; Sita of Treta Yuga and Yajnaseni of Dvapara" (Pradip Bhattacharya 108). Both of them are named after their father which again points out the heavy burden of patriarchy on their shoulders; Draupadi is known after the king Draupad (her father), whereas Sita is named after her father Janak, the king of Janakpur. It indicates towards the general plight of women in the society where their individualities are often times considered subservient to their male counterparts, conversely their mother have minimal or least influence on their personalities. In spite of all these, these characters prove out to be influential at the different stages and steps of the narrative. Moreover, the fancy names, which are assigned to them, are strong enough to expose the stiffening system of patriarchy rooted deeply somewhere in the psyche of the characters.

The various epithets which are used by different characters of the narrative unfurl the saga of relegation before us. For example, Draupad considers his daughter as the "Off-spring of Vengeance, or the Unexpected One", and "The Girl Who Wasn't Invited" which force to ponder on the objectified self of Draupadi, while her brother is named as Dhristadyumna; "Destroyer of Enemies". On the contrary the writers have celebrated the notion of nurturing strongly through the creation of characters like Dhai Ma (PI) and nature (SP) as the fostering mother of the mythic women. In the narrative (PI**),** Dhai Ma belongs to a working class, so she dismantles the preconceived notions related to the concept of mother and class. Conversely Draupad's wife Sulochana maintains a distance, owning to Draupadi's fierce past, present and future. Similarly, Sita (SP) is born out of the womb of earth, and likely to feel very much close and attach to everything that belongs to the world of nature. In the drama, nature becomes the prime cause of her excursion.

The text (PI) challenges the rituals which have been used as mechanics of control to tarnish the image of Draupadi. Accordingly in Tamil culture and tradition, she is celebrated as one of 'Amman goddesses' who symbolize energy, power and justice, and mothering faculties, and capable of protecting their subject from evil power. Likewise, Draupadi is considered as the guardian spirit of the innocent and destroyer of the sinners. Draupadi epitomizes the mélange of contrary powers, since she symbolizes dual personality of a woman who stands for the subordinate section of the society like women, children, Dalit and disables, while slays her enemy by her intense-inner fury. It seems that Divakaruni has caught the clue to procure fiery image of Draupadi from celestial fire to "change the course of history" (PI), and later on, to transplant the very image of fire in her personality to magnify her demeanour.

Divakaruni's Draupadi dismantles the ideal notion of the princess and heroine of the epic tradition, as she is a dark skinned heroine. She considers herself as the second self of the lord Krishna who is also known after his black beauty, and adore by women folk for his dark complexion. This makes Draupadi exceptional who breaks the barriers of race and class, she proclaims:

> Perhaps the reason that Krishna and I got along so well was that we were both severely dark-skinned. In a society that looked down its

> patrician nose on anything except milk-and – almond hues, this was considered most unfortunate, especially for a girl. I paid for it by spending hour upon excruciating hour being slathered in skin–whitening unguents and scrubbed with numerous exfoliants by my industrious nurse (PI 8).

In the novel, her bonding with Krishna is beautifully delineated by the writer and her friendship becomes exemplary. In the novel like a true confidant, he counsels her and guides, "A problem becomes a problem only if you believe it to be so. And often others see you as you see yourself" (PI).She isn't ashamed of her body; instead she is represented as someone who loves to flaunt her body. But it doesn't mean that she isn't aware of her uniqueness which is somewhere consolidating her strong bonding with Krishna. For Krishna, "No one can shame you, he said, if you don't allow it" which leads her to confess, "I felt for Karna was a singing fire, Krishna's love was a balm, moonlight over a parched landscape" (PI 356). Lastly, she realizes, "I am beyond name and gender and imprisoning patterns of ego. And yet, for the first time, I'm truly Panchaali" (PI 360).

Similarly the character of Sita (SP) is re-interpreted in the light of the contemporary theories which prove to be a shaping power behind the physiological and psychological makeup of Parameswaran .The whole drama is divided into the eleven scenes where she has represented Sita as a cheerful young lady who is keen and eager to explore different land and their inhabitants. She has dragged the legends of the past to the frame of her present world, where she attributes novel meanings to the archetypical character of Sita. Traditionally, she is known after her submissive and dutiful nature, but here, she is transformed into a carefree and human like woman character of *Sita's Promise* without losing the gist of religiousness.

The titles of the works are thematically loaded with various motives and motions of their writers, because they have invested and incorporated various existential and contemporary analytical inquiry into the titles themselves. The both texts are bearing the eponymous titles and the stories move around the pivot of female characters, who are confronting alienation and detachment in their lives. The dichotomous condition of their lives shows that they can't abscond from their realities. However, their conditions directly correlate them with the fluid identities of their writers who are far away from their homeland, but striving hard to be rooted both in the adopted and ancestral land their own.

The existential dilemma of Draupadi and Sita are in fact representing the inner dilemma and the struggle of their writers who also attempt to establish a co-ordination between two worlds; adopted land and land of birth at daunt of their own. For them, the world is an illusion, and they are forced by circumstances to carry their pseudo-identities which are hard to carry, but impossible to discard. The mythological characters are exposing the "*Mythia*" (illusion) of the contemporary world, where characters like Draupadi and Sita are deliberately moving against their drive to fulfill their worldly duties. The princesses are in fact leading camouflage lives, where they have to suppress their desires under the banner of the honour and dignity of their families which pushes them toward the state of oblivion. Meanwhile, the dilemma glorifies the very character of Draupadi and Sita, instead of turning them into ashes; it regenerates them into a phenomenal character of their world, and regenerating them out of their own remnants.

Draupadi feels like a tenant at her father and husbands' house. The palace is very tantalizing and perturbing image for Draupadi, which forces her to ponder on her own lot. She states, "I imagined my own palace, the one I would someday" (PI 130). Eventually, she is so much obsessed with the image of palace that it becomes the cause of her suffering and agony, which again validates her human like stature. In the case of Sita, she travels from the one place to another to propagate the message of survival and migration. She is being respected at the different place and by people of the different culture and tradition. Her brief, but fruitful stay in the lake Agassiz is significant in the sense that it foregrounds the theme of integration, accommodation and assimilation in the world. It also suggests that she is quite aware of her ethnical, anthropological, historical and geographical realities which equate her with her author's conditions.

Parameswaran has invigorated a dominant tapestry of the past and present through the mélange of the myth and realities. Her character traverses every ordeal of her life with gravity and demeanour of her own without losing her senses. She confronts the problem of her life in dignified manner. And in her life, she has been on exile on the two different occasions, but every time it is her choice, not an imposition. She has been in the close contact with nature; it was behind her first exile which was present in form of the artificial attire of a golden deer, and second time in the form of an artic tern which had lost its way. In the persona of Sita, Parameswaran is narrating the saga of a modern diasporic woman who is passing through the multiple stages of her life in multiple geographical and historical backgrounds to construct her own saga in her own language.

Through the analogy of artic tern, Parameswaran has tried to create an opportunity for the re-construction of the myth of the past in the contour of the present which is delineated succinctly by her through the incident of Sita's return to the land of Himavan. For Rama defines it, "An artic tern that divides its time between to North and South Poles making this flight of twice ten thousand miles each year" (SP 50). Here the tern provides an opportunity to Sita to promise, "I promise the children, I shall come again to this love land of lakes and blue skies and snow. I through my people shall surely come again and we shall build our temples and sing our songs with all the children of all the different lands who make their home" (SP 62).

In the novel Draupadi vociferously expresses her love and desire for Karna, and at times she does compare her husbands with her secret and unfulfilled love. She utters, "An insidious voice inside me said, Karna would never have let you suffer like this" (PI 99). For her, inner serenity and compassion is more important thing in her life than the shallow glamour and sparkle of a princess's life. She can sense the puffed and powdered realities of her palace where she doesn't able to relate herself with the people. She desires:

> When I had my own palace, I promised myself, it would be totally different. I closed my eyes and imagined a riot of colour and sound, birds singing in mango and custard apple orchards, butterflies among jasmines, and in the midst of it- but I could not imagine yet the shape that my future home would take. Would it be elegant as crystal? Solidly precious, like a jewel studded goblet? Delicate and intricate, like gold filigree? I only knew that it would mirror my deepest being. There I would finally be at home (PI 7).

The character of Sita and Draupadi are synonymous to their writers in the sense that they are caught in between the mirage of their dual identities, and find themselves locate like glabella between the eyes. Further Parameswaran had promulgated the term "Trishanku" to exemplify her unique position to describe the uniqueness her identity.

Inbothof the texts, the characters propagate the ultimate truth of the human existence, and every incident of their lives can be a lesson for the whole humanity .The texts are posing some valid, but vital questions before us to meditate on; how to lead your life in peace and harmony? What can be the possible repercussion of the act of vengeance? How would we make a sense of the things out of chaos? And lastly, how to accept the realities of your lives? For example, at one point of the narrative, Rama utters that "It is not for man to know his future. Man has been given memory so he can learn from the past, but he has not been given eyes to see into the future because it is best he accepts each day as it comes..."(SP 51). Draupadi's saga of vengeance verifies that she seems to be one among us, and her flaws and faults are very humane in nature which can be further validated by the yard stick of practicality. After her disrobing in the royal-court, she is incessantly living at the sharp end of thorns, which instigates her to take her revenge and remind her:

> What I'd suffered as a result in Duryodhan's sabha. Each night I recited the taunts of the Kauravasso that they stayed fresh in their minds. When we blew out our lamps, I tossed and turned on my bed, the rushes suddenly as hard as sticks, recalling Karna's face... Each dawn when I arose, sweaty with restlessness, I pictured our revenge, a fire-strewn battlefield, the air grim with vultures, the mangled bodies of the Kauravasand their allies-the way I would transform history (PI 199).

The act of disrobing is so much intense that it provokes the eminent scholar like Mahasweta Devi to re-narrate the saga in the garb of suffering of a tribal girl under the title of Dopti. From time to time, these characters have instigated scholar to re-interpret the realities of present in the light of the past of vice-versa. The texts count act of the creation and re-creation of mythology, folk tales and myths which is again bildungsroman saga of the central female characters. In the *Mahabharata* (Deadly war at the large scale) and Ramayana, there is a clash between the inner and outer world of these characters, whose lives are knotted in the subtext of the great epic narrative of India. Parameswaran is landing the contemporary scene and scenario on the stage through a concoction of the song, dance and drama, which is saturated in her indigenous mode and modulation of dramatic creation. Her dance drama is based on the mosaic of her memories. It opens with the invocation of Goddess Lakshmi, while music and dance pervade in the each and every scene of the drama. She is endeavoring to present the Indian Dramatic tradition, culture, dance and music before the rest of the world. Similarly, in the persona Divakaruni of Draupadi promulgates, "It was time I shook off my self-pity and did something. I resolved to form a separate court, a place where women could speak their sorrow to other women" (PL 323). She turns out to be a real savior (Amman Goddess) of widows of her city, and ensures the readers about the creation of a utopian world of women where they will be free, independent and safe from any sorts of dominance.

Works Cited

Aristotle. *Aristotle'sPoetics*. New York: Hill and Wang, 1961. Print.

Banerjee Divakaruni, Chitra. *The Palace of Illusions: A Novel,* London, Pan Macmillan, 2009.Print.

Bhattacharya Pradip. "Pancha Kanya" A Quest in Search of Meaning-Part II." *Journal of Human Values* 12.2 (2006): 107-136.

Chandra-Vaz, Urmi. "Indian Mythology is a New Medium of Choice for Feminist Narratives (and Its Working)". *Scroll.in.* 05 Feb. 2017, n.p. Web. 23 July. 2017.

<https://www.google.co.in/amp/s/amp.scroll.in/article/828515/indian-mythology-is-a-new-medium-of-choice-for-feminist-narratives-and-its-working.>

Cuddon, J.A. "Horizon of Expectation". *The Penguin Dictionary of Literary and Literary Theory*. Ed. UK: Penguin Books, 2014.

Diesel, Alleyn. "The Suffering Mothers: The Hindu Goddesses as Empowering Role Models for Women." Spec. Issue of *CSSALL*. 02 (2005): 35-59. Print.

Feder, Lillian. *Ancient Myth in Modern Poetry.* Princeton: Princeton University Press, 1977. Print.

Frye, Northrop. *Anatomy of Criticism*: *Four Essays*. Princeton, Princeton UP, 1957. Print. https://en.oxforddictionaries.com/definition/myth

Malinowski, Bronislaw. *Myth in Primitive Psychology.* New York: Norton, 1926. Print.

Parameswaran, Uma. *Sita's Promise: A Dance Drama*. New Delhi: Prestige, 1998. Print.

Pattanaik, Devdutt. Forward. *Sita: An Illustrated Retelling of the Ramayana*. By Pattanaik. New Delhi: Penguin, 2013. Print.

Rangaswamy, Padma. *Namaste America*. Pennsylvania: Pennsylvania State UP, 2000. Print.

Rich, Adrienne. "When We Dead Awaken, Writing As Re-Vision." *College English*. 34.1 Women Writing and Teaching. (Oct, 1972): 18:30. Web .10 April, 2018. Print.

Chapter - 25

Tracing the Distinctive Agendas of Dalits: The Socio-Political Injustice with Reference to Vijay Tendulkar's *Kanyadaan*

Abirami P.

Kanyadaan is one among the famous plays of Vijay Tendulkar. Tendulkar was a Marathi playwright and a social activist. His plays were mostly targeting the typical Indian society's discrimination and cruelty in the post independence and in the form seeking revolution and reformation for better future. Vijay Tendulkar was awarded the Saraswati Samman for the play *Kanyadaan*. Tendulkar himself says, "As its creator, I respect both Verdicts" because the most of the audience could not get the real purpose of this play. The audience misunderstood this play as anti-dalit play. To condemn both the play and the writer, they raised bad comments and thrown out their slippers to the artists while the play was staged. Vijay Tendulkar is famous for his controversies in the subject matters of his plays. *Kanyadaan* is the best example of the extreme controversy and sensitivity. The author himself stated about the play *Kanyadaan* is, "All my creative writing begins, not from an idea but from an experience, mine or somebody else's which then becomes mine. It was such an experience of another to begin with, that provided the starting point for *Kanyadaan*."

The social class system has followed since from the ancient India from the Vedic society as Varna according to the people's occupation as follows, Brahmins who are all being priests, scholars and teachers, Kshatriyas who are all being rulers, warriors and administrators, Vaishyas who are all being agriculturalists and traders and Shudras who are all labourers and service providers. These four classes have been following the professions by heritage and they have their own specific and suitable lifestyles. After the Vedic period, the four *varnas* have slowly demolished but the *jati* or caste system has emerged with thousands of branches. Commonly the socio-economic and political factors of the people were deciding factors of their status. The *varna* division is considered to be the positive division which helps them to ease their lifestyle. Contrastingly the caste or *jati* is the negative division which classifies people by their birth, colour and region. The people in the high ladder of the caste system were consciously suppressed those who are in the lower ladder of the caste. The caste ladder is consisting of socio-economical and political instrumentalities. Dalit or scheduled caste comes under the lower ladder.

In *Kanyadaan,* Vijay exhibits the upper caste Brahmin family and lower caste Dalit family to explore the controversial factors of their traditional and social behaviours. In 1983 when the play was first published the age old tradition of Brahmins were being strictly conservatives and deeply involved with religious ceremonies and customs. In *Kanyadaan*, the Brahmin couple was independent and ideal democrats. The protagonist of the play Jothy, being their daughter, brought up with independent lifestyle. Her parents' revolutionary ideas, especially her father's anti-caste ideologies, made up her mind to choose her life partner behind the social caste system. *Kanyadaan* produced with two Acts, five scenes and this has limited the characters.

The title *Kanyadaan* means that gift of a daughter. In Hindu tradition, the bride's parents give her to the bridegroom as a gift in the occasion of marriage. Traditionally the Hindu bride has no right to decide her life-partner either her marriage but here Jothy's case the Brahmin family accepts her life choice. While discussing about her marriage, Nath accepts blindly of Arun but her mother Seva asks tons of questions about Arun, his family, his occupation and his family's circumstances. As a mother, she insists her to analyze Arun's real behaviour and unhappy about Jothy's choice of partner only in the short period of time. But her infatuation and her father's anti-caste revolutionary ideology lead to her marriage with Arun.

Soon after the marriage, the scenario changed into tragedy. Arun, a Dalit young boy alike every other Dalit of seventies economically poor family background, unstable employment and brought up culturally diverse than a typical Brahmin family. Arun, alcoholic in the evenings and crosses his limits by scolding foul words and beating his wife Jothy. In his community consuming alcohol and using foul words are very common. But for Jothy, these are all cruel. Her inter-caste marriage is her own welcoming and self created problem to herself. When the two differently brought up person's tried to live together, these like problems are natural. In Jothy and Arun's case, they were diverse by two different cultures, customs and ideologies. Jothy's parents were educated, democrats, independent and they live beyond their caste system of Brahmins. They independently take part in their own interested areas like participating in rally, social welfare activities even in the other towns. They brought up their daughter as a democrat. As Nath says:

> ...Who stops you? We have democracy in this house and we are proud of it. Democracy outside and dictatorship in the home, we don't know these two-timing tricks...(P. 500).

By contrast to Jothy's family, Arun's parents were labourers, his siblings were uneducated and unemployed and they were all depends on Arun's earning for their survival.

The play, *Kanyadaan* depicts the problems of marriage and especially inter-caste marriage. This is more a play about the marriage customs and the modernity in marriage which doubles the problems in marriage life and less about the caste system in the society. This play could not show the discrimination and the ill treatment on the lower caste or Dalit people. Either this play has not given or insisted any of revolutionary thoughts or ideologies to improve the Dalit. This play is a story of a boy and a girl who got married of their independent choice of life and how they struggled and their burdens doubled because of their misunderstanding or overestimating each other and misjudgments in short period of time.

In the first layer, the author exhibits how the inter-caste marriages are in hard battle. Two couples in the play were presented with two different modes of life. Like a magnet if the Seva and Nath were south, Arun and Jothy were north. Contrasting lifestyles of the two different couples, the older couple also got married by their independent choice but they have similar interests and good understanding between them. They both were going out of town to do what they are interested in as a social activist. They respect each other genuinely and also their relationship. This is proven by Nath's words as:

> ... sending messages to one another cannot be called marriage. Isn't there a thing called co-existence? Eh? This is all too much of a rush, baba! This matter will have to be reviewed seriously sometime. (P.499).

Contrasting to the older couple, Arun and Jothy were two different persons have mostly dissimilarities. They have no proper understanding of their family, culture and their behaviours beyond everything; they have misunderstood of their individual identities. Psychologically a child can adopt and accept any form of culture and religion but for an adult, it is very hard to adopt new culture, religion and customs. This is the reality of Jothy and Arun's life. They were each individuals who were brought up in completely different and controversial cultural and traditional circumstances. She was admired by his poetry, not by him. He was interested on her because she is civilized, educated and earning. He needs her for his better survival and she was in living in the world of imagination of his poems. She said that she can do anything for him of his autobiographical poetry. Those literary skills and imaginary descriptions admired her a lot. When they joined together, their differences created the problems on their life and made their marriage complicated.

And in the second layer he focused on how the male and female characters struggle over their lives in different ways. In *Kanyadaan*, Jothy was beaten and abused by her husband and her earnings were goes under his control. She was beaten to worse to the extent of taking treatment in the hospital. Physically weak female has struggles to overcome this physical abuse of her husband. Like the common saying, female are emotionally fools, this is true in Jothy's case too. She accepted his husband and agreed to live together even after he mistreated and beaten her worse. In the other side Arun a male, he worked part time to his family's survival and to meet out the expenses of his studies. He was taken all the burdens of his family in his one shoulder. This is the case for many of the middle-class people who took all the family's responsibilities on their shoulders. That definitely led them to depression and alcoholism like Arun.

In the third layer, author gives a clean view on the caste system and its culture as a symbol or identity of their upbringing. India has created a huge distance and difference between people on the basis of caste and there is a custom of ill-treating the so-called lower caste people just because their birth is completely condemnable. In the sixties and seventies of India, the government systems were radically changing and people's life also in every dimension. The caste system is restricting the scheduled caste people in the name of their birth in a low-caste. To develop them from their lower status, the government has introduced reservation and subsidiary government schemes on each and every discipline of government and non-government sectors.

My personal opinion is that the caste system has almost diminished and has gone in most of our society. The leaders of the world have truly changed the state of lower caste into the common status. Abraham Lincoln demolished black slavery and in this twenty-first century the black Obama served as the president of the United States. In India too Dr B.R. Ambedkar like many other activists and leaders worked extensively and changed the black mark or negative aspect of looking at the lower caste people. We can see the lower caste people are shining and ruling in every department. The change has taken quite a lot of centuries but the struggles and efforts of anti-caste leaders are responsible for the success.

In this twenty-first century, nation has grown and accepted the people beyond their birth, color, culture, language, profession, and region. India had been governed by other religious people such as Dr A.P.J. Abdul Kalam is a Muslim and a scientist, Dr Manmohan Singh is a Sikh and a professor, and our current Prime Minister is a typical middle-class man and does not hold a degree. To the best example of all for the demolition of patriarchal and caste system of India is four times elected Chief Minister of Uttar Pradesh, Mayawati. She is a lady who broke all the patriarchal norms of the society and she is the Dalit lady who doubles her credit to rule the people beyond her birth mark. She is not the only one for this developed and nurtured society. Today's nation is modern and it is flexible enough to hold every diversion in one salad bowl for human prosperity.

Works Cited

Andelwar, Savita Laxmanrao. *"Vijay* Tendulkar's *Kanyadaan*: A Study in Social Transformation". *The Context*. Vol. 4 Issue 3 (January 2018).

Budholia, O.P. "Sociometric Adjuncts: Dalit Consciousness in Vijay Tendulkar's *Kanyadaan.*" *The Literary Herald: An International Refereed English E-Journal*. Vol.1. Issue. 2 (September 2015).

Tendulkar, Vijay. *Collected Plays in Translation*. New Delhi: Oxford University Press, 2004. Print.

Chapter - 26

Neoteric Dalit Ecoaesthetic Subaltern Rebellious Voice as Depicted in Bama's "Annachi": An Analysis

A.P. Pavithra Bhuvaneshwari

The only way to deal with an Unfree world is to be come So absolutely free that your Very existence is an act of Rebellion.

– Albert Camus

The creation of all things in the world including it is ascribed in the Bible, the Bhagavad-Gita and the Quran to God. This absolutely free and for infinite wise reason, he especially created man in this world. God has given man only the inestimable wealth resources to survive in the earth; still the man's unexpected death arrives. Man sustains and survives himself in the world using the God given wealthy resources even without the conscious that why he was created by God and made to be born in this earth. The sumptuous resources are given equally by God to all who are also created by God.

Men ignore themselves from gaining the knowledge that God has provided five senses to all men equally whom he created. Man utilizing his five senses, he defines and illustrates the world with his own created (i.e.) manmade prejudice philosophy such as man and woman, black and white, rich and poor, master and slave, employed and unemployed, literate and illiterate, normal and abnormal. They erected and molded an indestructible wall of prejudice philosophy with the broken rocks of universal equality and painted it by racism, inequality and caste system. The philosophies such as Marxism, communism and egalitarianism grew like a tree to give a fruit of equality to the world. The men in the world uproot those philosophies of tree with his sturdy axe of ambitious prejudice philosophy.

The flu of prejudice philosophy in the form of inequality, caste system, discrimination, racism, chauvinism etc. is spreading wide over the world. Predominantly, the flu of casteism and discrimination inaugurated its origination in India from ancient time onwards. As a consequence of this malignant flu, there spreads the disease of untouchability, discrimination, dalit discrimination, inequality by inferiorsing and dividing the position of human in the country. This disease has its core effect still this twenty-first century and it is evidenced through the recent news posted on June 15, 2019 in the Newspaper *The First Post*. The news bears the title "Casteism in Gujarat: Dalits across Hundreds of Villages Can't Get a Haircut Due to Year of Expression". The news moves on as mentioned below:

> Dalit men have been denied haircut by barbers in village of Gujarat. This is made common as a discriminatory practice followed so many years. It was only in mid-2018, that some Dalit youths from Trent village in Mandal Block of Ahmedabad district decided to complain to the block panchayat about this form of discrimination. But despite authorities, the barbers refused to cut the hair of Dalit youths. In fact, they preferred to close the shop instead of cutting the hair of Dalit youths. These cases of atrocities have been increasing in Gujarat, which have increase seventy percent. One of the men who was the part of the protest at Trent village against the barbers for their refusals to cut dalit men's hair, Ashok Parmar (26) said, "The barber shops in our village are still closed for Dalits. They only cut hairs of OBC's and other general caste men's either in their home or in his house." (*The First Post* June 15, 2019).

The instance and occurrence is a massive level and an act of shameful charge for Gujarat where Mahatma Gandhi was born and he is the man who was holding off specific number of campaigns to end the social boycott and discrimination of Dalits and Tribal people. And not only this, Gujarat is a place where our Prime Minister Narendra Modi started his political journey as a chief minister and it is the most sentimental place for Modi. Since it is unfair to say that they are aware that caste-based discrimination is against human right and is unquestionably, something, which Indian society should be ashamed of. Yet, this practice continues in Gujarat and the state claims to be a modern and progressive state in India.

To abolish casteism, so many NGO's, writers and social activists in each state aroused and through their programs and autobiographical narratives, they unearthed the feeling of suppression, oppression, and subjugation which bombarded their lives. In the words of modern critic

Raj Kumar, "Dalits apart from being "untouchable" they were also "un seeable" "un approachable" and un hearable y most upper caste communities".

Those details engrave themselves with a sharp weapon of casteism and climbed the steps of education to gain and promote awareness to reclaim their human dignity and self-respect. Those writers and social activists arise like a fountain from the dry land of casteism where they fertilize themselves as well as their people through their writings and activities where they have always been insisting and laying a rigid foundation of truth and power. Indian society is primitively caste-orientated which is formulated by man, not by God or Goddess of Hinduism.

The sweetness of modern education had been flavored on the post-Independence Indian Dalits who recognized the potentiality of education in an additional way of thinking and organized a new literary movement. The movement started in Maharashtra, the homeland of Ambedkar. It is important to realize that Ambedkar had established the people's society in Bombay in 1945, and started Siddharth College hoping that education would explore a new platform for Dalits. His famous call "educate" "unite" and "agitate" was being spiritedly followed by Dalit group of writers.

The seed of Dalit literary movement was sown by Dr B.R. Ambedkar and then little by little, it sprouted and laid a deep penetrating root and finally, it grew into a huge Baniyan tree which not only gives shelter by creating and promoting self-respect among Dalits but also lifts up dalit consciousness and Dalit aesthetics among the writers emerging all over India.

Dalit writers penetrated and fixed a strong root and grew boldly where they kept a fierce step by challenging and interrogating the upper class domination in the new emergence of dalit literature in recent times. Few writers unmask the "dalit consciousness" through their autobiographical narratives. Such as Omprakash Valmiki's *Joothan,* Hazari's *Untouchable: The Autobiography of Indian Outcaste,* Laxman Mane's *Upura,* Vasant Moon's *Growing up Untouchable in India*, Susmita Bhave's *Pan on Fiery*, Bama's *Karukku* and Urmila Pawar's *The Weave of My Life*.

"Dalits Aesthetics" spring out, when Dalit communities in various Indian states have been producing literary works such as poems, short stories, novels, dramas, and autobiographies and signifying centric essence of untouchability, poverty, oppression of caste, repression and revolution. The fundamental aim of dalit literature is to furiously assassinate the man-made caste system and ideologies in Brahminical Hinduism. The aspirated hope of every dalit writer is to bring forth and lay standard basement of casteless society in India.

The term Dalit "Ecoaesthetic" which means ecology (i.e) dalit environment and aesthetic which surrounds dalit aesthetic where dalit environment and dalit aesthetics are unique idiosyncratic in itself because dalit literature is all about depicting, signifying, portraying, representing and epitomizing the every dalit individual and his life's encounter in a bowl of hot soup is shaped and carved in a realistic mode.

The dalit endure and confront certain painful events in his life such as crushing poverty, harassed ignorance economic exploitation and chained illiteracy, ceaseless rejection of human equal rights, pessmistic perception of stereotyped taboos is the situation which only dalits could witness from the deep of their mind and heart emotions.

"The Dalit environment and Dalit Aesthetics" could the understood and experienced and it could be delineated only by a dalit writer by birth. In the beginning, caste related issues were explored and analyzed by the non-dalit writers and reformers in the social area without even intensely realizing and apprehending the pure dalit point of view. Notwithstanding, in the literature of non-dalit writers, Dalits are always picturised as victims, suffers, loser, tragic fatalities and rarely as a rebellion, revolutionary, activist.

Those writers, who does not belong to dalit community, and are progressive and revolutionary writers like Premchand, Mulk Raj Anand, T.S. Pillai, N.S. Khandekar and several others depict dalits under the grudge of sentiments tied up with emotions of anger, pity, and melancholy which are the predominant and supreme feelings of dalit. Non-dalit writers portray their life based on their sympathetic and empathetic feelings.

Dalit Literature arises from a cultural conflict, where the significant mode of a dalit writer is to bring forth the changes in India through his revolutionary writing in a rebellion tone. A dalit writer wants equality and social justice. It should be done to everyone including the poor and the downtrodden. According to many dalit writers, only a dalit writer by birth can have the sensitivity and genuine that is dalit aesthetic writer. In the words of Tarachand Khandekar:

> Dalit writing by dalit writers is as a letters of their own blood. They are the natural outburst of the feelings and thought that have been denied expression for a long time.

The writings of dalit writers are the faithful outcome of their life's exploit encounters where they feel that their rational visions and reactions should be remolded into art which truthfully signify the raw dalit aesthetic sense in a pure way without adding any substitute identity and essence in it. Dalit writers accurately and originally bring forth their lives, environment and situations interconnected with their dalit character. These writers are creating a new dalit environment with a dalit aesthetic sense based on the ideas of liberty, equality, and human freedom.

In furtherance to make their rebellious voice heard, Dalit writers have operated with all literary forms, such as dalit poetry, dalit autobiography, novels, short stories, and drama using their own carved dalit language and dalit ecoaestheics is clearly viewed as dalit environment and experience which could be honestly fulfilled by a dalit wrier which this concept of dalit ecoaesthetic is applied to the dalit writer Bama's short story "Annachi" in Tamil "Kusumbukkaran". The protagonist of this short story is a rebellious person who is not violent but uses his tongue as a violent weapon comically as a word play to the arrogant upper community masters. Through this rebellious protagonist Bama brings out the dalit conscious and captures depicting the dalit environment and use of her dalit language in her short story "Annachi" brings out the concept of dalit ecoaesthicism.

Bama, also known as Bama Faustina Soosairaj, is a Tamil Dalit feminist writer. As a committed teacher and novelist, she rose to fame with her autobiographical novel *Karukku* (1992) which revolves around the joys and sorrows experienced by dalit Christian women in Tamil Nadu. Subsequently, she wrote two more novels *Sangati* (1996) and *Vanman* (2002) along with two collections of short stories *Kusunbukkaran* (1996) and *Oru Thattyum Erumaiyum* (2003).

Bama was born in 1958 as a Faustina Mary Fatima Rani in Roman Catholic family belonging to Paraiyar community from Pudhupatti near Chennai. Later she accepted "Bama" as her pen name. Bama's ancestors were from the dalit community and worked as an agricultural labourer. It was the dalit background and environment of Bama as a dalit writer incorporated her tragic encounter in her novels. But in this short story "Annachi" she rises out the rebellious tone in a revolutionary mode. She had a determined feel for her people and writes about her own parents and ancestors as a labourer in the upper caste field. She expertly captures the dalit environment and paints it by her local dalit language of her place and addresses the hypocrisy of the caste system.

The title of the short story *"Annachi"* is a respectful term "elder brother". The story surrounds around young dalit youth called Ammasi who is quiet the hero and the hero worshipper among the youth and a great deal of disturbance and nuisance among his family and community people, and a "scorpion sting" among the upper caste community people from the lines of the story as follows:

> This fellow seems to be a mischievous one. Though his father and mother were such innocents, looks how this donkey born to them had grown to be such a nuisance". Even as Madathi said this with a great deal of anger, Muthurathinam went further. "The boys from that family are all like this. This others at least you can adjust to but this Ammasi, no adjustment possible in his case, such a head strong fellow!
>
> (Bama's "Annachi").

Bama creates a dalit environment through the names of the characters, village names and by expressing the physic of Ammasi in their language where the reader could bring the picture of village and characters in front of their eyes. The names of the characters are Thayamma, Madathi, Muthurathinam, Irulayi, and the dalit environment language and words have been used such as Emma, Kenda Fish Smile, Kamma Bank, Eimachan, Koolh, Elai, Netiyakallu, Ayya, Adey, Eppa, Chinnayya, Annachi.

Bama's sense of dalit aesthetics revolves around the dalit young youth called Ammasi who is quite the hero among the young and thorn in the flesh of elders of his community. He has a strong sense of self and asserts his rights to face the upper castes. Bama compiles two instances in the story in the first instance; he refuses to get up in the bus to give his seat to the landlord whose field his father works. Bama's rebellious tone voiced through the tone of Ammasi as follows:

> "Still sitting, even after recognizing me? Get up, let me sit." I said I will get down at Nettiyakallu and I will keep sitting then. You can sit after that.
>
> "Elai... Nettiyakallu is right here, okay? Get up da, and stand aside While you Ayya is standing".
>
> "You said Ayya? My Ayya is working in Chandra sekran field at this very moment. When did you become my Ayya? I will not get up even if you stand on your head!"
>
> (Bama's "Annachi")

The second instance Bama created is the conflict between Ammasi and Jayshankar Naicker for calling him "Annachi" as elder brother. The Naicker was full of black rage that a low caste boy called him, the upper caste men as Annachi as a blood relative. This conflict finally ended with Ammasi use of an abusive word against Naicker. This made Naicker call for panchayat in order to punish Ammasi. But Ammasi in the panchayat boldly and courageously faced the panchayat and made everyone awe-struck with his intellectual and self-knowledge argument it is as follows:

> Ammasi too, responded gravely, "There's nothing wrong with what I said. Did I call him mama Machan, trying to create relationship and asking for the hand of girl? I only called him "Annachi" elder than me. If he is younger I call him "Thambi".
>
> (Bama's "Annachi")

Bama concludes the story in the old woman Poovathi's voice that the philosophy of universal equality is told through the funny proverb. As it follows:

> It is just what the old woman Poovathi, says, when a donkey shits is there a difference between what it shits first and what it shits last?`Shit is shit. All men are just men, so saying Ammasi is walked away.

To conclude, it may be admitted rather undoubtedly that the concept of dalit ecoaesthetic is discussed with Bama's "Annachi" where the protagonist Ammasi is depicted as a revolutionary person who reacts against upper caste communities and it clears project the dalit environment with conflicts, name of person, addressing, the person and places. And hence it culminates with a point that only a dalit writer by birth could use the fruit of dalit ecoaesthetics in their writings.

Works Cited

Ambedkar, B.R. *The Untouchables - Who Were They and Why were They Become Untouchables?* (1948). New Delhi: Prestige Books, 1998. Print.

Aston, N.M. *Dalit Literature and African Literature*. New Delhi: Prestige Books, 2001. Print.

http://en.m.wikipedia.org>wiki.

https://pratillpi.in> annachi-Bama

https://sotosay.word press.com>...

Lalmungthani Melody, *"From Oppression to Liberation through Education". Critical Essays on Dalit Literature.* Ed. D. Murali Manohar. New Delhi: Atlantic, 2013. 10-18. Print.

Mukherjee, Alok. Reading Sharankumar Limbale's *Towards an Aesthetic of Dalit Literature: Histories, Controversies and Consideration*. New Delhi: Orient Black Swan, 2010. Print.

Rajkumar. *Dalit Literature and Criticism, Literary / Cultural Theory*. New Delhi; Orient Black Swan: 2019. Print.

—. *Dalit Personal Narratives: Reading Caste, Nation and Identity*. New Delhi: Orient Black Swan. 2010. Print.

Chapter - 27

African American Sojourn – An Attempt to Subvert the Literary and Power Traditions of the Dominant Culture

Dr S. Jayanthi

African-American literature is written by African-American writers of African origin and it focuses on the themes which are, directly or indirectly, related with the theme of racism, slavery, identity crisis and struggle for freedom. The female Black writers' contribution is very significant in African-American literature. African-American literature can be defined as works by the people of African descent who have been the resident of the United States of America. This literature highlights the problems of black people, their hardships, culture, and history. The writers of African-American literature were a very sensitive realist, that's why they took those social and racial issues which were directly related with the life of the people. Inequality was one of the major problems at that time because the Black people were the victim of the Apartheid and the slavery has made the lives of the people very miserable. African-American literature constitutes an important part of the African diasporic literature. This literature is different from the post-colonial literature because it has been written by those writers who were living in the same nation and belonged to a minority group.

African-American literature traces its origin to the works of the late 18th century writers such as Phillis Wheatley, Gwendolyn Brooks, Fredrick Douglass, Paul Laurence Dunbar, Charles R. Johnson, James Baldwin, Fran Ross and Derrick Hughes. It flourished during the period of Slave Narratives and the Harlem Renaissance. Many Black authors such as Alice Walker, Toni Morrison, Ralph Ellison, Maya Angelou and Ntozake Shange etc. are considered the main writers of the United States. African-American

Literature is an important ingredient of American literature. It explores the pains and problems of the Black marginalised people.

African-Americans were considered incapable of intellectual production and their works were not acknowledged. This inspired Black writers to prove that they also have the equal rights like other European American authors. Henry Louis Gates, Jr. opines in this context, "...It is fair to describe the subtext of the history of black letters as this urge to refute the claims that because blacks had no written traditions they were bearers of an inferior culture" (44). However by refuting the claims of dominant culture, African-American writers were showing their writing skills and were trying to subvert the literary traditions of the state and it give more room to the racial discrimination and identity crisis.

African-American literature presently exists as a unique entity and it has its own place due to the autobiographical elements, unique style of storytelling and the strong voices of oppression and Marginalization. Both Jazz and hip hop are wonderful artistic examples and these were developed in isolation which eventually revitalized American culture. So far as African-American oral culture is concerned, it is rich in different genres and especially in poetry and has spiritual overtones, African-Americans gospel music, blues, and rap. All these kinds of characteristics and themes can be easily seen in different works in African-American Literature. It resists Western literary theory to analyze African-American literature. In this context Henry Louis Gates Jr., argues, "My desire has been to allow the black tradition to speak for itself about its nature and various functions, rather than to read it, or analyze it, in terms of literary theories borrowed whole from other tradition appropriated from without" (qtd. in Sinha and Ghosh 30).

Many African-American writers have tries to provide different horrendous and bitter experiences of African-Americans. The first two centuries of the African diaspora's sojourn in the United States of America were relates with the African-American folklore and Slave Narratives. The aim and objective of these Slave Narratives were to shed light on the pitiable plights of the Black people who were living their life under the heinous act of slavery. The abolition of the slave tradition was to bring forth the diabolic consequences, hazards and horrors of American slavery. Keeping all this in view, it was emphasized to abolish American slavery. Apart from it, African-American folklore gives additional insights into African-American thought.

William Wells Brown, Harriet Wilson, Martin R. Delany, Victor Sejour, George Moses Horton, Lucy Terry, Frances E. W. Harper and James M.

Whitfield are few writers who maintained, nurtured and developed American poetry spearheaded by a noted poet Phillis Wheatley. Wheatley was a revolutionary person who produced the proofs of her poetry in the court. Paul Laurence Dunbar, "the Poet Laureate of the Negro race", an appellation coined by Booker T. Washington, is kwon as the most important and signatory figure in the African-American literature after Wheatley and before the Harlem Renaissance of the 1920s and the 1930s. The era's most high-flying political figure was Washington, who gave contradictory remarks from Du Bois. Du Bois adopted more stimulating and challenging attitude to end racial discrimination, Washington believed that the Blacks also should be given equal status like other White woman.

In spite of the groundwork laid by earlier generations, a shift turn came in African-American literature because it was the time of development of art, culture and literature. There was a lot of development in intellectual field and political spheres. This period is also known with another name the New Negro Renaissance. The Harlem Renaissance developed a new kind of environment in America with the black cultural identity in fifteen years. It was the period of African-American art, culture and literature. This movement is related with few names such as Jessie Redmon Fauset, Langston Hughes, Wallace Thruman, Nella Larsen, Rudolf Fisher, Countee Cullen, Arna Bonlemps, and Zora Neale Hurston. James Weldon Johnson, Jean Toomer, and Charles S. Johnson were the mentors of this movement.

Langston Hughes' poetry is groundbreaking in African-American literature. His poetry collection *The Book of American Negro Poetry* (1922) was appreciated by many authors and critics of the time. The poetic works of Gwendolyn Brooks and Robert Hayden belong to the post World War II. Brooks became the first African-American to win the Pulitzer for her poetry, thus setting new standards for modernist poetry. Nikki Giovanni and Sonia Sanchez were other female poets well known during the 1950s and the 1960s. Giovanni's poetry is dynamic and dramatic which empowers her view on what it is to be black and to be a woman.

1960s and 1970s were two dynamic and productive decades in the history of African-American literature and the arts. In these years the black women artists and writers gave full vent of their emotions in their works of arts or in the novels and poetry. Black theater was also used by several black male and female artists as a literary vehicle to propel African-American literature into a new era.

Woman, the creator of life, a source of regeneration has in the present scenario found a voice to voice the voiceless. She has chosen a mode to give vent to her suppressed emotions and feelings. Helene Cixous says about *ecriture feminine* in "The Laugh of the Medusa". It is a bid to find a language to enable woman to analyse the injustices of patriarchy and women's resistance to them. She observes:

> Woman must write herself: must write about women and bring women to writing, from which they have been driven away as violently as from their bodies…woman must put herself into the text-as into the 1world and into history-by her own movement. (875).

Madhu Dubey argues in *Black Women Novelists and the Nationalist Aesthetic* (1994) that "…without the 'sheer possibility of blackness' that came out of nationalist thought, the focus of contemporary black authors on black community would be rendered most; a contemporary text's foregrounding of previously neglected issues more often than not argues for a cohesive black community, together varies from text to text" (112). In the works of Alice Walker, for example, one may find examples of her womanist aesthetic, which essentially calls for "black women, especially those most marginalized by race, caste, and class to have their voices heard and their histories read via literature and other forms of creative discourse" (112). In the pursuit of this aesthetic, Alice Walker revived the novels of Zora Neale Hurston in the early years of 1970. Neale Hurston's *Their Eyes Were Watching God* (1937) also is about the women and their position. Alice Walker and other women novelists' such as Toni Morrison, Ntozake Shange, Toni Cade Bambara, Maya Angelou, Audre Lorde, Gloria Naylor, Jamaica Kincaid, and J. California Cooper have given the clear glimpses of the themes and the contents of the Afro-American literature.

The Nobel Prize was conferred to Toni Morrison, the first African-American writer, for the first time. She has written many novels out of which *The Bluest Eye* (1970), *Sula* (1973), *Song of Solomon* (1977), *Tar Baby* (1981), *Beloved* (1987), and *Jazz* (1992) etc. are her best-selling and well-known novels. Frances Harper's *Iola Leroy* (1892) and Toni Morrison's *Tar Baby* (1981) are about the probelsm of black women and their marginalised position in the society.

Y. S. Sharadha's novel *Black Women's Writing* refers to Chris Weedon's *Feminist Practice and Post-Structuralist Theory*, where he makes a case for the appropriation of recent French theories of language and culture to analyse the injustices of patriarchy, which has falsified and distorted the female experience. In the light of these theories, women writers have created real images of women presenting sexual and social pressure with special accent. But the literature by women writers was unknown, neglected, and denigrated as it revealed a basic truth of African-American society. The 1960s saw a rise of militant theatre with Amiri Baraka to give voice to "the maligned *other*" (78).

Theatre has also played a main ole and it has cast a good impact on the minority class of America. The term "black theatre" is about the theatrical output of the black writers. Mance Williams holds the view in *Black Theatre in the 1960s and 1970s*:

> ...plays during the 1950s expressed a new form of protest, one that not only exhorted Black people to standing for their rights but warned whites that Blacks would settle for nothing less than their full share of the American Dream. (112).

From 1916 to 1935, there are nine main Black women playwrights who have written about the problems of the Black people. Alice Dunbar Nelson, Angelina Weld Grimke, Georgia Douglas Johnson, Mary Burrill, Myrtte Smith Livingston, May Miller, Ruth Gaines-Shelton, Marita Bonner and Eulalie Spence were the legendary figure of that period. These writers have dealt with the feminine perspectives and their works give a notion that a "New Negro" is emerging in America. These writers have focused on the One-Act play.

In the early years of American drama, the White playwrights used some Black images which supported slavery. Many Black playwrights have militated against such distortions fashioning their own truths about Blacks. The plays of black women between the 1950s and the 1980s portrayed the same themes as the black dramatists with a different view in a feminine perspective. Much different from the male writers Childress, Shange and Hansberry etc. have given a wide range of female characters and they have depicted them in a different way. Their heroines are bold and there is no submissiveness in their voice. Her heroines are much challenging and ground-breaking. These female characters present a different kind of image in the society.

Alice Childress, the first Black woman playwright, makes aware of the many sides of racism and prejudice and challenges blacks and whites to change it. *Florence* (1950), *Trouble in Mind* (1955), and *Wine in the Wilderness* (1969), are her important works. Lorraine Hansberry's play *A Raisin in the Sun* was staged in 1959 and the playwright got name and fame due to her writing skills. Hansberry became the first Black woman whose play was presented on Broadway. Lorraine Hansberry's play *A Raisin in the Sun* has its longstanding appeal of an American Dream and the family longs for a better life for them but their race becomes a hindrance. Three generations of women have been depicted in the play. Lena's husband dies and she starts heading her family. Walter's wife, Ruth shows resistance and she keeps revolting to her husband's ideology. Beneatha, a college student, never accepts the subjugated status of women in the society and she challenges Walter's patriarchal dominance.

Ntozake Shange, along with Alice Childress and Lorraine Hansberry, is an outstanding black woman playwright characterized by a vision typically feminine and dissimilar from of numerous black male dramatists of the period. In the book *Diving Deep and Surfacing: Women Writers on Spiritual Quest* Carol P. Christ writes:

> Shange is acutely aware of the nothingness experienced by women in a society defined by men. But Shange is also aware of a double burden of pain and negation suffered by women who are black in a society defined by white men – where black women are not even granted the ambivalent recognition some white women receive for youth and beauty or for being wives and mothers of white men. Shange's poem also reflects the double strength black women have had to muster to survive in a world where neither being black nor being woman is valued. (97).

She takes the lead from Hansberry and seems preoccupied with broadening the American theatre to include African rituals. Her theatre pieces generally do not conform to traditional dramatic structure and it is difficult to detect a noticeable progression of action or character. Addressing the issue of dramatic structure in Shange's pieces, Sandra L. Richards in her article "Conflicting Impulses in the Plays of Shange" states that her plays are a series of poetic monologues interrupted at times by conventional dialogue (75). As an African-American woman feminist and artist, she creates an effective poetic drama and has shown on the American stage that black females are worthy of heroic stature and literary exploration.

Thus, African-American writers have highlighted the problems of the African-American psyche through its literature. Theirs' is a different voice that makes the study strike a different note in terms of the genre selected and the narrative techniques used and their purpose as a writer. They make a call for the blacks to first understand themselves, and this self-understanding is considered to be the first step to drive them towards independence. These writings are intended to boost the self-confidence of the black brethren rather than self-hatred bordering on inferiority complex. It reveals an all-inclusive outlook that is quintessentially humane, non-discriminatory and edifying.

Work Cited

Christ, Carol P. *Diving Deep and Surfacing: Women Writers on Spiritual Quest.* Boston: Beacon Press, 1980. Print.

Cixous, Helen, Keith Cohen, and Paula Cohen. "The Laugh of Medusa." *Signs* 1.4 (Summer 1976): 875-893. Print.

Dubey, Madhu. *Black Women Novelists and Nationalist Aesthetic.* United States of America: Indiana University Press, 1994. Print.

Gates, Henry Louis. Jr., ed. *Race Writing and Difference.* Chicago: University of Chicago Press, 1986. Print.

Richards, Sandra L. "Conflicting Impulses in the Plays of Ntozake Shange." *Black American Literature Forum*, Vol.17 (Summer 1983): 73-78. Print.

Sharadha, Y. S. *Black Women's Writing: Quest for Identity in the Plays of Lorraine Hansberry and Ntozake Shange*. New Delhi: Prestige Books, 1998. Print.

Sinha, P.K. and Jagadish K. Ghosh. *History of American Literature.* New Delhi: Commonwealth Publishers Pvt. Ltd., 2011. Print.

Williams, Mance. *Black Theatre in the 1960s and 1970s.* Westport, Conn: Greenwood Press, 1985. Print.

Chapter - 28

When I Hit You: Marginalised Coming to the Fore

Dr Arti Chandel

Avadesh Kumar Singh shares the definition of "Marginalization" of International Geographical Union, as "The temporary sate of having been put aside of living in relative isolation at the edge of system (cultural, social, political or economic), in mind, when one excludes certain domains or a phenomenon from one's thinking because they don't correspond to the mainstream philosophy" (2). Literature expresses various discriminatory practices prevalent in society on the basis of social, political, economic, cultural and gender bias. *When I Hit You* or *A Portrait of the Writer as a Young Wife* is Meena Kandasamy's second novel. The text under study easily falls under the category of feminist writing, the way Meena depicts the struggle of an Indian wife to be a writer, to voice her experiences, along with the trauma of a marriage based in inequality, torture, brutality and violence, makes the novel more complicated and challenging, shaping it into a writing of the marginalised gender, *the second sex*. Earlier it was believed that nature not man is responsible for women's subjugation. Evelyn Reed views this as "a falsification of natural and social history. It is not nature, but class society, which lowered woman and elevated man. Man won his social supremacy in the struggle against and conquest over woman" (58-66).

The term Marginalization is inclusive of the group of people or a person that is forced to live at the margin or periphery of society due to cultural, historical, social, sexual or economic factors or reasons. "Man, as the Renaissance slogan had it, was the measure of all other things in the universe: while the Western norms of dress, behaviour, architecture, intellectual outlook and so on provided a firm centre against which deviation, observations, variations could be detected and identified as Other and marginal" (Barry: 67). As the story unfolds, the newly married young woman does not wish her imaginary lover to imagine her "as a woman with shining eyes furiously typing away something on a laptop, a something which she will erase as evening begins to stalk her doorstep" (98). The reason is that "That's the image of a wife as a writer" but she is "not a writer except in these brief snatches of time" (98). Here, the intense wish to be a writer is overtly expressed, yet it seems that wife and writer are two paradoxical, hence incompatible relationships. Moreover wife is not a relationship; rather it is a profession, which is to be fulfilled with competence and dedication.

R.S. Pathak rightly suggests that the marginal has no other option but to speak. "It has to speak, voice, not hide its tears, fears and angst and wrath in as many forms as possible. Tongue, if unused, is a fleshy burden, tentamounting to its own detonguing. Moreover, marginals cannot for long persist with their monologue of identity or difference. It has to disidentify itself and open itself to intervening positive influences for larger identity" (15). Voice or say is not permitted to those at margins. The subalterns are not permitted to speak, hence there is no record, no evidence of what they feel, experience or think, in fact, they do not have the language to express themselves. They go through the ordeal of shame and insult. Language is used as a weapon to further silence the victim by the victor. The protagonist informs in the very outset of the novel that though it is the story of her life, her failed marriage because she was "being routinely beaten and it had become unbearable and untenable…to keep playing the role of the good Indian wife", yet her mother "does not talk about the monster who was… husband, she does not talk about the violence, she does not even talk about the actual chain of events that led to … running away" (3). The only thing that the author wishes is to take responsibility over her life, hence she decides to write her story, despite the fact that she loves her mother, she asserts "authorship is the trait I have come to take very seriously" (9). She loathes the attempts of her mother at stealing the story of her life and building her own episodes around it. The unnamed first person narrator declares that such an action is "plain plagiarism" and the most stunning truth is that her mother is "stealing from a writer's life" (9). The first and foremost lesson that the protagonist has learnt as a writer, is: *Don't let people remove you from your own story*" (9). This lesson is not just learned by the writer of the novel, rather it is learnt by the wife, interchangeably by the writer as a wife as well as the wife as a writer in the process: the woman, the wife, the individual, who is forced to the periphery, while the centre is being occupied by the man, her husband. The process is not as simple as it appears to be.

A complex and complicated process is involved and followed by the subjugator, comprising of a series of events. Thus, writing the story of one's own life not only relieves the novelist of the agony and torture that she has gone through in her brief marital life, but also facilitates her to take hold of the authenticity of the events of her life, as Kamala Das has declared: "I have written several books in my lifetime but none of these provided the pleasure the writing of my story has given me" (3).

K. Satchidanandan says, "Women's function in the patriarchal society is primarily one of negation ... Her very act of writing almost inevitably breaks the set rules and norms of the status quo" (107). *When I Hit You Or, A Portrait of the Writer as a Young Wife* is not the story of an uneducated, unprivileged, ignorant, poor girl, in fact the narrator is highly educated:

"A Doctorate in Philosophy, the only daughter of well to do parents, both of whom are College lecturers, a feminist in ideology, in the process of being a writer, as she is in the middle of writing a novel, when she got married. The narrator has been time and again told by her parents to be silent, whenever she is beaten up by her monstrous husband. Her father informs her: "Silence is peace. You cannot make peace until you hold your tongue" (156).

When the daughter complains again and wishes to come back to her parents, the father warns her: "If you break off your marriage, every one in town will mock me" (156). For the narrator: "To stay silent is to censor all conversation. To stay silent is to erase individuality. To stay silent is an act of self-flagellation..." (161). But silence does not work the way it was desired by her parents. It kills the protagonist gradually on the one hand, while the husband takes it for her sexual involvement with other men. Along with beatings, another ordeal begins for her, as the husband starts raping her every night in order to punish her for her sin. It is writing that saves the wife, as it is the prerequisite of her survival. Sandra Gilbert and Susan Gubar opine the same: "What is most important to me must be spoken, made verbal and shared, even at the risk of having it bruised or misunderstood. What I most regretted were my silences...my silence had not protected me. Your silence will not protect you" (225).

The subjugation and control starts with the husband manipulating the young wife for deactivating her Face book Account, then knowing her email password through exhortation and himself managing her messages and mails, getting a local number for her to avoid the roaming charges of Tamilnadu SIM card and advising her not to share her new number with anyone except her parents. He curtailed her internet access to three hours a week that to in his presence, as he carries the USB dongle with him all the time. Though the budding writer in the wife foresees it as an attempt to kill the writer in her, her parents find nothing objectionable to it and rather supports him, especially the father telling her the same thing: "The internet is your drug" (60), as the husband states earlier: "*You are addicted*" (59). Then the millennium statement by both of her parents come: "Your husband is doing it for your own good" and this is the declaration the narrator confides that "When I hear 'your own good' I am reduced to being a child again. I do not argue anymore. I go silent" (60).

The social stigma that is associated with the girls or women who suffer failed marriages is immense and all the blame is put on the women. The females ponder over many questions before opting for divorce, weighing the torture and insult that their parents may endure after they come to live with their parents after separation from their husbands. There are plenty of questions that perturb them such as: what the people will say or think? The same happens with the protagonist of the novel, who, despite the recurrent inner voice that urges her to '*Walk out*' of the horrendous marriage, did not leave her husband, as there had been another voice, residing in her and asking her:

> "How you know the world will laugh at you for a month-long marriage. Even that is not as cruel as the sight of the sad faces of your parents. Disgraced. You have given them nothing but disappointment. The defeat they will carry in their eyes for the rest of their days. Never again the same pride. Never again the easy trust. Never again will the way they say your name be the same. No more will they carry their dreams on your shoulders. (61).

The wife's mental state is difficult to be narrated, there is dilemma within her, as confusing and contradictory thoughts crowd and conflict her mind. She is concerned with the fact that she will live alone, without any companion or a relationship all through her life after her separation from her husband, and she might blame herself, her *haste, hot blood, sharp tongue* after a considerable number of years, her not giving a chance of rectification to her husband etc. She is perplexed as she does not know whether she will be able to forgive him after all, and finally, she decides to *fight* rather than *flight.* But what kind of fight she can fight, being almost imprisoned as a wife? She is alone, a stranger in that town, without her own phone, without a job, without the freedom to connect to the people even on social media, not knowing the local language of that town, there is an endless list of reasons for the wife's suffering and enduring the torture passively. Her situation is different from other women, as every woman's situation is different; hence she asserts that there is no definite answer to the question, "What prevents a woman from walking out of an abusive relationship?" (65). The old-school feminists' theory of economic independence fails to answer this specific question in her case.

Things started to worsen when the husband started beating the wife for nothing, initiating it by accusing her falsely followed by her refusal and an obvious argument leading to verbal and physical abuse. Her utilizing the free time between household chores for writing is also disliked by him, so when she was asked to write an essay on sex surveys for *Outlook*, rather than taking her writing seriously, he showered a torrent of abuse on her, saying that she was asked to write the essay on sexuality because she had "the wide ranging experience of having fucked men who are twenty years old, thirty years old, forty years old, fifty years old, sixty years old, seventy years old" (75). He, in fact declares that the writer like her who writes in English, serves the purpose of a bridge between the colonizer and the colonized, hence "the writer who writes in English, this bridge – she is the whore" (74). This was not enough, he further went on accusing her of selling her body, calling it elite prostitution, "where men do not get to touch you, but they masturbate to the image of woman you represent" (76). And then there are suggestions that the wife has "slept with the entire editorial team at *Outlook*" (76). To stop her from keeping the deadline or in fact to discourage her spirit of writing, he forcefully takes out the laptop and leaves it in Mangalore while traveling to his village for a marriage, taunting her: "Should I remind Writer Madam that she is also a wife?" (76).

The techniques and tools employed by the husband are typical of a controller, subjugator, exploiter, possessor or owner. At one time, these are: railing at the wife, slapping her, throwing her laptop across the kitchen, forcing her to delete the manuscripts, a non-fiction book-in-progress, as somewhere in the pages of it she has written the word 'lover'. But she opts just not listening to or responding at his accusation of her of carrying her past into their present. She is rather already in future thinking of writing all about the present moment and all his atrocities, and thus escaping the cruel moment where the slaps only when what is written by her is deleted, thus forced to argue about freedom of expression with her husband. She maintains the power of writing, thus: "I am someday going to be writing all this out … that gives me hope, I just have to wait for this to end and I can write again, and I know that because I am going to be writing about this, I know that this is going to end" (87-88). She poses a significant question that by deleting an email a book-in progress, a random user-generated reference on Wikipedia, or/and the history of all the devices her phone has paired up with will he be able to delete what she has felt for someone? "If the material does not exist, does the memory go away as well?" (88) The oppression, the exploitation, the subjugation is reciprocated by the wife and the writer by writing the word 'lover' repeatedly and also writing letters to the unknown, unseen, unheard lovers, and it gives her pleasure as she tells that she does this because of "The defiance, the spite. The eagerness to rub salt on his wounded pride, to reclaim my space, my right to write" (88). The wife finds it easier to write poetry, but now the husband finds it problematic again, vehemently arguing that if she puts her pain in words, their temporary misunderstandings, fights and unhappiness will forever doom their relationship. When he writes of his mistreatment and cruel behaviour towards her and is confronted by the wife the reader comes to know of his duplicity, as he utters: "'Your poems blame me. My poems blame me… Your poems label me and put me in a box, my poems struggle to move past my weaknesses" (83). Pathak aptly opines: "The question is then not whether the Subaltern can speak but whether such space is created out of the patriarchal discourse where a Subaltern may safely voice its hope and fears. If such a clearing of space is not made then the marginal must attempt to create such space for themselves. Thus, "[M]marginal people must learn to preserve themselves, sigh at least to register their existence and their disapproval of their suffering" (15).

The tyrannical husband controls the wife's sexuality, as he does not allow her the pleasure in marital sex, a small involuntary moan from her upsets him, not like a lover who wants to hide it from neighbours, but because he denies her any sexual pleasure as he does not think it proper for a woman. Whenever it happens he commands her to shut up and stops the act in order to punish her to keep her pleasure before him. So she learns to be silent and still, as her husband orders her to control in an angry voice. In the absence of love, understanding and politeness on husband's part, the wife who gets nothing but battering, insult, loathing and abuse from him, is reminded of the soft, kind, polite and loving words of her 'One True Love' and though she considers it a thought-crime as per her husband, neither she feels guilty nor she is afraid of his beatings or belt-lashings. The writer-wife softly converses with her pseudo-Marxist husband about her sexual moans as inevitably human, telling him that they are language of how she feels during sex, the emotive function of the language among other functions. But "sown by patriarchy, watered by feudalism, manured by a selective interpretation of Communism – a woman should not moan. That is how history steals her voice" (154). All these are the typical and tested tools for the suppression of female voice and sexuality. The last and most unexpected one comes the wife's way, when the husband reveals that he will skin her scalp and escape untouched by anyone. This finally compels the parents to advise their daughter to come back to them, whenever he threatens her life. The time arrives all ripe for the wife to leave him with dignity and integrity, when he questions her on the issue of a call from an unknown number. Before that moment the husband seemed to live in a fool's paradise for a brief period of time, believing that the wife was bearing his child, though the wife tried every single traditional kitchen item and recipe to avoid the pregnancy, as she is determined not to bear the child of a man whom she does not love. Here, the writer within her takes hold of the situation by provoking the husband and disclosing his long-preserved secret of his failed marriage before marrying her and reminding him that he had abandoned his Comrade friend's body to the enemy for the sake of his life. Beaten and bruised, she finally speaks the truth on his face: "Don't tell me how brave you are. A brave man doesn't run. A brave man doesn't rape and hit his wife. You … are not a brave man" (212). On being threatened for life, she waits for his verbal and physical abuses to end, and then carrying her passport, ATM card, laptop and phone, she leaves him with dignity.

Language is the greatest and most convenient tool that facilitates a man to insult, mistreat, objectify, demean and dehumanize women. The husband mistreats his wife by name-calling her liberally, at which the narrator is deeply shocked: "The coarseness of my husband's insults makes me cringe. I'm ashamed that language allows a man to insult a woman in an infinite number of ways" (171). Sukhmani Roy puts her view point in this connection a: "feminist writers and critics recognize language as of major tool to woman's oppression and realize the necessity of reshaping language in order to allow woman an entry into the symbolic order, feminist writes like Virginian wolf and marry Daily have recognized the unsuitability of manmade language which either trivializes or altogether silences women" (198). The language is the weapon that the wife uses strategically for her liberation. The language allows her to write the smallest and cruellest detail of her subjugation within the marriage, but it is her language not his.

The narrator confides that though during her College, she gets the male attention in plenty, she handled it diplomatically, which helped her get rid of most of it, but it did not help her in 'the Quest for One True Love'. The reader feels the female urge, the innermost desire a woman has, which is the desire to be loved, cared and respected by at least one man, her love; and unlike men, women desire for emotional love, which leads to sexual intimacy and union, culminating into ecstasy, bliss, similar to spiritual experience. This female desire to love and being loved makes the narrator affirm in the last sentence of the novel: "I am the woman who still believes, broken-heartedly, in love" (249).

Works Cited

Barry, Peter. *Beginning Theory*. 2nd ed. Manchester University Press, 2004. Print.

Das, Kamala. *My Story*. New Delhi: Sterling publishers, 1988. Print.

Gilbert M Sandra and Susan Gubar. *The Mad Woman in the Attic: The Woman Writer and the Nineteenth-Century Imagination*. Yale University Press, 1979. Print.

Kandasammy, Meena. *When I Hit You Or, A Portrait of the Writer as a Young Wife*. New Delhi: Juggernaut Books, 2017. Print.

Pathak, R.S. *Indian English Literature: Marginalized Voices*. Ed. Avadesh Kumar Singh, New Delhi: Creative Books, 2003. Print.

Reed, Evelyn. *The Myth of Woman's Inferiority. Fourth International*. 1954. 15(2): 58-66. Web. 13. Mar. 2011.

Roy, Sukhmani. 'Of Language and culture in Post-modernism and Feminism condition contexts'. Ed. Shirin Kudchekar. New Delhi: Pencraft, 1995. Print.

Satchidanandan, K. *Indian Literature: Positions and Propositions*. Delhi: Pencraft International, 1999. Print.

Singh, Avadesh Kumar and R. S. Pathak. *Indian English Literature: Marginalised Voices*. New Delhi: Creative Books, 2003. Print.

Chapter - 29

When 'She' Smiles: Deontology in Indian *Puranas*

Dr P. Bala Shanmuga Devi

This presentation aims at seeing how women are marginalized and treated as the other in the Indian *puranas* which supposedly is to be the highest form of guidance for the society for ages to come. A random study of marginalized female characters from the *Ramayana* and *Mahabharata* is taken up and empowered characterization of a smiling Sita in *Adbhut Ramayana* is also taken up in juxtaposition to the crying former.

> There is no creature more sinful, O son, than women. Woman is a blazing fire. She is the illusion, O king, that the Daitya Maya created. She is the sharp edge of the razor. She is poison. She is snake. She is fire. She is, verily, all these united together.
>
> (*Mahabharata*, Bhishma, 13.40)

It seemingly appears true that women have been ancestrally marginalized in all avenues be it deontological, familial, societal, academical, humanistic, legal and others. There are still numerous ways in which women remain marginalized. There are every day instances of how our children are learning from the world around them as well as from the *puranic* tradition that women are far less important than men. Every day when we pull out our money bills, we take it for granted that it's men who are noteworthy, but isn't it true that there are some notable women and it's high time that we see them also? In most of the religions God is "He." Although the same is true in all the main religions of the world, this was not always the case. Archaeological evidence for Goddess worship being the earliest form of religion especially in Indian ethos is seen. There are many theories as to how the men took over and the women allowed them to, but soon we see female sexuality being demonized along with the sacred 'She'. The 'He', on the other hand, has been uplifted and put on a gleaming pedestal. Could it be that men were fearful of the power of women and thus ingrained patriarchy in our culture to an extent that it's considered normal and don't even realize it's all around them?

It can be easily noticed that women are and have been ancestrally marginalized in all avenues. There is always a debate on how they were treated in ancient times and how they were treated in the Vedic Period and how it turned out to be in the subsequent eras that followed. But it is to be noted that justification of howsoever 'she' has been treated is extended stating the fact that her subservience and patient endurance of every other pain inflicted upon her was mandated to ensure smooth functioning of the family and in turn the society. So, in all ages, woman is expected to swallow pain in silence and wallow in misery with her tears shed in secret and her smile flashed in public, and the man always takes credit for the progress of the family and she lives a life of secondary citizenship, and in most cases just a refugee in her own household. The *Garuda Purana* explicitly states that "Wicked persons, artisans, slaves, defiled ones, drums and women are softened by being beaten; they do not deserve gentle handling" (1.109.31). On the other side of the coin, it must be noted that 'she' is not actually always as she appears to be. There had been very strong instances that women exhibited strength beyond the means and understandability of the respective men in question. Their resistances were recorded at the time they chose to be appropriate enough and when it did happen men appear to be helpless to stop them. The vitality and vigour that is seen is explanatory enough that the women can be stopped only when they themselves chose to.

Gods and Goddesses are invariably represented with all smiles. No Goddess is seen shedding tears. But in *puranic* stories we see the vice-versa and the layman is led to think that the women are weaklings and a stereotypical women is one for whom virtues and sufferings are inseparable. The much deep-rooted Indian patriarchal misogynist tradition characterizes virtuous women as only weeping and chooses to stay as underlings. The status of women in the household is definitely to be looked into. According to ancient Indian practice marriage is a sacrament. It was not considered as a contract which led to procreation. The vital purpose was the union of two families. The term *dampathi* suggested that the husband and wife were regarded as the joint heads of the household with the wife enjoying more or less equal powers to her husband and destined to march together for eternity ensuring eternal progress. The wife is identified with the Vedic Hindu's House and home the very foundation of a household.

> The Rig-Vedic hymns present portraits of a noble band of ladies illustrating the high position enjoyed by women in the Vedic Ages as seers and sacrificers, their independence and courage, and their womanly love and conjugal devotion. The girls received education like boys and went through the *brahmacarya* discipline. The Atharva-Veda observes how a bride had no chance of a good match, if she had not been educated as a *brahmacarini.* Women studied the Vedic literature like men…Women performing the *sandhya* or offering sacrifices by themselves, unaccompanied by their husbands, figure as late as the time of Ramayana. (11.20.15) (Gupta 203-204).

Patriarchal traditions that emerged in the later stage invested the husband with greater powers in household affairs and restricted the power of the woman to such an extent that she slowly grew subservient and the concept got embedded slowly and strongly in the psyche of the society that it led to complete disaster in the position of the status of women with eternally painful circumstances for the women in question. Unfortunately, these standards have declined primarily due to the influence of foreign invaders, either militarily or culturally. These foreign invaders who invaded and dominated India looked at women as the spoils of war to be taken like a prize. Decay of the spiritual standards crept into Indian Vedic culture. Emphasis on the development of individual self-reliance to dependence on and service to others came into vogue. Thus, the pursuit for truth, and the spirit of renunciation and detachment were replaced by selfishness and possessiveness. And in due course of time women were viewed and treated as less divine and widely considered as objects of gratification and as a property to be possessed, controlled and also exploited. It was juxtaposed with what Bhishma stated, "O ruler of the earth (Yuddhisthira)! The lineage in which daughters and the daughters-in-law are saddened by ill treatment, that lineage is destroyed. When out of their grief these women curse these households, such households lose their charm, prosperity and happiness" (*Mahabharata*, Anushashanparva, 12.14).

Ethics here has been given a new colouring of obedience to duty and to God. In most deontological systems, morality is characterized by a focus upon and strict adherence to independent moral rules. These moral rules are meant to regulate the ways through which those duties are to be carried out. When any woman or man follows his or her duty, he or she is by definition behaving morally and is defined as a deontologist. Failure to adhere to such codes of conduct defined one as immoral. And it so happened that the codes of conduct were more stringent and binding for women more than that drawn upon men. Deontological ethical theories included those imposed on Divine Command, Duty Theories, Rights Theories, Contractarianism and that on Monistic Deontology:

(i) Divine Command Theory: The most common forms of deontological moral theories those which derive their set of moral obligations from a god. According to many Christians, for example, an action is morally correct whenever it is in agreement with the rules and duties established by the Christian God.

(ii) Duty Theories: An action is morally right if it is in accord with a given list of duties and obligations.

(iii) Rights Theories: An action is morally right if it adequately respects the rights of all humans (or at least all members of a given society). This is also sometimes referred to as Libertarianism, in that people should be legally free to do whatever they wish so long as their actions do not encroach upon the rights of others.

(iv) Contractarianism: An action is morally right if it is in accordance with the rules that rational moral agents would agree to observe upon entering into a social relationship (contract) for mutual benefit. This is also sometimes referred to as Contractualism

(v) Monistic Deontology: An action is morally right if it agrees with a single deontological principle which guides all other subsidiary principles (Cline, "Deontology and Ethics").

Criticism arises as to lack of clarity regarding conflicts between moral duties. A *puritanic* deontological system prevents one from telling lies even when it would account to saving a life but also instructs the same person from doing harm to others. Virginity is very much taken into account but a young woman is permitted to serve a sage in whichever way he wishes if the father deems fit or the elders of the family think so. Occasions where the morality of the action is questioned is also not clearly defined. Rightly saying the deontological system is based upon absolute principles and absolute conclusions. In reality, moral questions often involve gray areas where we have typically conflicting duties, interests, and issues that make things difficult. Hence the question of which duty is to be followed regardless of the consequences is still hanging like a Damocles' sword. Then the million dollar doubt of the applicability of the codes of conduct in various ages or eras or centuries also arises. One is perpetually in doubt of which moral duty should be abandoned and what should be retained also arises.

An insight into the these codes of conducts followed or overlooked in the *puranic* tradition with reference to few characters of the *Ramayana* and the *Mahabaratha* is undertaken in this research paper. Most of the inferences are the author's personal views which are open to criticism. A cursory glance at a few female characters who took things at their stride is highlighted against the deontological view that permeates most of our *puranas*. A few random examples are taken up for study.

Gandhari and Kunti of the *Mahabaratha* are revered as the royal mothers and every effort they take is always towards the betterment of their respective spouses and their children. Draupadi is a whole package of awe and wonder. Dhamayanti is a personification of sacrifice and *patini* incarnation. Similaly Sati, Sita and so forth are Goddesses on earth who stand as a personification of the deontological ethics which held good then. Savitri, Anasuya, Ahalya, Arundhatee, Maitreyi, Gargi, Madalasa and others also have gained great importance with divine deontological significance. It is said simply reciting their names removes sins.

But these all seem to have a tinge of marginalization. The male always stood taller and stronger. The women were always supposed to ensure that her whims and comfort stood secondary to all the men in her life. Kunti was victimized by both her fathers, shamed by her illegitimate son Karna and left at a lurch by her husband who walks in to death carried by lust towards Madri, and had to struggle for ever to see her five sons secure a position in Hastinapur. Bhishma Pitamaha also said, "The teacher who teaches true knowledge is more important than ten instructors. The father is more important than ten such teachers of true knowledge and the mother is more important than ten such fathers. There is no greater guru than mother" (*Mahabharata*, Shantiparva, 30.9). This is more than truth in the case of Kunti. She has always been the pivotal point of all the affairs around her. Her 'men' depend on her for umpteen affairs and never once we do see her 'smile'. The making of some lives is extremely in the hands of others. That was the case of women in the times of the *Mahabharata*. Their happiness or sorrows were decreed by men to whom supposedly they belonged to. Men directed and women suffered. Gandhari and Draupadi drank deep of sorrow though they both lived as queens. Kunti is given away by her father Shurasena to Kuntibhoja as a gift who wanted her to serve the Brahman sage called Durvasa and in turn loses her actual name Pritha. Service here meant personal service doing all his bidding, even sharing his bed if he so desired. The pleased sage bestowed Kunti with mantras and a long series of event that followed forms the great part of the story of the *Mahabharata*. Her own father gives her away to a friend. Her adoptive father gave her in marriage to an impotent man. And that husband chooses to risk his live out of lust for Madri, his beautiful younger wife. Kunti had planned to ensure kingship for her sons as Pandu will eventually be crowned the king. Had he been alive he would have spared Kunti of her hardships of loosing palatial life and live a long strive strewn livelihood. And Yudhishtra, her eldest sons is a weakling who gambles all her security off and later on it is with great difficulty that she persuades him to fight for their rights. Bhima once laments when he sees his mother sleeping on the forest floor after walking for miles but "Kunti, however, would not have judged herself to be badly-off at all. She had foiled the plot of her son's rivals. As a Kshatriya woman that was enough for her" (Karve 53).

It is Kunti who wanted Draupadi to be the wives of all her five sons to ensure their unity. She encourages Bhima to beget sons with a *rakshasa* woman who help them in their ultimate war against the Kauravas. Her plans are such that howsoever Duryodhana tries to set them against one another, it fails. Her impartial care of the five ensured their unity. Her will has been unbending in all phases of her hardships extreme though they were. All her deprivations were because of the men around her, yet she 'smiles' through her hardships very staunchly and stands tall in whatsoever might be the circumstances. Doubtless, Kunti's heart too was made of steel. When she died, waiting in yoga pose awaiting the forest fire to consume, she did die as she lived, unbending with a 'smiling' heart.

Draupadi too had been a source of unity and solidarity. As long as Draupadi lived it had never been possible to separate the brothers. It was she who frees the brothers after Dharma gambles and puts everyone's honour at stake. Her troubles are human, wrought upon her by her five husbands. She was the wife of the five but bereft, the daughter of a king but bore her burden like an orphan, she had brave allies but she was alone. When dishonour was levied upon her, she saw her husbands and fathers-in-law watching in silence. Undue blame is put on Draupadi that she was the cause of the Great War when she laughed at Duryodhana. When Draupadi 'smiles' it opens a Pandora box of all troubles. Her 'smile' invigorates the fury of Duryodhana leading to plenty of consequences. So the happiness or 'smile' of women is always not so positively interpreted in the *puranic* tradition also. The war actually was ensured when the blind elder prince was denied kingship owing to his blindness. When all that the Pandavas could do was to beg for a piece of land Draupadi seeks vengeance with the heart of a wounded lioness and she stays so till her death perfect in judgement both during peace and during war. She was not spared of a single pain, be it the problem of her honour, or that of a rival wife. And she stood an exemplary model of deontological codes of conduct whatsoever, despite the fact she questions about legal technicalities when Dharma gambles off everything. Dharma never forgives her for questioning his rights in open and is considered a serious violation of deontological codes of conduct. Yet Draupadi stays put. She refuses to accept the fact that her 'smile' or laughter evoked the wrath of Duryodhana. Even on the verge of death "Draupadi smiled. Bringing Bhima's face close to hers, she said with her last breath, 'In our next birth be the eldest, Bhima; under your shelter we can all live in safety and joy'" (Karve 105).

Sita on the other hand, having been discovered from a furrow and thus named Sita though has so many speculations attached to her birth, is also believed to have grown up as a warrior princess. The stoic poise with which she endures troubles demands more mental agility than her 'tears'. She is one who stands as an exemplification of staunch deontological image of an ideal wife. Her priceless and princely upbringing has no say at all after she marries Rama. The *Ramayana*, principally the story of one man and Sita's parents or relatives no longer exist after she is married. It is as if she is an orphan though the greatness of her father, a ruler of the Janakas had been exemplified earlier. If Laxman is an ideal brother his idealness stops there. What is to happen to his wife who is left without the presence and love of her husband though she stays in a palace. Rama is a deontological ideal man. But he takes Sita to the forest and casts her off during pregnancy. And he keeps crying thereafter. Reference can here be taken from *Abdut Ramayana* a Vaishava Shakta text wherein Sita never cries but in the peak of her glory keeps herself in 'smiles'. It could also be interpreted that the twelve years in the forest was simply a long honeymoon for Sita. She enjoyed herself in the idyllic setting as she gradually transforms from a little girl to a mature women deeply in love. She gives herself completely to Rama without being surrounded by the bustle of servants, by her father-in-law and three mothers-in-law. This proximity and love that Sita had extended to Rama makes the discrimination that he extended to her after returning from Lanka, impossible to accept. Rama had plenty of rooms to understand the person that Sita was. Hence it makes her abandonment unacceptable. Her tears do not touch Ayodhya. They are only hers to carry. But in *Abdut Ramayana* she is not the crying queen. Sita 'smiles' very often. She acknowledges the weakness of Rama and the fact that he is no match for the all powerful Ravana again makes her 'smile'. The *Kavya* tradition speaks of the heroine getting into trouble and the hero going and saving her. Sita insists that Rama come and save her rather than by the emissaries in tune to the deontological tradition. Yet, after Rama reaches Lanka, in *Abdut Ramayana* she identifies that Rama cannot save her with his powers. Hence, when the ten headed Ravana falls unconscious and the thousand headed Ravana emerges and leaves Rama breathless, she takes the form of *Mahakali* and stops 'smiling'. Her anger in all extremity is threatening even to Rama. When Sita exhibits her anger, her true potential is a surprise to the man who had lived with her for such a long period and is well beyond his understanding. He had never seen this form of Sita. He had never known that his wife had such powers. The world of discrimination speaks of women only in terms of beauty and duty. Other features of her personality are totally unseen by her spouse as well as by those around her. So when her anger, at the prospect of Rama getting hurt puts her to *Viswaroopa* and causing havoc to the thousand headed Ravana as well as to the entire demon army, stays unquenched and she is beyond the recognition of Rama himself that he humbly asks who she was. He praises her by reciting her one thousand and eight names staring with Sita and ending with Akasamurti. At Rama's request, Sita resumes her human form and Rama recites twelve verses all of which express adoration and worship and leads her to Ayodhya to be his queen. Never does Sita sheds a single tear. It is ultimately Rama who 'weeps' so much that the river Vaitarani is created and fills up the depleted ocean. She is in fact amused when sages praise Rama for having killed Ravana for she doesn't find it praiseworthy. Her divine serenity puts aside all the discrimination levied upon her and is always in 'smiles'.

Thus, this paper is just a bird's eye view of the discrimination levied upon women in yonder ages especially that during the *puranic* age as revealed in the *puranic* texts. An attempt to see how women were discriminated and how they beat all such odds is also seen. There is more room for such analyses in abundance in many more of the *puranas*.

Works Cited

Cline, Austin. "Deontology and Ethics." *Learn Religions*, 25 June 2019, learnreligions.com/deontology-and-ethics-249865.

Gupta, R.C. *The Wonder that is Hindu Dharma*. B.R. Publishing Corporation, 1987, pp. 203-04.

Karve, Irawathi. *Yuganta*. Orient Longman Limited, 1974.

Razvi, Sulaiman. "Women in Hinduism." *Word Press*, 5 June 2015, vedkabhed.wordpress.com/ 2015/06/05/women-in-hinduism-2/.

Chapter - 30

Theorizing the Subaltern Representation as a Genre

Dr B. Manivannan

A Subaltern is literally a person of inferior rank or a junior officer. It is the term first introduced by Antonio Gramsci, the Italian Marxist thinker and in later postcolonial theory the word represents the largely unorganized under classes and so they are subordinated groups. It has been further popularized by Edward Said, Homi Bhabha and Gayatri Spivak. Bhabha and Spivak are Indians but have settled in the west writing their critiques on subaltern.

In Notebook 3, p 14, Gramsci first uses the term "subaltern" with regard to social class. He writes, "Subaltern classes are subject to the initiatives of the dominant class, even when they rebel; they are in a state of anxious defense." It is in this sense that subaltern groups are subordinate to a ruling group's policies and initiatives. (qtd. in Marcus Green) Subaltern is of social strata born out of politico-economic coercion. Gramsci substituted a civic society or political society within the wider social totality and here political society donated the coercive elements whereas civil society the non-coercive. Hence, Gramsci came out with the famous formula "state = political society + civil society. In other words, hegemony protected by the armour of coercion" (Andrew Milner 69). Thus, this paper is an attempt to explore more in to theoretical discussion across postcolonial concepts in general and between subaltern history and literature in particular.

The word subaltern emerged with Gramsci and its significance in the context of history and culture has been remarkably felt since the postcolonial studies began to enunciate it academically. The first part of this paper aims not only at studying historical legitimacy involved in subaltern studies but also establishing of the view that subaltern theory is more Indian than any other western countries; it is neither Eurocentric, nor Anglo-American.

The second part discusses how the motif and theme of the text are represented providing certain form for the product of subaltern discourse as a new genre. So a subaltern text involves both history and generic representation in making a literary kind of its own. For, history explains the role of politics in society and politics in culture, vice versa and genre schemes the process and product of literature.

A group of historians initiated the subaltern studies to check elite dominants all form of patriarchy started from colonial history to the oppression of women. The word subaltern widely had the connotations to underscore feminist politics, post colonialism and cultural studies. The meaning of subalterning became very close to the "politics of the people" who for the first time felt themselves active agents of their own history on paper at least. Subaltern Studies was launched in 1982 under the editorship of Ranajit Guha as a critique of the two dominant approaches to history – writing in South Asia. One is colonialist and other nationalist but both are of elitist so rejected. Subaltern studies attempted to recover that space of politics where marginal groups were dominated. They are still system less people, had tried to assert their own initiative.

In the international scenario, the origin of postcolonial theory can be traced to Said's *Orientalism*. It is a scholarly account not of orient itself, but of how British and French scholarship had constructed the orient as 'other'. Robert J.C. Young argues:

> For Said, *Orientalism* was a discourse in Foucauldian sense of the term an enormously systematic discipline by which European culture was able to manage and even produce the orient,...during post – Enlightenment period and Said concluded that the major element in European culture is precisely the idea of European identity as a superior one in comparison with all the non-European peoples and cultures. (385).

Said's understanding of western construction of the east drew the attention of Bhabha and he thought the logic of colonial discourse was to explain the colonized as population of degenerate types on the basis of racial origin. It also sets up a basic split in the construction of other men which itself led to a kind of ambivalence. In the words of Bhabha, the colonized; imitation of the colonizing white man's image has actually operated in history as mimicry. The effect is that the hybridized existence of the colonized and subaltern who accepts the claim of the dominant that there is an ordinary reason and authority to dominate. Thus, a subaltern history may well conduct itself a subaltern agency to provide the subaltern subject; but the issue is whether the subaltern can save an anonymous space for him/herself. While tracing the dalit history in India Milind Wakankar focuses on the sixteenth century Indian poet Kabir 'who defied caste and religious distinctions in his impassioned verses (3) and further asserts:

> …a resurgent dalit (untouchable) movement has sought to claim for Kabir the status of a dalit God or a dalit thinker. 'Dalit' or 'downtrodden' is how empowered untouchables prefer to address themselves. Kabir's stems from his 'loss of caste' as a weaver, a *julaha*, but also from his explicit references to caste distinctions in his poems. (3)

One of his poems (translated by Tagore) openly declares the poet's casteless stand:

> For the priest, the warrior, the tradesman,
> and all the thirty-six castes,
> alike are seeking for God.
> It is but folly to ask
> what the caste of a saint may be; (2).

Here, it is notable that how Nandanar as an untouchable Saiva Saint, Kannappa *Nayanar*, a subaltern tribe (found in *Periya Puranam*) were blessed by Lord Siva. Thus, Kabir defines subalternity in terms of divine order. This is how Mahatma Gandhi called untouchables *Harijans,* sons of the God. But the irony is that this dalit subalternity is vigorously articulated by a Tamil dalit poet Mathivanan:

> Though
> Everything is possible
> I'm not going to do
> Anything,
> Except this:
> This mask of disgrace
> That's locked on me
> To show that I am 'low' and you are 'high' –
> This superior face
> That you are wearing –
> These masks
> I'll go on tearing. (*The Oxford India Anthology of Tamil Dalit Writing*7)

And at the level of practical politics, Gayatri Spivak advocates, the subaltern studies group…must remain committed to the subaltern as the subject of history. As they choose this strategy, they reveal the limits of the critique of humanism as produced in the west (Spivak, 1987: 209). Spivak also reveals her notion that 'strategic essentialism' by which what she insists subaltern people must be conscious of ruling over dominant discourse.

By 1986, there appeared the historical materialism approach that threw light on "Eurocentric, metropolitan and bureaucratic systems of knowledge". This was a post-modernist turn which created two groups one still loyal to the history from below model and the other more radical exploring the 'myth of rights". Here one cannot forget Gayatri Spivak's collaboration with Ranajit Guha for the selected subaltern volume that neglected the transformation. Spivak's seminal essay, "Subaltern Studies; Deconstructing Historiography" was timely in theorizing both 'peasant consciousness' and 'gender consciousness.' She also raised the very valid question 'can the subaltern speak'. This indicated that the subaltern was problematic category trying to occupy the speaking position; 'subaltern speak' could be of dominant discourse as well as disagreeing voice and it is felt by the subaltern theorists that there is a demand for substituting act for speech (336).

Ranajit Guha's early representation on some aspect of the historiography of colonial India from the first volume of subaltern studies sets the tone for the collection of images by tracing roots of Indian nationalism in the colonial enterprise.

The next few subaltern representations are basic and one such essay written by David Arnold links subalternity to its Gramscian origins and points out disengagement in terms of Indian politics. Raj Chandavarkar's critique on the Indian working class; Chris Bayly's contribution is more critical to emphasize the autonomy of the peasantry which is not helpful to make historical because he says "every subaltern is an elite to someone lower than his". Rettamalai Sriniasan's "A Brief History of My Life" briefs the socio-political formation of 'Adi Dravidar' community.

In the recent years, there is many a rationalist working on subaltern issues. To name a few, Sudesh Mishra who has written a prose work on the Indian emigrant to Fiji, Kaushik Ghosh's review on 'primitive' and premodern; Indrani Chatterjee's images on colour, gender and slavery describing the creation of half-caste in Indian context; Sundar Kaali's effective call for the 'not-for-a-moment silent' subaltern politics that puts together early Indian textual traditions; Ishita Banerjee Dube's discussion on *Mahima Dharma*, a subaltern religious movement in Orissa; Vijay Prashad's argument on the language and vision of India's freedom from the point of view of dalit politics; Christopher Pinney's study of whether "magical realism' as an attitude towards reality is representational techniques used by the colonized; Quadri Ismail's interrogations on the claims of Tamil nationalism in Srilanka; Tejaswini Niranjana's writing on the "new woman" in contemporary Indian cinema; Flavia Agnes' critical attempt on the colonial and nationalist histories of the Hindu Law of Marriage and women's property; Raj Gouthaman's "Dalit Protest Culture: The First Stage; Land: Woman's Breath and Speech" penned by P. Sivakami and so on. Even the subaltern genre finds its space in film scripts like "Parierum Perumal" (a Tamil film) focusing on both caste subalternity and caste diversity.

The list can never be ended and the subaltern studies are very much encouraged by the Indian Universities and the new historicism is academically viable to address may subaltern issues in the Indian sub-continent; thus what Indians do to subaltern history is significant.

Now the second part of this paper tries to theories about the subaltern literary form; it is a generic approach that attempts to redefine the subaltern text as subaltern genre. Though genre has its etymological roots in the Latin word' genus' means kind, it still remains as an undefined term. It is as complex as the term culture. Genre is relatively conditioned by the literariness of a text." Tzvetan Todorov" as pointed out by Heather Dubrow, "maintains that what is central to that genre is not the subject matter per se but rather the state of mind it induces; an uncertainly about how the events are to be interpreted" (86).

Benedetto Groce the Italian philosopher, argues in his work "Estetica" that knowledge takes two forms; The intuitive that is achieved through the imagination; the logical which is obtained through the intellect the former consists of knowledge about individual phenomena and produced images, ... the latter concentrates on universal phenomena and produces no images but concepts (83).

According to Croce, the generic categories lead the reader/audience move from an intuitive to a logical response to that work and the two relationally cannot coexist (84). Thus, every true work breaks generic laws. Hence, Genre is concerned for change and this change influences the mode of writing on particular issue. But are they true genre representations of subaltern literature? It can be applied to a work of art focusing on any subaltern problem.

The subaltern literature is a wide spectrum in which the subject matters are as varied as they are: dalit feminist writing, gay literature, postcolonial writings and so on. Thus, by forming a logical response to a work or by theorizing a subaltern work there is a possibility of the birth of dominant discourse that may be generic and it would answer for the Spivak's question 'Can Subaltern Speak?" And, the expectation/demand is that not only subaltern speak but can he/she speak coherently? And also how and what he/she speaks for form and context respectively determine what is generic of subaltern literature. This generic representation is undoubtedly done through the choice of the language that comprises cultural, ethnic, ritualistic and dialectic attributes. In this context Sharaddha Chatterjee reflects:

> Since language – being in the realm of the symbolic and structuring the unconscious – has a function of always being Other than what it represents in speech, or in this case, writing, writing comes to encompass not only that which is written, but also that which is hinted at in the interstices between words. One way to engage with the form of the letter is to employ the use of the metonym (the part standing in for the whole), which Lacan (1957/2006) claimed was similar to Freud's concept of 'displacement'. (Sharadha 72).

For instance, still magical realism is the generic code of Latin- American literature and thus, the subaltern history could provide paradigms of knowledge, that inform and shape cultural and literary texts and also the genre study in turn generates new paradigms of knowledge about subaltern literature.

Works Cited

Chatterjee, Sharaddha. *Queer Politics in India: Towards Sexual Subaltern Subjects/ Description: Abingdon, Oxon*. New York: Routledge, 2018. Print.

Dubrow, Heather. *Genre: The Critical Idiom.* London: Methuen 1982. Print.

Green, Marcus. "Gramsci Cannot Speak: Presentations and Interpretations of Gramsci's Concept of the Subaltern". *Rethinking Marxism*. Volume 14, Number 3 (Fall 2002).

Milner, Andrew and Jeff Browitt. *Contemporary Cultural Theory: An Introduction* (3rd Ed). London: Routledge, 2002. E-book.

One Hundred Poems of Kabir. Trans. Rabindranath Tagore. Assisted by Evelyn. London: Underbill Macmillan and Co., 1915. E-book.

Spivak, Gayatri. "Subaltern Studies: Deconstructing Historiography." Ranajit Guha (ed.). *Subaltern Studies IV: Writings on South Asian History and Society*. New Delhi: Oxford University Press, 1985. 330-63. Print.

—. *In Other Worlds: Essays in Cultural Politics*. New York: Methuen. 1987. Print.

The Oxford India Anthology of Tamil Dalit Writing. Ed. Ravikumar and R. Azhagarasan. New Delhi: Oxford University Press, 2012. Print.

Wakankar, Milind. *Subalternity and Religion: The Prehistory of Dalit Empowerment in South Asia.* New York: Routledge, 2010. Print.

Young, Robert J. C. *Postcolonialism: An Historical Introduction*. London: Blackwell, 2008. E-book.

Index